BRITAIN'S ECONOMIC PROBLEM REVISITED

Also by Robert Bacon and Walter Eltis

THE AGE OF US AND UK MACHINERY

Also by Robert Bacon

CONSUMER SPATIAL BEHAVIOUR

A FIRST COURSE IN ECONOMETRIC THEORY

DEMAND PRICES AND THE REFINING INDUSTRY (*co-author*)

Also by Walter Eltis

GROWTH AND DISTRIBUTION

THE CLASSICAL THEORY OF ECONOMIC GROWTH

KEYNES AND ECONOMIC POLICY (*editor with Peter Sinclair*)

CLASSICAL ECONOMICS, PUBLIC EXPENDITURE AND GROWTH

BRITAIN'S ECONOMIC PROBLEM REVISITED

Robert Bacon

and

Walter Eltis

Foreword by

Robert Skidelsky

First edition (*Britain's Economic Problem*) 1976
Second edition (*Britain's Economic Problem*) 1978
Third edition (*Britain's Economic Problem Revisited*) 1996

Published by
MACMILLAN PRESS LTD
Houndmills, Basingstoke, Hampshire RG21 6XS
and London
Companies and representatives
throughout the world

ISBN 0–333–64770–X hardcover
ISBN 0–333–64771–8 paperback

A catalogue record for this book is available from the British Library.

10 9 8 7 6 5 4 3 2 1
05 04 03 02 01 00 99 98 97 96

Printed in Great Britain by
Ipwich Book Co Ltd
Ipswich, Suffolk

Contents

Great nations are never impoverished by private, though they sometimes are by public prodigality and misconduct. The whole, or almost the whole public revenue, is in most countries employed in maintaining unproductive hands.... Such people, as they themselves produce nothing, are all maintained by the produce of other men's labour. When multiplied, therefore, to an unnecessary number, they may in a particular year consume so great a share of this produce, as not to leave a sufficiency for maintaining the productive labourers, who should reproduce it next year. The next year's produce, therefore, will be less than that of the foregoing, and if the same disorder should continue, that of the third year will be still less than that of the second....

The effects of misconduct are often the same as those of prodigality. Every injudicious and unsuccessful project in agriculture, mines, fisheries, trade, or manufactures, tends in the same manner to diminish the funds destined for the maintainance of productive labour. In every such project, though the capital is consumed by productive hands only, yet, as by the injudicious manner in which they are employed, they do not reproduce the full value of their consumption, there must always be some diminution in what would otherwise have been the productive fruits of the society.

Adam Smith, *An inquiry into the Nature and Causes of the Wealth of Nations* (1776) II 3

Foreword to the Third Edition by Robert Skidelsky

I.

The 'Bacon and Eltis thesis', as it is known, has been one of the most influential attempts to explain the relatively slow postwar growth of the British economy. First proclaimed in a newspaper article in 1974, and elaborated in three newspaper articles in 1975, it was a sophisticated variation of the traditional view that the more of a nation's resources the state took in taxes, the less would be left over for producing wealth. The 'thesis' came at a watershed in postwar economic life. In the main European countries, governments were spending about 10 per cent more of their national incomes in the 1970s than they had in the 1960s; at the same time the real annual growth rates of their economies had halved. The juxtaposition of these two facts suggested that the 'growth of the state' was in some sense hindering the growth of wealth. In Britain this idea struck a particularly resonant chord. Not only had Britain been growing slower than France, Germany and Italy; but the British problem seemed to have the unique feature that 'the shift in employment from industry to services, and public services in particular, had no equal in any other large Western developed economy' (1st edn and also pp. 11–12 below).

Bacon and Eltis divided the economy into a market sector which produces goods and services for sale and a non-market or tax-financed sector. (This was not equivalent to the division between the private and public sectors, since the market sector included those parts of the output of the nationalised industries covered by sales.) The market sector had to produce sufficient output to satisfy its own consumption, investment and export needs plus a surplus to satisfy the consumption and investment requirements of the non-market sector. Bacon and Eltis argued that any undue expansion of the non-market sector was bound to 'crowd out' market sector consumption, investment, and exports. There would be a double effect: the claims on marketed output would grow, and its capacity to meet those claims would shrink.

This, they say, is what happened in the 1960s and 1970s. The pre-tax share of marketed output claimed by those who did not produce it rose from 41.4 per cent in 1961 to 60.3 per cent in 1974; at the same time there was a transfer, through a sequence of recessions, of a third of the market labour force into the non-market sector, in accordance with the pseudo-Keynesian doctrine that the government should be 'employer of the last resort'. This left 'too few producers' of wealth. Because non-market employment was tax-dependent, taxation had to rise substantially. In practice, workers could pass on any taxes aimed at cutting real wages, so profits, industrial investment and net exports were squeezed. The economy was trapped in a vicious circle of slowing growth, rising unemployment, accelerating inflation and deteriorating external balance.

Bacon and Eltis concluded that the choice lay between shrinking the non-market relative to the market sector, to allow taxes to be cut, and the share of profits net of tax to be restored or nationalising the investment function. Economists can 'support the allocation of investment resources through the market, or they can support Left policies of higher public spending, but they cannot have both. And the British people must decide, either to strengthen the market sector so that it can function effectively, or to support the Left' (1st edn and also p. 116 below).

In the year the book was published (1976) the Labour Prime Minister James Callaghan announced that the government would no longer try to maintain full employment by inflation and public sector job creation. The government started a policy of export-led growth by forcing down the exchange rate, which it combined with tough incomes policies. Large public expenditure cuts were designed to slash the budget deficit and push back labour into the market sector. Chapters added to the second edition of the book (1978) deal with this (short-lived) attempt to reverse the structural maladjustment of the British economy, and parallel American and Canadian experience of public sector growth. The collapse of the Callaghan strategy in the 'winter of discontent' in 1978–79 led to the election of the Conservatives under Margaret Thatcher. She pursued Callaghan's aims by different methods. The linked objectives of Conservative macroeconomic policy were to end inflation by cutting money-supply growth and to reduce the growth of the tax-financed sector by capping central and local government spending and eliminating subsidies to loss-making industries. Supply-side policies to speed up growth included cutting marginal tax rates, privatisation and trade-union reform.

Between 1979 and 1989 the British economy grew almost twice as fast as between 1973 and 1979 and faster than all the industrial economies except Japan. Profits recovered, there was a marked acceleration in manufacturing productivity growth, and inflation was much lower. The question is how far this improved performance was due to reversing the structural impediments to faster growth identified by Bacon and Eltis in the mid-1970s.

In their new chapter in this volume 'Bacon and Eltis after 20 Years' the authors admit that the Thatcher governments failed to cut real public spending in the manner which Healey and Callaghan had done between 1976 and 1978. But they restricted its rate of increase – mainly by cutting public sector capital investment programmes – so that, with the faster real growth of the 1980s, it was almost 4 per cent lower as a share of GDP in 1989–90 than in 1978–79. Though there was a modest shift back from tax-financed to market sector employment (largely due to the effects of privatisation), the consumption of the tax-dependent sector actually grew faster than that of the market sector. Further, the tax burden increased slightly between 1979 and 1989, the reduction in the share of public spending in GDP being used to eliminate borrowing.

Professor Crafts has argued that the much improved British economic performance of the 1980s cannot be attributed to structural changes, since these did not happen. The return to normal profit levels in industry has resulted from the curbs on real wage pressure provided by high unemployment and faster productivity growth, the latter made possible by scrapping inefficient plant and restoring managerial prerogatives. This conclusion casts doubt on whether Britain's problem of slow growth in the earlier period was caused by the 'crowding out' of private-sector investment by tax-financed consumption. Crafts shows that between 1965 and 1974 rising taxes hit market sector consumption more than market-sector investment, 'a much less damaging outcome than was discussed by Bacon and Eltis'. One explanation for this is that rising tax rates will tend to raise unemployment rather than lower profitability, except temporarily. By the same token it is only in the relatively short interval when unemployment can be kept below its 'natural rate' that increased public-sector employment is bound to be at the expense of private-sector employment. Unemployment had drifted up from 2 per cent in the early 1960s to 5 per cent by the mid-1970s; after 1979 manufacturing industry shed 1.5 million jobs. Where unemployed resources can be brought into use, additional claims by both the public and private sectors can be met. (N. Crafts and Nicholas Woodward, *The British Economy since 1945*, 1991, pp. 63, 270, 285.) Apart from this, the jobs shed in the private sector were largely among males, while those gained in the public sector were largely among females. 'The latter group could not obviously have been robbed from manufacturing – unless, that is, they had changed sex in the process.' (William Keegan, *Mrs Thatcher's Economic Experiment*, p. 36)

There is some tendency, then, nowadays to say that the Bacon–Eltis 'thesis' caught a temporary anti-statist fashion, that the expansion of the tax-financed sector was not the main cause of Britain's slow growth, and that the Thatcher 'escape', which did not rely on any real shrinking of public spending and moreover was incomplete, disclosed what the real problems were: namely, overpowerful trade unions which inhibited efficient working of plant and productivity growth, appeasing monetary policy, inflexible relative wages, managerial incompetence and deficiencies in research and development and education and training. In other words, the long-run British 'disease' was low productivity growth and this was independent of the share of tax-financed consumption. In their new chapter Bacon and

Eltis acknowledge that higher productivity growth, enabling real wages and profits to grow together, created a 'positive sum game' in industry. But the sources of this higher productivity growth are largely unexamined.

Nevertheless, Bacon and Eltis are able to salvage one crucial part of their thesis. The Thatcher governments refused to create new public sector jobs to offset the rise in unemployment in the market sector. This enabled them to cap the tax burden, and this, in turn, undercut the main source of trade-union militancy which the first edition of the book had identified: resistance to higher taxes. It was, they claim, the new assurance that increases in gross pay would be reflected in rising real take-home pay which was the main factor in creating an industrial relations climate favourable to efficiency and productivity improvements. This tax achievement was unique in the OECD European countries. In Continental Europe government outlays and receipts were, by 1989, not only much higher than in Britain, but were higher than they had been in 1979, and had risen compared to Britain's in relative terms. With taxation growing as a ratio of personal incomes, average living standards remained flat in France and Germany over the decade, leading to the kind of industrial militancy Britain experienced in the 1960s and 1970s. (Bacon and Eltis might have added that productivity growth halved in these countries in the 1980s, whereas in Britain it doubled.) In Sweden, where the government remained employer of the last resort till 1985, public spending reached 65 per cent of GDP that year, and since then Swedish governments have shuffled 'between intolerable taxation, unsustainable borrowing, exploding public expenditure and growing unemployment, because [Sweden's] market sector can no longer provide a sufficient level of employment to sustain the standard of living...to which the Swedish people have become accustomed'.

Bacon and Eltis conclude their new chapter by saying that the 'destabilising sequence' which they identified in Britain in the 1960s and 1970s could recur if public spending were again allowed to cream off most of the fruits of growth and government returned to being an employer of the last resort. That the three main political parties *say* they are determined that this should not happen is the clearest evidence of the influence which their book has had.

II.

The importance of a set of arguments is liable to outlive the occasion which gave rise to them. The general question which Bacon and Eltis raised (or rather restated) concerned the role of the state in the production of wealth and the limits of taxation in a free society. Whatever the validity of their explanation of Britain's slow growth rate – and it must be remembered that they were only trying to explain the *deceleration* of an already relatively slow growth rate over a short period of time – their thesis has a much wider general significance. They offer a fertile set of ideas for understanding the global 'marketisation' of economies which has occurred since the early 1980s as well as the 'fiscal crisis' of the state which led up to it. Two ideas in particular are worth emphasising.

In the first place, Bacon and Eltis were the first mainstream economists in the West to produce a structural theory of macroeconomic imbalance. Hitherto it was only the Marxists and neo-Marxists who had contended that macroeconomic problems such as rising inflation and unemployment, widening budget deficits, and rising public debt were rooted in structural pathologies, though they saw these as arising from the nature of the capitalist system. By contrast, orthodox economists tried to promote technical solutions to the problems of inflation, unemployment, and slow growth within the limits of the mixed economy as it had evolved, or was evolving. It was the enormous merit of the Bacon and Eltis thesis that it broke with this approach without assuming the inevitability of, or necessity for, collectivism. In their argument, statism, not capitalism, was the villain of the piece. By posing the alternative between freedom and collectivism so sharply, they helped arrest the muddled British creep towards collectivism and create an intellectual climate favourable to Thatcherism. Helped by the 'success' of the Thatcher experiment in Britain, market-promoting 'structural adjustment' became the orthodoxy of the 1980s; in the Communist world, where the state owned the whole economy, it led to the restoration of capitalist market relations. The crucial role of ideas in this whole development needs emphasising.

The second contribution of Bacon and Eltis was to revive the notion of tax resistance. In their account workers refused to pay the higher taxes levied to finance increased social spending and public sector employment, shifting the burden to employers, who tried to pass it on to the consumer in higher prices. Who ends up paying the 'inflation tax' depends on the relative bargaining power of capital and labour, and different groups of workers. This, I think, still provides the most convincing structural explanation of the inflationary pathology as it developed from the late 1960s onwards. (The *locus classicus* of this kind of analysis is Colin Clark's article, 'Public Finance and Changes in the Value of Money', *Economic Journal*, December 1945.)

In the first two editions of their book, Bacon and Eltis saw workers as irrational. As voters they demanded higher levels of social spending (the so-called 'social wage'); as employees they refused the taxes to pay for them. But the authors also doubted whether the real 'outputs' of these services grew in line with their inputs. 'This might help explain why workers apparently failed to take the increase in the 'social wage' much into account in their wage bargaining' (1st edn and also p. 15 below). Bacon and Eltis return to this theme in their new chapter. Here they identify health-care and education as 'superior' goods, the demand for which rises faster than national income. If a society determines that these will be provided by the state, the government will need to increase spending on them more rapidly than the national income rises if it follows the preferences of its population. This implies that taxes will have to rise faster than national income, thus reproducing the destabilising sequences of the 1960s and 1970s.

In the 1980s the British government managed to increase the ratio of GDP spent on health (and other public services, but not education) by cutting other items of expenditure, but it is not clear how far this rebalancing can go. Health-care and education are widely regarded as 'underfunded', though there is no great eagerness to pay higher taxes to remedy this situation. Bacon and Eltis still attribute the perception of 'underfunding' to disappointment with outputs, to be remedied by improving 'value for money'. 'The underlying perception', they write, 'is that the financial inputs the UK public services receive are now appropriate in relation to the national income...'. I doubt if this perception is universally shared. Many parents who educate their children in private schools spend almost twice as much on education as the government spends per child in state schools without being twice as rich. Are these parents myopic, or does more spending, in fact, produce better quality – such as smaller class-sizes?

Bacon and Eltis skirt round the problem. They acknowledge that a 'good deal of expenditure on health and education could be arranged through the private sector' but say that 'in practice all OECD governments take responsibility for establishing minimum standards out of national and local budgets'. A guarantee of minimum standards, though, does not require governments to finance increased expectations which accompany rising personal incomes, especially if the expectations rise faster than the incomes.

Now that governments have abandoned their role as 'employer of the last resort' the main pressure to expand the tax-financed sector will come from the growing demand for 'superior' goods. If this is not to reignite the destabilising sequence of tax resistance, tax shifting, rising inflation and rising unemployment, a way will have to be found of meeting an increasing proportion of this demand from private sources. Having got rid of pseudo-Keynesian finance, we are left with the genuine crisis of the Welfare State.

Robert Skidelsky
May 1995

Preface to the First Edition

In September 1974 Bruce Page, a managing editor of the *Sunday Times*, came to Oxford to talk to us. He had just read our NEDO research monograph, *The Age of US and UK Machinery*, where we arrived at some very surprising conclusions about productivity in British industry.[1] We had made a detailed comparison of the machine tools in Britain and the United States, and we found that those in Britain were no older on average than those in the USA, that Britain had expanded investment in the most up-to-date machines as fast as the USA, and that the United States lead in numerically controlled machine tools was only about three years. But each American worker produced between two and three times as much as each British worker. As the American workers did not use newer or better machines in any way we could detect from the detailed evidence we analysed, how did they do it? We concluded that the answer was that Britain used more men to work the same machines, and ran them for fewer hours per week. If Britain had 50 per cent more men per machine, and got one-third less output from each machine, the lower productivity level would be fully explained.

These propositions were surprising in 1974 but there is widespread agreement today that the *overmanning* and *underproduction* we wrote about then are among the crucial weaknesses of British industry. The 'Think Tank' (Central Policy Review Staff) published a report on the British car industry in December 1975 which arrived at similar conclusions.[2] British assembly lines with the same machinery as European ones needed up to twice as many man-hours to assemble cars, and at the same time, far less output came from each assembly line. There is thus definite evidence of both overmanning and underproduction in the car industry, and there is little doubt that the position is similar in other industries.

But in September 1974, when we met Bruce Page for the first time, we did not think that this was the only weakness in the economy. We had further evidence about British industry that was startling and disturbing. Its labour force was declining rapidly, so the workers, who each produced markedly less than Germans, Frenchmen and Americans, were also becoming fewer at an alarming rate. At the same time growing numbers were being employed in the public services who produced nothing at all that could be sold at home or overseas. Our figures showed that if Britain solved the overmanning problem, the numbers who actually produced exportable goods would fall still more drastically and in all probability the extra workers made redundant would simply swell the numbers in the public sector whose needs for capital equipment, imports and durable consumer goods had to be met largely from declining industry. We were beginning to appreciate the powerful implications of this line of argument, and how much of the deterioration in the British economy it could explain.

Bruce Page found our new propositions interesting. He had been thinking along rather similar lines himself for some time. The British economy was in crisis in the autumn of 1974 and everything seemed to be going wrong. Our propositions appeared to give a comprehensible account of what was happening and why. He encouraged us to write a short article setting out our argument, and 'Budget Message for Mr Healey: Get More People into Factories', was published in the *Sunday Times* on 10 November 1974. Interest in the article was considerable and we were encouraged to work out our new theory fully and thoroughly, and to do the detailed statistical work that was needed for a full account of how the structure of the economy had deteriorated.

Our theory had several important features. One central proposition was that part of the economy produced a surplus that made it possible for the remainder to function. If the surplus-producing sector grew rapidly, the economy grew rapidly: if it declined, the economy collapsed. We needed to work out the full theoretical implications of a leading surplus-producing sector of this kind. Also, for our statistical work, we needed to know exactly where all the inputs of the surplus-producing sector came from and where its outputs went: what fraction was sold overseas, what fraction was reinvested, what fraction was consumed within the surplus-producing sector itself, and so on. We therefore needed to develop a theory which made use of input-output analysis, and the very particular theory of growth and development we had in mind.

By a curious coincidence one of us had just completed two years' research on the great French physiocrat economist and scientist, François Quesnay, who wrestled with precisely the same problems in the eighteenth century.[3] Wassily Leontief said he was following Quesnay when he constructed the first input-output table for the United States economy and Adam Smith would have dedicated *The Wealth of Nations* to him if he had lived till 1776. Quesnay, a farmer's son, believed that agricultural rents provided the surplus which supported the Court at Versailles, the French aristocracy, the armed services and the church. Their often luxurious consumption depended on the surplus that the farmers produced, but agriculture could only produce enough to buttress the *Ancien Régime* if the farmers used expensive farm capital. Without this they could only produce enough to feed themselves, with nothing left over for the Court, the church and the aristocracy. But French governments taxed farmers heavily, who then had to sell their farm capital to pay the taxes with the result that they produced less and provided a smaller surplus for the King, who responded by raising taxation still further, which made the farmers still poorer. If Quesnay was right, the French monarchy was in a vicious circle which could only lead to financial collapse, as it did in 1789, fifteen years after his death. For his full analysis of an extremely sophisticated model, he needed an input-output table for the French economy which showed the complete relationship between agricultural inputs and outputs. He published this, his famous *Tableau Économique*, and according to one account Louis XV himself set up some of the type for one of the editions, for printing was one of the King's relaxations, and Quesnay lived at Versailles where he was one of the King's doctors.

Our view of Britain's crisis was to a startling extent similar to Quesnay's account of the crisis of the *Ancien Régime* in France. But in Britain the surplus-producing sector was not agriculture. In our article of November 1974 we thought it was industry, and our theory there was physiocratic, with industry the leading sector. We therefore followed Lord Kaldor in believing that the growth of industry was of vital importance to the economy, but for markedly different reasons.[4] In a leading article on 15 April 1975 *The Times* perceptively called those who believed that deindustrialisation was Britain's main problem 'physiocrats'. But we were becoming aware in December 1974 and January 1975 that to assume that only industry provided the trade and investment surplus on which the rest of the economy lived was a crude oversimplification. Over one-third of Britain's exports consist of services, so in February 1975 in an article that was widely discussed and commented upon,[5] one of us set out our basic argument with a 'tradable' sector consisting of all the firms, farms and offices in Britain that sell goods and services overseas; and this sector had to provide a sufficient export surplus to cover the import needs of the rest of the community. As there was rapid growth in Britain's public services, which export nothing, in 1961–74, the economy's 'non-tradable' sector was getting larger all the time, so there was increasing strain on the 'tradable' sector which resulted in inflation and a deteriorating balance of payments. We moved from the crude physiocracy of industry supporting the economy to our new position partly as a result of a series of extremely helpful and stimulating conversations with Max Corden, the Reader in International Economics at Oxford, who, while he disagreed with much that we were then saying, carefully and patiently took us through our theory step by step to bring out every implication of the argument.

We made out final transition from the idea that the 'tradable' sector fulfilled the vital surplus-producing role to a realisation that everyone who produces anything 'marketed', i.e. *that is sold* at home or overseas, produces a potential surplus. As the whole nation's exports and investment are sold, and everything that is privately consumed in addition, the economy's 'market' sector has to provide for all of these.

If it produces too little, exports or investment or private consumption or all three are bound to suffer. We appreciated the power of the distinction between 'market' and 'non-market' sectors when we read Jack Johnston's important article, 'A Macro-Model of Inflation', in June 1975.[6] We appreciated that the borderline Johnston suggested was the correct one, and with it our theory was complete and coherent.

By June 1975 the *Sunday Times* was convinced that we had something to say that should be widely discussed. To our great pleasure we were invited to write three articles of 6000 words each for publication in the autumn. Before we sat down to write our account of the British economy for a readership of almost four million, we thought it essential that what we said should be internally consistent, and that everything should add up. We therefore wrote an account of the economic theory we had developed, and this is published as Chapter 5 of the present book. We could only go ahead and write our articles for the *Sunday Times* when we knew that what we were saying was compatible with a coherent economic model, and indeed contradictions would have become rapidly apparent if we had been without a theoretical account of what we were saying. A version of the theory we have used and developed which differs in several respects from Chapter 5 was accepted for publication in the November 1975 issue of the *Bulletin of the Oxford University Institute of Economics and Statistics*,[7] and we owe much to Teddy Jackson, John Knight and Michael Surrey, the editors, for their patient and constructive criticism, advice on presentation, and much else, not least their permission to reprint a version of the article in book form so soon after its first appearance.

With the theory worked out, we were in a position to publish for the *Sunday Times*' much wider readership. Here we owe a great debt to Harold Evans, who edited the first article himself, to Ron Hall who edited the second and third, to Malcolm Crawford who corrected many errors, and to Rosemary Righter who edited our 'Reply'. The articles benefited greatly from Harold Evans's and Ron Hall's editing. We have retained some of their contribution in the versions we publish here as Chapters 1–3, and those who know both versions may well feel that we should have retained more.

The opening sentence of the first article in which economists and economic advisers are divided into 'structuralists' and 'tinkerers' we owe to Bruce Page and Machiavelli. Bruce Page advised us that a first sentence was crucial if 6000 words were to be read, and he drew our attention to the striking sentence with which *The Prince* opens.[8] We took his advice.

We were greatly assisted in preparing the articles for publication in this book by the extremely helpful comments and criticisms that the *Sunday Times* published. We are very grateful that those whom the *Sunday Times* invited to participate in the debate took so much trouble to understand our argument and probe for its weaknesses. We hope that some of these have now been removed as a result of their contributions.

Our final step before the publication of this book was to bring together some of the fundamental implications of our argument. These like the main argument are very simple, and our summary of them is published here as Chapter 4. This shows exactly how growth in the economy's non-market sector must put pressure on workers and companies, and with what results. This chapter follows directly from the three initial chapters, and those who have studied no economics should find it almost as easy to read as our original articles. The final Chapter, and the explanation of the charts with which the book concludes, are intended for economists and written in the language of the subject, so they are likely to be comprehended only by those who have studied economics for one or two years. But the chapter is not difficult as economics articles go, and many who read the first four chapters will find that they can follow a good deal of the final chapter.

We received a lot of letters after the publication of the original articles, and many of these gave us great pleasure. What interested us particularly were the letters from overseas. It is our impression that people in several other countries believe that there are elements in our theory that apply to their countries. It is our intention as a next step in our work to obtain international data comparable to what we publish here for Britain, and we shall hope to test the theory against this wider information. It is our belief that it may help to explain much that has happened in several countries.

In conclusion we must thank our research assistant, Nick Prescott of Magdalen College, Oxford. He worked for us right through the summer of 1975, producing all the data we needed for the *Sunday Times*' articles and tabulating it with great care. Then in November and December he helped to prepare the tables that we publish here. His comments on our work have been useful, and he has saved us from many false trails. Finally we must thank Mary Gisborne and Sybil Owen of the Oxford University Institute of Economics and Statistics for typing the articles we published in 1975, and some of the chapters of this book. They made it possible for us to meet our deadlines.

Robert Bacon
Walter Eltis
January 1976

NOTES

1. R. W. Bacon and W. A. Eltis, *The Age of US and UK Machinery*, NEDO Monograph 3, September 1974.
2. Central Policy Review Staff, *The Future of the British Car Industry*, HMSO, December 1975.
3. See W. A. Eltis, 'François Quesnay: A Reinterpretation, 1. The Tableau Economique; 2. The Theory of Economic Growth', *Oxford Economic Papers*, vol. 27, July and November 1975.
4. Lord Kaldor's argument is set out in *Causes of the Slow Rate of Growth of the United Kingdom* (inaugural lecture), Cambridge University Press, 1966.
5. Walter Eltis, 'How Public Sector Growth Causes Balance-of-Payments Deficits', *International Currency Review*, vol. 7, January–February 1975.
6. J. Johnston, 'A Macro-Model of Inflation', *Economic Journal*, vol. 85, June 1975.
7. R. W. Bacon and W. A. Eltis, 'The Implications for Inflation Employment and Growth of a Fall in the Share of Output that is Marketed', *Bulletin of the Oxford University Institute of Economics and Statistics*, vol. 37, November 1975.
8. 'All states and dominions which hold or have held sway over mankind are either republics or monarchies.'

Preface to the Second Edition

We have been delighted that so many have found the first edition of *Britain's Economic Problem* interesting and provocative of thought. We have taken the opportunities provided by a second edition to make several additions. The charts and tables of the first edition have been brought up to date, for a year has passed since it was published, and we have added two new chapters.

In 'First Steps Towards a Solution' we outline and explain the policies which Britain has followed in its efforts to alter the structure of the economy in favour of industry and commerce, and we assess their chances of success. Exports have begun to grow rapidly, but many are disappointed that this has not yet led to growing output and employment. It must be emphasised that policies for structural change are bound to act slowly. In our opinion Britain's new policies stand an excellent chance of success if they are persevered with. Moreover, there is now agreement between many senior Labour and Conservative politicians on several of them including the need to control employment in the non-market sector.

A second new chapter, 'The Problem in Canada and the USA', examines two countries where public expenditure has grown as quickly as in Britain. The chapter includes a number of comparisons between Britain, Canada and the United States, and it seeks to explain why both the North American countries are beginning to experience difficulties similar to Britain's. We are of course less familiar with Canadian and United States statistical sources, but we have received much help and advice. We are especially indebted to Professor John Sawyer, Director of the Institute for Policy Analysis in the University of Toronto.

Canada and the United States are not the only countries which have faced problems because of rapid non-market sector growth. In our future research we hope to examine other countries, including in particular Australia and Sweden.

We have benefited greatly from the lectures and seminars which we have been invited to give in universities, banks and companies in Britain, Italy, Canada and the United States. We have learned much and several who heard us will notice that they have influenced the new chapters. Opportunities to give lectures or seminars based on the North American chapter, in Ottawa, New York, Washington, St Louis, Los Angeles and Bermuda were especially valuable.

Finally, Walter Eltis owes a special debt to the Department of Political Economy of the University of Toronto where he was a Visiting Professor in 1976–77. Toronto, with its large Political Economy department and its marvellous libraries, has been an ideal place in which to pursue and develop new ideas.

Robert Bacon
Walter Eltis
August 1977

Bacon and Eltis after 20 Years

The first edition of *Britain's Economic Problem: Too Few Producers* was directed especially at the UK. In 1975 when the 'Declining Britain' articles on which we based the first three chapters were published in *The Sunday Times*, UK inflation had reached 25 per cent, public-sector borrowing was 10 per cent of GDP and public expenditure 48 per cent of GDP. Unemployment was rising rapidly, and we believed that many of our academic colleagues would regard this as *the* problem which required immediate attention. That would have led many of them to advocate a recovery package involving further increases in public expenditure and job-creation in the public sector. We believed that view would be supported in Harold Wilson's Cabinet which was replete with economics graduates with first-class honours degrees from leading UK universities, who had been taught (and in some cases had themselves taught) in the 1930s, the 1940s and the 1950s that sufficient fiscal expansion could always solve the problem of unemployment.

The analysis we presented in *The Sunday Times* in 1975 and in the first edition of *Britain's Economic Problem* in 1976 emphasised that extra public expenditure would eventually need to be financed by higher taxation, and that trade unions would have the power to pass some of this on, so that it would increase the real cost of labour to industry and commerce. With a higher cost of labour, private-sector industry and commerce would cut employment and, more significantly, employment-creating investment, so still more jobs would need to be created in the public sector to contain unemployment at an acceptable level. We predicted that, in the economic conditions which prevailed in 1975–76, the further pursuit of public-sector job-creation would produce conditions where inflation would continue to accelerate, and the employment the public sector had to provide to contain unemployment would grow. With inflation at 25 per cent in 1975, and the budget deficit at 10 per cent of GDP, that would have led rapidly to complete financial destabilisation, which had become endemic in many non-OECD economies, and from which there was no reason to believe the UK would be exempt.

We summarised our fear of this very real danger in perhaps the most significant paragraph in the book:

> As the unemployment figures rise, extra jobs can only be provided outside industry and only the government can provide jobs where there is no prospect of profits. Hence, governments are tempted to provide still more jobs in the public services, and as they raise taxation to pay for them, in due course company profits and workers' living standards are further squeezed with the result that there is still more pressure against company profits in industry. In consequence industry invests still less, more industrial workers become redundant and still more workers need to be fitted into the public sector. This ever-accelerating spiral leads nowhere except to total economic collapse and it is so deep-rooted in structural maladjustment that it is in no way amenable to tinkering. (p. 24)

This quotation embodies the three central propositions on which our theory is based. These are:

1. An increase in public-sector employment as a ratio of total employment, or indeed in any kind of extra public expenditure as a ratio of total output in the economy, can result in an increase in the real cost of labour or capital or both to the private sector.
2. Any increase in the cost of labour or capital in the private sector will reduce the equilibrium level of private sector output and employment below the level that would otherwise be achieved.
3. Any reduction in the equilibrium level of private sector employment will increase the amount of employment the government will need to provide in the public sector if it has an employment target which it seeks to sustain.

These three central propositions were based on a distinction between the sector of the economy which is tax-dependent and the sector from which all taxes ultimately derive. As nationalised industries are in the public sector but are also potentially capable of paying taxes and financing non-taxpaying social services, the actual distinction had to be slightly different from the conventional public/private-sector dichotomy. The sector of the economy which does not market its output is the tax-dependent one. None of it is financed by selling its output, so it must be entirely financed from taxation or borrowing. The sector which markets its output (which includes all private-sector industry and commerce plus the nationalised industries in so far as they cover their costs) is the one from which the government must ultimately derive all tax revenues.

Our propositions therefore became (i) that any increase in the relative size of the non-market sector would require extra taxation; (ii) that this would raise costs and so reduce output and employment in the market sector; and (iii) that the containment of unemployment would then require still more employment in the non-market sector, where governments could create jobs without regard to their financial viability.

When our argument was first published in 1975 and in 1976 there was ready agreement that the three strands in our theory corresponded to recent developments in the British economy. Employment in the non-market public sector had risen more than 50 per cent in the previous 13 years and because this was tax-dependent, taxation had had to rise massively. We encapsulated this in our remark that blue-collar workers were having to pay a level of taxation which used to be paid by bank managers and university professors. It was also well understood that market-sector employment and especially that in manufacturing industry had been declining, and that industry had been insufficiently profitable to finance a significant level of new capacity-extending investment. It was a matter of elementary logic that the creation of still more non-market-sector employment would further increase the burden of taxation on the market sector.

THE POLITICAL REACTION TO OUR ARGUMENT

Because these propositions on which our theory was based made sense to our readers in public life, it was strongly supported in 1975 and in 1976. It was not intended to be and it was not actually regarded as a theory of the Right. In our third *Sunday Times* article, which formed the basis for Chapter 3 of *Britain's Economic Problem*, we set out 'A Left Solution' which we associated with the economics of the interventionist wing of the Labour Party, and 'A Right Solution' which we associated with the economics which Keith Joseph and Margaret Thatcher were beginning to advocate. The burden of our argument was that the market sector, private industry and commerce, was becoming too weak to generate the investment and employment the economy required. It would be for the electorate to decide whether the solution lay in greater intervention to strengthen what industry could achieve, plus a higher 'social wage' in the form of increased social services which workers would have to moderate their wage demands to accommodate; or in considerably lower taxation to allow industry and commerce to grow faster, using their own resources. The electorate decided between these approaches and on other equally significant questions a few years later in 1979. Before then, one of us had had more sympathy with the 'Left Solution' while the other preferred the 'Right Solution'. The argument was intended to be politically neutral.

When our *Sunday Times* articles first appeared in November 1975, they were supported from both sides of the political spectrum. Denis Healey, the Chancellor of the Exchequer in Harold Wilson's Labour government, wrote in a subsequent issue that, 'The "Declining Britain" articles have provided the most stimulating and comprehensive analysis of our economic predicament which I have yet seen in a newspaper. ... I strongly support their basic proposition that ... a faster growth in our manufacturing output will require more investment in industry; this will not be possible unless we limit the increase in the claims on the nation's resources which are made by public and private consumption', while Lord George-Brown who had presided over the preparation of *The National Plan* in 1964–65 wrote in *The*

Sunday Times that 'One of the many valuable contributions by Bacon and Eltis to any useful debate on "The Way Ahead" is to enable us to make a fresh evaluation. ... I agree pretty wholeheartedly with the authors' own choices of what we should do now. ... One thing there can be no disputing: we must have really massive cuts in Government expenditure on non-productive items.' Harold Wilson himself remarked in the House of Commons immediately after our 1975 articles were published that Whitehall had 'too many chiefs and too few Indians'.

There was similar support from what was then the Conservative Opposition. Sir Geoffrey Howe, the Shadow Chancellor, wrote in *The Sunday Times*, 'I have no doubt that we need to proceed broadly in the direction of the "Right" solution, foreshadowed by Bacon and Eltis'. Lord Blake underlined our influence on the Right in *The Conservative Party from Peel to Thatcher*. He quoted a statement by '[t]he economist John Redwood' that, 'if recent policies are extrapolated, the public sector will consume the whole of the gross national product before the end of this century' and added, 'An important book on this subject appeared in 1976 – *Britain's Economic Problem: Too few producers*. It was written by two Oxford economists – Robert Bacon and Walter Eltis – who argued that the rising amount of resources devoted to unmarketed goods and services as compared with those that were bought and sold was increasing inflation and unemployment while reducing investment and growth. The book was serialised in the *Sunday Times* and had much influence on Conservative policy-makers' (p. 323).

David Butler and Dennis Kavanagh picked up the way in which our argument was supported by both the main parties when they wrote in *The British General Election of 1979* that, 'Conservatives seized on these findings as their explanation of de-industrialisation and inflationary pressure in the economy; Bacon and Eltis seemed to confirm the wisdom of their policies for holding back the public sector, reviving private enterprise and cutting direct taxation. The gradual change in direction of the Labour government's economic policy also appeared to heed this analysis.'

The publication of our 'Declining Britain' articles in November 1975 and the first edition of our book in April

1976 preceded the economic crisis of 1976, the IMF visit and the massive public-expenditure cuts that followed. Real public expenditure was cut more than 8 per cent between the fiscal years 1975–76 and 1977–78, the largest reduction made by any government over a two-year period. The IMF visit is clearly the principal explanation of the extent of these cuts, but the reception of the 'Declining Britain' articles and the subsequent book, as well as the absence of an effective answer at a level policy-makers would be aware of, may have contributed to the creation of an intellectual and political climate where government could more easily depart from the previous Keynesian orthodoxy.

Lord Blake added to his account of the influence of our book that 'the argument was far from being accepted by all or indeed most economists' (pp. 323–4). If that was so, their dissent was not presented in a manner that influenced either Labour or Conservative party policy.

THE ECONOMIC IMPACT OF THE TIGHTER CONTROL OF UK PUBLIC EXPENDITURE

The containment of the growth of public expenditure was central to the policies of the Conservative governments which succeeded Labour in 1979. None of these cut real public expenditure in the manner that Harold Wilson, Denis Healey and James Callaghan had achieved between 1975–76 and 1977–78, but by restricting its rate of increase they reduced the ratio of general government expenditure in GDP by 4 percentage points from 44 per cent in the cyclical peak of 1978–79 to 40 per cent in the cyclical peak of 1989–90. The policies adopted sought to control the growth of public expenditure in a variety of ways including the application of tight cash limits to contain pay and employment in central and local government.

Figure 1 shows that there was a very clear upward trend in the ratio of government expenditure to GDP until 1975. Since then there have been large fluctuations, with peaks in the recessions of 1980–81 and 1992–93 and troughs in the cyclical peaks of 1978–79 and 1989–90. Since 1975 the trend has been downwards with the current share close to that experienced in the early 1970s. Within this overall pattern there have been important sectoral changes. The

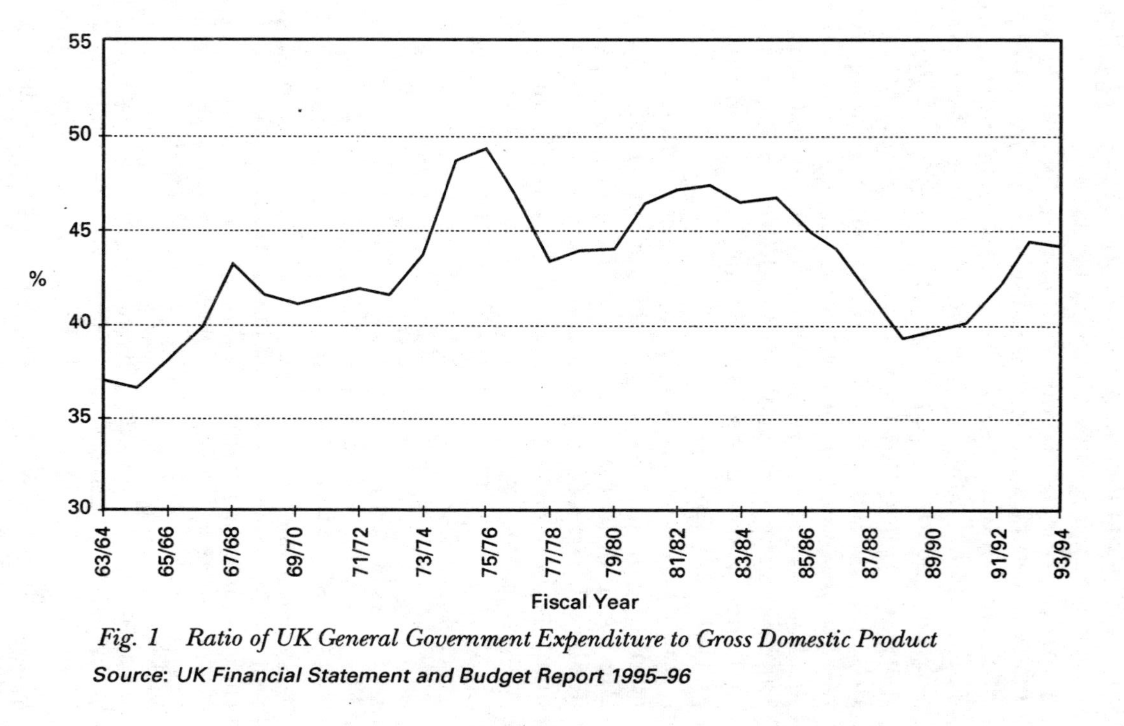

Fig. 1 *Ratio of UK General Government Expenditure to Gross Domestic Product*

Source: UK Financial Statement and Budget Report 1995–96

fall during the 1980s was achieved, despite large increases in social security and health programmes. These were counteracted by significant reductions in defence, subsidies to industry, capital spending and debt interest.

In the first and second editions of *Britain's Economic Problem*, we placed some emphasis on the growth of employment in the market and the non-market sectors. Those in the public sector who produce no marketed output depend on tax revenues from those who produce marketed output (mainly in the private sector) to finance their employment: or on government borrowing which will increase taxation in the future. We argued that there would be a strain on resources and an escalation of public expenditure as a ratio of GDP if the numbers producing marketed output declined while the numbers in the non-market sector increased.

Table 1 shows what happened to market and non-market employment in the years after the publication of the 'Declining Britain' articles on which our original argument was based. The table shows market and non-market employment in the cyclical peak years of 1961, 1969, 1973, 1979

Table 1 *Non-market and market sector employment in the UK: 1961–89*

	1961	*1969*	*1973*	*1979*	*1989*
Non-Market Sector					**Thousands**
General Government	3 558	4 198	4 878	5 384	5 255
Public Corporations	605	408	378	344	62
Total Non-Market	4 163	4 606	5 256	5 728	5 317
Market Sector					
Private Sector	19 303	19 010	18 279	17 944	20 379
Public Corporations	1 591	1 662	1 512	1 721	770
Total Market Sector	20 894	20 672	19 791	19 665	21 149
Non-Market/Market	20.0%	22.3%	26.6%	29.2%	25.1%

Source: CSO: Employment in the public corporations is included in the non-market sector to the extent that they receive subsidies and incur financial deficits.

and 1989. In 1975, 1976 and 1979 we argued that at cyclical peaks employment in the non-market sector can only be increased without causing an acceleration of inflation if it is correspondingly reduced in the market sector, i.e. that at cyclical peaks the economy is at or above its sustainable employment level. Inflation was accelerating in both 1979 and 1989 so at both these cyclical peaks, unemployment was below its non-accelerating inflation or 'natural' rate. The OECD estimates that in 1979 the UK's 'natural' rate of unemployment was 6.6 per cent and its actual rate 5.0 per cent, while in 1989 its 'natural' rate was 8.8 per cent and its actual rate 7.2 per cent. Hence, in both these cyclical peak years, market-sector employment could not be increased without quite considerable reductions in non-market employment. Over the cycle from 1979 to 1989 considered as a whole, the OECD estimates that the natural rate of unemployment averaged 9.3 per cent while the actual rate averaged 10.0 per cent, so the economy was run with perhaps 0.7 percentage points more unemployment than its equilibrium rate because of the priority the government attached to bringing inflation down.

Table 1 shows some fall in the ratio of non-market- to market-sector employment from 1979 to 1989. Non-market employment declined 7 per cent because there was a fall of 2 per cent (129,000) in those who worked for central and local government, and a decline of 82 per cent (282,000) in those employed in the non-market element of the public corporations, mainly as a consequence of the extensive privatisations in the Thatcher decade. In all, non-market employment fell 7 per cent. In the same period, market-sector employment grew 7 per cent (by 1,483,000). Private-sector employment rose 12 per cent (by 2,435,000), and employment in the market element of the public corporations fell 55 per cent (by 951,000). The large swing between 1979 and 1989 in the inter-sectoral head-count had a relatively modest effect on the public expenditure totals. Between 1979 and 1989, total employment incomes in central and local government grew 125.3 per cent, while total employment incomes in the whole economy increased 124.2 per cent, so the share of central and local government in aggregate wages and salaries actually increased: the 2 per cent net reduction in general government employment may have disproportionately involved lower-paid staff. In addition, a good deal of the employment swing the table shows reflects the direct and indirect effects of privatisations, which had a more significant impact on the government's capital account than on its current account and therefore lessened the extent to which it could correspondingly reduce taxation.

The 4 percentage-point reduction in the ratio of public expenditure to GDP was most strongly influenced by reductions in public-sector investment, in defence expenditure, in debt interest, the virtual elimination of subsidies, and the elimination of the borrowing needs of the newly-privatized public corporations. Walter Eltis showed in 1982 how the most powerful net effects of public expenditure cuts on the rest of the economy are produced by cuts in capital spending and in actual purchases of goods and materials, and it is these that had the greatest impact between 1979 and 1989.

The opportunity to cut taxation or borrowing which the 4 percentage-point reduction in the public expenditure ratio opened up was entirely used to reduce borrowing, so the proportion of current resources the non-market sector purchased scarcely altered. In 1979 we developed a table in the *Economic Journal* which showed how marketed output was divided between purchasers in the non-market and the market sectors from 1961 to 1973. In Table 2, we extend this series to include the cyclical peaks of 1979 and 1989.

Table 2 Where marketed output (net of capital consumption) was purchased (%)

	1961	*1969*	*1973*	*1979*	*1989*
Non-market sector	33.7	36.8	39.8	42.2	41.2
Market-consumption	56.1	51.5	51.8	48.2	53.3
Business-investment	7.8	7.4	7.1	4.9	9.4
Investment in dwellings	2.3	3.5	3.5	3.2	3.5
Inventories	+1.5	+1.3	+2.3	+1.6	+0.7
Exports less imports	–1.4	–0.5	–4.5	–0.1	–8.1

Table 2 shows that the principal shift from 1979 to 1989 was from the balance of payments to market-sector consumption. Those who produced marketed output consumed a higher fraction, and the personal savings ratio actually fell from 9.6 to 5.8 per cent of disposable incomes. In the 1976 and 1978 editions of *Britain's Economic Problem* we provided an account of the 'Barber Boom' (now in Chapter 2 below) where bank credit exploded and public and private consumption soared, investment rushed into the housing and property markets and the balance of payments was destroyed. In the 'Lawson Boom' at the end of the 1979–89 decade, there was the same over-rapid growth of bank lending because of low real interest rates and further deregulation of the banks. This again encouraged personal borrowing and investment in the housing and property markets. As the personal savings ratio is made up of saving (mainly contractual) for retirement less the dissaving of personal borrowers who seek to anticipate future incomes, a large burst of dissaving due to over-optimism by borrowers and eagerness of banks to lend explains the 4 percentage-point fall in the aggregate personal savings ratio.

But in the Lawson Boom, because there were not competing pressures on resources from the non-market sector, business investment in industry and commerce was extremely strong, which helps to explain why the private sector was able to create more than 1½ million new jobs in the decade.

PUBLIC EXPENDITURE IN THE UK AND IN EUROPE

It is important to examine how the development of UK public expenditure compares with other countries in the European Union. The information the OECD provides does not permit a sufficient breakdown of the data to provide a series comparable to our Table 2, but there is internationally comparable information on public expenditure and taxation as ratios of GDP. Table 3 compares general government outlays and current receipts in 1979, 1989 and 1993. The series for outlays omits some capital-account public expenditure items, so it shows UK public expenditure falling from 40.9 per cent of GDP in 1979 to 37.5

per cent in 1989, in place of the fall from 44 to 39¾ per cent of GDP which CSO statistics indicate.

It will be evident that of these 13 European economies where all but Norway are in the European Union, the UK's public-expenditure ratio was the lowest in its cyclical peak of 1989 and the second lowest in the most recent year, 1993. In 1989 general government outlays were below the average of the other European economies by 11.9 per cent of GDP and were still 11.1 percentage points below the average of the other 13 in 1993. The UK cut its general government outlays ratio by 3.4 percentage points between 1979 and 1989 while the 13 other European economies increased theirs by 3.5 per cent of GDP.

The UK's ratio of general government receipts to GDP was the third lowest in 1989 and the second lowest in 1993 when it was 12.3 percentage points below the average of the

Table 3 *Total outlays and receipts by general government as a ratio of GDP*

	OUTLAYS			*RECEIPTS*		
	1979	*1989*	*1993*	*1979*	*1989*	*1993*
Austria	48.2	49.0	52.9	45.8	46.2	48.7
Belgium	57.7	55.0	56.7	50.2	48.8	50.1
Denmark	53.2	59.6	63.1	51.5	59.1	58.7
France	45.0	49.1	54.8	44.1	47.9	49.0
Germany	47.2	44.8	49.4	44.6	44.9	46.0
Greece	30.7	44.5	48.1	28.0	30.0	34.6
Ireland	43.8	40.6	42.9	34.3	38.9	40.5
Italy	41.6	51.3	56.2	31.5	41.4	46.6
Netherlands	53.3	53.8	55.8	49.7	49.1	52.6
Norway	49.5	53.5	57.1	50.8	54.9	54.4
Portugal	36.2	41.7	53.2	30.0	38.7	45.2
Spain	30.1	40.9	47.6	28.3	38.1	40.1
Sweden	60.0	58.3	71.8	57.1	63.7	58.3
Average of 13	45.9	49.4	54.6	41.9	46.3	48.1
UK	40.9	37.5	43.5	37.7	38.5	35.8

Source: OECD

other 13. In 1989, at the UK cyclical peak, UK government receipts, that is, taxes and social security contributions, were 6.4 percentage points below Germany's and 9.4 percentage points below France's.

The immediate effect has been that in the 1990s, the UK has had lower rates of income tax, corporation tax and above all payroll taxation on the employment of labour than either France or Germany. Overall UK tax rates did not fall between 1979 and 1989 (in Table 3 they rise by 0.8 per cent of GDP) but in successive UK budgets special emphasis was placed on reducing marginal rates of taxation, so that by 1989 the UK had the lowest rate of corporation tax in the European Community (33 per cent against 52 per cent in 1979) and a marginal rate of income tax of 40 per cent when this had been 83 per cent (on earned incomes) in 1979. Average tax levels are also now far lower in the UK, as Table 3 underlines.

Just how these lower UK tax rates have influenced comparative economic performance is a complex question. Lower taxation is one of several considerations which have attracted to the UK 40 per cent of the US and Japanese investment which has come to Europe since the Second World War. By 1992, foreign-owned companies employed 18 per cent of the labour, produced 23½ per cent of the output and were responsible for 31½ per cent of investment in UK manufacturing industry. The average productivity gap between UK and French and German manufacturing industry was halved during the 1980s, when productivity rose more than 40 per cent in the UK and about 20 per cent in France and Germany.

With rapid productivity growth and virtually no overall increase in taxation as a ratio of GDP, the average net-of-tax earnings of employees in UK manufacturing industry grew 3.1 per cent per annum from 1979 to 1989, while the profits of non-North Sea industrial and commercial companies increased 4.3 per cent per annum faster than the GDP deflator. There were significant industrial relations benefits from this rapid increase in both wages and profits which created what game-theorists refer to as positive-sum game conditions. Betting on horses is a negative-sum game where there are winners and losers, and losses in general to punters and bookmakers together because of the tax on betting. British industry managed to play a positive-sum game in the 1980s and employees, managers and shareholders were each able to take more money out of the economy each year because of the large growth in net-of-tax incomes which they were able to generate.

Not surprisingly, game theorists have discovered that the solution to positive-sum games is generally cooperation between the players, while in negative or zero-sum games, where some can win only if others lose, conflict is inevitable. We showed in the first and second editions of *Britain's Economic Problem* that in the 1960s and the early 1970s the share of GDP which government took was growing so rapidly that what remained for the private sector net-of-tax scarcely increased. It was no wonder that in those decades workers struggled with employers and with other groups of workers to achieve a rising standard of living in an environment where all could not enjoy this. The result was endemic conflict in which wages grew faster than profits, some gained, others lost, and strikes were frequent. In the 1980s employees were able to raise their net-of-tax private consumption by 3 per cent per annum without cutting into profits. As a consequence cooperation to achieve successful production offered more than industrial action could possibly deliver, and at the same time the cost of industrial action to individual unions was raised and the support they would receive from secondary action by other unions was greatly weakened by new industrial relations legislation. The private-sector trade unions soon became aware of the significance of these developments. A further favourable result from the creation of an environment where net-of-tax incomes grew significantly year after year was that unions increasingly cooperated with managements to eliminate the overmanning and restrictive practices which had been tolerated in the 1960s and the 1970s. It is now universally understood that all can gain from more efficient production. One of us was Director-General of the National Economic Development Office from 1988 to 1992. In that time he never heard any trade-union leader remark that increases in productivity would destroy jobs. He heard many union complaints that much of British industry was investing too little, training too little and spending too little on research and development, which was holding back living standards and competitiveness. The language of the unions had become entirely one of the need to improve productivity and to cooperate to achieve this to the greatest degree managements would allow.

In France and Germany, in contrast to Britain, the average annual growth in real net-of-tax earnings has been less than half a per cent per annum in the decade from 1979 to 1989. In both these countries personal taxation and other deductions have grown as a ratio of personal incomes, so take-home pay has increased less rapidly than the incomes employees received from their companies. An additional squeeze on the wages workers actually receive has been due to the continual rise in employers' social security contributions, together with a tendency for real wages to rise more slowly than productivity. In Germany there have been the added costs of reunification. The net effect has been that while most French and German workers are well-paid, their average living standards have risen extremely little in the last ten years. French and German trade unions have therefore begun to develop the attitudes the UK used to have in the 1960s and the 1970s when employees gradually realised that they could only gain significantly higher living standards by getting larger pay increases than others, which was most readily achievable through the threat of industrial action. In France and Germany in the 1990s, the new frustrations are beginning to show with more frequent and extensive strikes.

While these have all but disappeared in the UK private or market sector, there are areas of the public sector where the 'cash limits' used to control public expenditure have been set so low that negligible real income growth has resulted. This has produced precisely the zero-sum conditions which used to prevail in the private sector and it has naturally led to a continuation of union militancy.

If the private market sector is achieving rapid productivity growth, it should be possible to increase levels of pay in the non-market public sector at parallel rates. There is no statement in the 1976 and 1978 editions of *Britain's Economic Problem* where we suggest that individual levels of pay for those who produce unmarketed public services should be held back in comparison with pay in industry and commerce. If real output is growing fast enough in private industry and commerce to permit positive-sum wage bargaining, the same should be attainable in the public sector through the restoration of pay arbitration based on fair comparisons. By 1995 it has been learnt that responsibility for the control of inflation rests on effective monetary and fiscal policies, and if the aggregate of pay increases is successfully contained by these, it will not be inflationary to allow the 20 per cent of employees in central and local government to enjoy the same average rise in living standards as the 80 per cent in the private sector.

The UK's new combination of positive-sum conditions in the private sector and zero- or negative-sum conditions in some of the public sector can be seen as a fundamental tension between two broad principles which influence the relative size of the public sector. The first is that the private sector will only function effectively if net-of-tax real incomes advance sufficiently rapidly to permit the establishment of positive-sum conditions for those who work in industry and commerce. This requires an adequate rate of productivity growth, while a sufficient fraction of the fruits of growth must be retained by those who produce in the market sector. But there is a second principle which is also important.

Evidence from a variety of countries, as surveyed by Norman Gemmell in 1993, shows that as families become richer they spend growing fractions of their incomes on health, education and personal security. These are actually describable as 'superior' goods and services, because the rich spend a higher fraction of their incomes on them than the less well-off. The expenditure elasticity of demand for health, education and personal security, i.e. *the proportional increase in demand for these divided by the proportional increase in aggregate expenditure* exceeds 1. If a society determines that these will mostly be provided by the state, then its government will need to increase their provision more rapidly than the national income if it is to follow the preferences of its population.

The consequent international tendency for public expenditure ratios in GDP to grow is sometimes referred to as

Wagner's law. Adolph Wagner, a late-nineteenth-century German economist, believed that redistributive social welfare was itself a 'superior' good and that for this and a number of further reasons (set out in Gemmell (1993)) public expenditure would increase as a share of the national income as an economy's incomes per head grew. In the late twentieth century this 'law' has fitted Europe well, but not the US and Japan. But it is evident that, if taxation and public expenditure ratios show an ever-rising trend, because a wealthier economy redistributes more, a point will come where that development will produce economic destabilisation. Even if there is sustained majority political support for continuing redistribution, those whose economic actions are also guided by personal motivations will be aware that the rates of return from tax evasion and tax avoidance are all the time increasing as average tax rates rise, while the net-of-tax returns from productive investment and employment decline as the adverse impact of taxation on industry and commerce increases. To continually increase the rate of return from tax evasion and avoidance and reduce the return from productive investment and employment must eventually undermine an economy's growth potential. This is an error which the US, the thriving Pacific Rim economies and since 1976 the UK, are becoming careful to avoid. The 'law' of ever-rising *redistributive* taxation should be resisted, but not the wishes of a population for a greater supply of 'superior' goods such as education, health and personal security which families would themselves buy more of as their incomes grew if they were not predominantly provided by the state.

In theory a good deal of expenditure on health and education could be arranged through the private sector, but in practice all OECD governments take responsibility for the establishment of minimum standards out of national and local budgets. Increasing provision of health and education is therefore likely to impose a rising trend on these items of public expenditure. The cost of other public expenditure categories such as national defence and industrial and agricultural subsidies may fall, as they did from 1979 to 1989, so a rising overall trend in public expenditure is potentially avoidable, but a population's desire for improving health, education and personal security (which is independent of whether it also wishes to redistribute more: it may or it may not) is likely to exert some upward pressure on public expenditure.

There are therefore tensions between the need to create positive-sum conditions in the private sector and the need to provide the rising standards of health, education and personal security which families' revealed preferences indicate. With the high rate of productivity growth which much of Europe achieved in the 1950s and the 1960s it was possible to achieve both. Thus, from 1965 to 1977 West German non-market expenditures rose one-and-a-quarter times as fast as marketed output, but private consumption and investment were still able to grow at annual rates of almost 4 per cent and 2 per cent. That combination of some growth in the public expenditure ratio and a quite rapid rate of increase of real personal consumption may have come close to tracking the preferences between private consumption and the public provision of health, education and other public goods which German electorates desired at that time. In contrast, in Britain over this period, public consumption and investment grew twice as fast as marketed output per head and almost four times as fast as private consumption and investment. That almost certainly represented a faster shift in favour of government provision of health, education, and other public goods than implicit preferences called for, and this over-rapid shift in favour of the public services reduced the private sector to near zero-sum conditions, with the consequences we set out in the 1976 and 1978 editions of this book.

From 1979 to 1989 the relative rates of growth of public provision and private rewards for UK market-sector producers were reversed. With a falling ratio of public expenditure to GDP, the provision of public goods and services grew less than private consumption and investment. This slower growth in public expenditure may have compensated for its over-rapid expansion in the previous 20 years, so the relative growth of the two sectors may have come close to following the underlying preferences of the population, if the period from 1961 to 1989 is considered as a whole. After 1979 it was central to Conservative Party strategy to reduce the growth of public expenditure in relation to the national income, and it won four successive general elections when its intention to break away from former trends cannot have been clearer.

Despite the fall in the ratio of total public expenditure to GDP from 1979 to 1989, spending on health and 'public order and safety', mainly police and prisons, actually increased as ratios of GDP. Public expenditure on health grew one-and-a-half times while real expenditures on 'public order and safety' increased more than twice as fast as GDP. These estimates of real rates of increase do not allow for the 'relative price effect' that expenditures on public services are usually subject to more inflation than the majority of private-sector purchases. Private- and public-sector purchases are both deflated by the economy's general rate of inflation, but nominal expenditures on health and law and order both grew faster than GDP, and the evidence from family expenditure surveys that families spend more on these as their real incomes grow refers only to their nominal expenditures. There is no evidence that families correct for the 'relative price effect'. Hence the growth of public expenditure on health and personal security from 1979 to 1989 may well have corresponded to family preferences as revealed by personal expenditure patterns.

But in the continual pressure to reduce public expenditure from 1979 to 1989 education grew two-thirds as fast as GDP, although it is universally regarded as a 'superior' good. That has been largely made good since 1989, for in the 14 years from 1979 to 1993 considered as a whole, the share of public expenditure on education in GDP rose, and it has increased one-and-a-half times as fast as GDP to conform to the private perception that this should grow faster than expenditures in general. In the longer 14-year period from 1979 to 1993, expenditure on public order and safety grew four times and expenditure on health more than twice as fast as GDP.

Since 1990 total public expenditure has grown substantially relative to GDP but its level is still well below the European Union average. Social provision for the unemployed and for those on low incomes automatically rises when the economy is in recession, so the increase in total public expenditure since 1990 has had a significant cyclical element. The government intends to return to the lower 1990 ratio as the economy recovers with reductions in the overall cost of personal social benefits. It expects to be able to continue to shift public expenditure in favour of health, education and personal security while reducing total public expenditure as a share of the national income. The evidence indicates that the Thatcher and Major governments have so far managed to increase the share of total public spending in what many would regard as the areas where there is most justification for a growing share, and this development is likely to continue.

There is nonetheless a widespread belief that public health, education and law and order have been under-provided for. This is despite the evidence from the national accounts that public expenditure on these has grown sufficiently faster than GDP to reflect the preferences of the population. The above argument suggests that families would not have increased their relative expenditures faster than the government if the decisions had been theirs.

The widely voiced dissatisfaction with some of these services most plausibly reflects the way in which the police, the prisons, the national health service and state education have been organised and managed, which government has come to recognise as the key issue which deserves attention. The introduction of the 'Citizen's Charter' in 1993, which sets out the quality of service which individuals are entitled to receive, and the increasing freedom to manage internal budgets within health and education are directly concerned with the quality of the public services, and the priority the government attaches to this.

We reiterated in the 1976 and the 1978 editions of *Britain's Economic Problem* that extra resources had been poured into health and education, that a high fraction of these had been channelled into administration, and that consumers had not perceived commensurate improvements at the sharp end. We quoted from a study by Max Gammon which showed from official National Health Service (NHS) statistics that from 1965 to 1973 the number of occupied beds in NHS hospitals in Great Britain had fallen from 451,000 to 400,000 while the number of administrators and clerical staff in the Hospital Service had increased from 48,000 to 72,000. These series cannot be extended on a precisely comparable basis, but current official series show that the available beds in English NHS hospitals were 435,000 in 1966, 391,000 in 1976 and 231,000 in 1992/93. The number of administrators, managers and clerical staff in the NHS in England almost doubled from 83,000 in 1974 to 152,000 in 1992. The trend which Max Gammon originally diagnosed has therefore continued relentlessly through Labour and Conservative governments and many Secretaries of State for Health. Only those who require hospital treatment, and their families, can judge whether the very substantial reduction in the number of beds in the last thirty years, and the continuing increases in managerial, administrative and clerical staff, has provided a satisfactory availability of beds for those who require emergency treatment, operations and continuing care.

The significance the Citizen's Charter attaches to public perceptions of whether the hospital service is advancing or declining shows how the most important public expenditure issues now centre on how the public services are administered and organised and not on the rates of growth of financial expenditures. It is becoming increasingly recognised that we must learn to measure the *outputs* of public services, the levels of literacy and mathematical attainment in our schools (where there are comparative international studies), the proportion of crimes 'solved' by the police, the extent of hospital waiting-lists and whether these are growing or declining. If *inputs* into these services advance, that is, if there are more teachers, more policemen and more employees of the NHS, but numeracy and literacy fail to advance, as many crimes remain unsolved, and hospital waiting-lists remain as long, the public will not accept that the *output* of these services is improving. These have become the issues that matter.

The UK's present strategy is to seek to reconcile constraints over financial *inputs* into public expenditure with improvements in the quality of *outputs* by adopting management techniques which increase value for money. The underlying perception is that the financial inputs the UK public services receive are now appropriate in relation to the national income, and that the higher standards of provision the public desires will be best delivered through improvements in management.

The policy of maintaining a near-stable share of public expenditure in GDP (apart from the fluctuations inherent in the cycle) reflects the difficulties the UK experienced in the last thirty years from over-rapid change. Too fast an increase in public expenditure left workers facing slow or zero growth in what their real wages would buy, which led to frustration and zero-sum behaviour. At the other extreme, over-rapid reductions led to zero- and even negative-sum conditions among those who provided certain public services, which created frustrations and resistance of a different kind. The adverse pressures from too little private or too little public consumption are most easily containable in a rapidly growing economy where both can be increased at rates which command general assent.

The particularly damaging scenario with which our book is concerned is one where increases in the public expenditure ratio first produce worker frustration, and go on to damage investment, the productive base and the economy's underlying rate of growth. That gradually makes it more difficult for a society to satisfy its aspirations for private and public consumption, and if pushed relentlessly, goes on to create a situation where the frustrations from inadequate growth of private consumption and the necessity for cuts in public consumption are encountered at the same time.

We shall now explain in more detail than in 1976 and 1978 exactly what occurs when an economy departs from adequate growth in the resources available to private industry and commerce.

THE DEVELOPMENT OF OUR UNDERLYING ARGUMENT THAT EXCESSIVE NON-MARKET GROWTH DESTABILISES ECONOMIES

Our underlying theoretical argument was based on three propositions: that a fraction of tax increases will be passed on, that the consequently higher cost of labour will reduce market-sector employment, and that a reduction in market employment will force taxation up further because workers no longer employed in the market sector will be an added burden on the finances of the state. If these effects are sufficiently powerful they can produce the complete destabilisation which threatened the UK in the 1970s, but which was averted by the re-establishment of control over the growth of public expenditure in 1976 and in 1979. Our academic argument rests on the power of these propositions. We begin with whether higher taxation will actually raise the real cost of labour.

There is now much econometric evidence which indicates that a fraction of tax increases is passed on. This was summarised by Robert Bacon in 'The Effects of Public Employment and Other Government Spending on the Rate of Wage Inflation' in 1980, and in a further survey, 'Real Wages and Taxation in Ten OECD Countries', which Anthonie Knoester and Nico van der Windt published in 1987. A 1990 OECD study found that, on average, for 16 OECD countries, a 1 per cent increase in the 'tax wedge' (the excess of the total amount companies pay to employ a worker over what the tax system allows the worker to receive) induced an immediate increase in labour costs of ½ per cent. Virtually all well-based wage equations show that changes in the direct taxation of wages influence the pace of wage increases, while changes in indirect taxes and employers' social security contributions influence these through their effect on prices, which will be wholly or partly passed on into higher wages. There are three significant transmission mechanisms.

First and most simply and directly, the supply curve of labour is universally seen as depending upon expected real earnings net of tax. An increase in the taxation of wages will reduce what workers receive at the previously established real wage. Workers will supply less labour at that wage if there is any sensitivity of the supply of labour to the rewards of the worker. The new equilibrium between the supply of labour and the wage will be at a level where companies pay more but workers receive less than in the previous equilibrium where there was no taxation of wages. Empirical evidence does not suggest that there is much sensitivity of the supply of labour to the real wage, but there is some, so higher payroll or income taxation is associated with a lower supply of labour and a higher cost of labour to companies.

Robert Bacon shows how the argument can be generalised so that workers are influenced both by the part of the real wage which is available to buy marketed output, and also by the social wage (the public services they benefit from) and in addition by the availability of leisure. In this broader and more general approach, there is still some tendency for higher taxation to reduce the supply of labour and increase its cost to industry and commerce, unless the increase in the social wage is seen as a greater priority than increases in the market wage.

A second consideration which leads to the passing on of some taxation of wages is based on the influence of workers' expectations. Their supply of labour will depend on the real net-of-tax incomes they expect to receive in the 'year' for which they are bargaining. In order to continue to enjoy the same real standard of living, they bargain for pay increases which cover the price increases they anticipate (the current rate of inflation if their expectations 'adapt' to immediate experience), plus whatever further pay increases they would require to cover additional deductions from their paypackets or salary cheques. Employees will therefore enter wage negotiations with a larger target increase if tax deductions are growing. Employers will face strong resistance to increases which fail to compensate for higher taxation, and the bargains that result will be influenced by this. The argument is often extended to suggest that workers' wage demands are based, not merely on what they believe will produce a specific net-of-tax real wage, but in addition they will expect a real wage which grows in line with what they have received in the immediate past. Again, rising taxation will add to the wage increases they require to achieve any target net-of-tax real wage path.

A third line of argument, much present in the earlier editions of this book, suggests that, in addition to what has been said so far, the pace of wage increases is influenced by whether wages are above or below the level at which the labour market is in equilibrium. If the wages which workers seek run ahead of the real wages the economy can deliver because aggregate demand is limited through monetary and fiscal policy, growing unemployment will result. This will pull back the pace of wage increases, so employees' efforts to pass taxation on will raise unemployment rather than wages. Any developments (through government action or equilibrating market forces) which re-establish the 'natural' level of unemployment will at the same time have to establish the higher real wages workers require in order to pay higher taxes.

These theoretical lines of argument and others like them have led to a plethora of wage equations which have been widely tested and are compatible with the view that employees pass a fraction of tax increases on through higher wages. We can now examine the first of the three fundamental relationships which have the potential in combination to produce economic destabilization: the connection between an increase in taxation, and a consequent increase in the real cost of labour.

For this presentation of the argument, it will be assumed that an economy has a uniform proportional rate of tax of T which is levied on all incomes. A uniform rate of tax of T levied on all outputs (value-addeds) would have quite similar general effects, since if employers could not pass an increase in T on in higher prices, workers would pay none of the higher taxation unless money wages *fell*, while if employers could raise their prices in response to higher indirect taxation, workers would recover part of tax increases if they could raise money wages. In the example which follows, T is raised by 1 percentage point because there is an initial increase in public expenditure by 1 per cent of GDP, and the budget is balanced. If the wage (and therefore the cost of labour) is W before tax, it will be $W(1 - T)$ after tax, and if taxation rises by 1 percentage point, the proportional fall in the wage after tax is the increase in tax, $0.01 W$, divided by the original pre-tax wage of $(1 - T) W$. Hence the proportional fall in net-of-tax wages is $0.01 W$ divided by $(1 - T) W$, or $0.01/(1 - T)$. Net-of-tax wages therefore fall by the 1 per cent increase in taxation times a multiplier of $1/(1 - T)$. The size of this multiplier will be 1.18 if T is 15 per cent, 1.67 if it is 40 per cent, 2 if it is 50 per cent, and 3 if it is 67 per cent. We therefore have the important proposition that a tax increase will reduce net-of-tax wages by a multiple of the increase in taxation. This multiplier of $1/(1 - T)$ means that in a highly-taxed economy like Sweden where taxation takes almost two-thirds of the national income, $1/(1 - T)$ will approach 3. With a multiplier of 3, an increase in taxation of 1 per cent of the national income would reduce net-of-tax earnings by 3 per cent. A Swedish worker earning a money income of 300 Kronor would have only 100 after tax if incomes were taxed at a rate of 67 per cent, and a tax increase of 1 per cent on his total income of 300 would remove a further 3 Kronor from his paypacket, and leave him with a net-of-tax income of 97 instead of 100, a reduction of 3 per cent.

The equivalent multiplier will be about 2 in most of Europe where taxation averages 50 per cent of GDP, perhaps 1.67 in the UK where it averages 40 per cent, and little more than 1 in an economy like Hong Kong, where average taxation is only 15 per cent.

If a fraction, $Ç$, of tax increases is passed on in higher wages, then an increase in taxation by 1 per cent of all incomes will raise the cost of labour $Ç/(1 - T)$ per cent. If $Ç$ is 1 so that tax increases on wages are fully passed on, then a 1 percentage point tax increase would raise the cost of labour 3 per cent in an economy with 67 per cent taxation, 2 per cent in a typical European economy and 1.2 per cent in an economy like Hong Kong. If $Ç$ is ½, so that workers are able to pass on half of tax increases, a 1 percentage-point tax increase would produce an increase of up to 1½ per cent in the cost of labour in an economy like Sweden, a 1 per cent increase in Western Europe, and a 0.60 per cent increase in Hong Kong. In general we can write:

Elasticity of cost of labour with respect to taxation $(E_{W/T})$ equals $Ç/(1 - T)$ (1)

The second link in the potential destabilisation chain is that an increase in the cost of labour will reduce market-sector employment. Here we can use the concept of the elasticity of substitution between labour and capital, *the decrease in the quantity of labour which is employed (relative to capital), divided by the relative increase in the cost of labour.* If the elasticity of substitution between labour and capital is – ½, a 1 per cent increase in the relative cost of labour would produce a ½ per cent fall in the amount of labour employed. Estimates of the elasticity of substitution between labour and capital have virtually always found a figure of less than 1 (Sato (1970) and Arrow, Chenery, Minhas and Solow (1961)), so a 1 per cent increase in the relative cost of labour is almost invariably associated with a fall of less than 1 per cent in employment. If we write $\tilde{o}$ for the elasticity of substitution between labour and capital, and $E_{N/W}$ for the elasticity of market sector employment with respect to the cost of labour, then in general:

Elasticity of market sector employment with respect to the cost of labour ($E_{N/W}$) equals $\tilde{o}$ (2)

This equation understates the full adverse impact of a higher cost of labour on the employment the market sector provides. The impact of the elasticity of substitution between labour and capital shows what the fall in employment will be when the market sector's capital stock is at a particular level. In 1976 and 1978 we also emphasised the way in which tax increases which workers pass on reduce net-of-tax profits and market-sector investment. This will have an adverse *dynamic* impact on the market sector's capital stock and the employment it can provide, which will therefore fall more sharply than is indicated by expression (2) which describes a *static* movement along a given production function.

The third link in the potential destabilisation chain is between a fall in market-sector employment and the consequent need to increase taxation, either to provide alternative public-sector employment for newly-redundant workers, or else to finance their unemployment. If the marginal product of labour in the market sector is β times its average product and 1 per cent of market sector employment is lost, then β per cent of the tax-paying part of the economy will cease to function. Taxation would need to be raised by β percentage points if a worker made redundant in the market sector is employed in the public non-market sector (in existing office accommodation) at a similar wage. If those made redundant in the market sector are merely allowed to become unemployed, they might cost the state as little as one-third of their former marginal products. If the state takes the view, which used to prevail in Sweden, that the government normally acts as employer of last resort, such workers will be found employment in the public non-market sector at a cost to government finances which would correspond at least to their previous marginal product in the market sector. If the state had to provide new capital installations in addition it would have to provide total funds which exceeded workers' previous marginal products. If the alternative public sector provision is μ times as expensive as the private-sector provision that is eliminated by increased taxation, and the elasticity of the rate of taxation the economy requires to balance its budget with respect to the level of market sector employment is $E_{T/N}$, then in general:

Elasticity of the tax rate with respect to market sector employment ($E_{T/N}$) equals $-\beta\mu$ (3)

The full destablisation sequence has the three elements that (i) tax increases raise the cost of labour, (ii) increases in the cost of labour reduce market-sector employment, and (iii) reductions in market-sector employment cause an increase in taxation. This will start the whole sequence off again and produce a second round of the same developments, and after that a third. A significant question is whether the second round of tax increases which come at the end of (i), (ii) and (iii) will be larger or smaller than the initial increases, and whether the tax increases which subsequently set off a third round are larger or smaller than those which set off the second. If the tax increases that set off each round become progressively larger, the economy will explode into destabilisation. Alternatively, if the tax increases in the second round are significantly smaller than those in the first, the sequence will in due course diminish to insignificance. The dynamic sequence could be *explosive* with tax increases becoming larger in each successive round, or *damped*, with tax increases continually diminishing.

Whether the tax increases which set off the second round are larger than those which initiate the process will depend on the size of the three links in the dynamic chain. Thus the initial tax increase raises the cost of labour by a multiple $E_{W/T}$, the elasticity of the cost of labour with respect to taxation. This extra cost of labour then reduces market-sector employment by a multiple $E_{N/W}$, the elasticity of market-sector employment relative to the cost of labour. This reduction in market-sector employment then goes on to increase taxation by the further multiple $E_{T/N}$, the elasticity of taxation with respect to market-sector employment.

The extent of the increase in taxation that initiates the second round will be the initial increase in taxation times the combined effect of the three elasticities. Hence:

Increase in taxation that initiates the second round equals the increase that initiates the first times $E_{W/T} \times E_{N/W} \times E_{T/N}$ (4)

We can use the statements we derived for the three elasticities, $E_{W/T}$, $E_{N/W}$, and $E_{T/N}$ in expressions (1), (2) and (3) to derive a numerical value for (4) which tells us whether the potential destabilisation sequence will be explosive or damped:

Increase in taxation in the second round equals the increase that initiates the first round times $-[Ç/(1-T)]\,\tilde{o}\,\beta\,\mu$ (5)

So the sequence will be explosive if $[Ç/(1-T)]\,\tilde{o}\,\beta\,\mu$ exceeds unity. Let us begin by considering what values these might have in a British sequence with the economy as it is developing in the 1990s. It could be suggested that the trade unions have become quite weak so that Ç, the proportion of what workers lose from tax increases that they are able to pass on could be as low as 0.3. Taxation itself is close to 40 per cent of GDP, so $1/(1-T)$ may be about 1.67. The elasticity of substitution between labour and capital, $\tilde{o}$, is perhaps about – 0.6. It appears close to this in many studies, while μ, the budgetary cost of supporting those who lose their jobs in the market sector as a ratio of their former wage might be quite low, perhaps as little as 0.4, because such workers are not found alternative government employment and unemployment benefits have become a low fraction of earnings. The marginal product of the workers who lose market-sector employment might be about 0.7 times the average product of labour in the market sector, so β might be about 0.7. In all, with these assumptions, $-[Ç/(1 - T)]\ \tilde{o}\ \beta\ \mu$ would come to $0.3 \times 1.67 \times 0.6 \times 0.4 \times 0.7$ which equals 0.084. With an economy that follows that description, an initial increase in taxation would set off an echo sequence which was perhaps one-twelfth as great. That would indicate that there is no present risk of a destabilisation sequence.

We can contrast this with the situation which prevailed in the UK in 1975 when we published the 'Declining Britain' articles which formed the basis for the first edition of *Britain's Economic Problem* in 1976. At that time the trade unions were far more able to pass taxation on than in 1995 so *Ç*, the proportion of a tax increase which is passed on may have been as high as 0.6 as against the 0.3 we are supposing in 1995. *T*, the proportion of taxation in GDP, was similar to the present 40 per cent. At that time workers made redundant in the market sector were found equally well-paid work in the non-market sector and the cost to the state was not merely the provision of a public-sector income equivalent to their former wage. Paying newly-employed public-sector workers the same wage would have made μ equal to 1.0, but capital costs also had to be incurred to provide office blocks and other appropriate accommodation in the public sector. This will have raised μ to perhaps 1.3. Thus the total cost of employing an extra worker in the public sector was perhaps 1.3 times the level of income the marginal worker received in the market sector. $\tilde{o}$, the elasticity of substitution between labour and capital, and β, the ratio of the marginal product of labour to the average product, will have been similar to their assumed values in 1995, – 0.6 and 0.7. With these assumptions, $-[Ç/(1 - T)]\ \tilde{o}\ \beta\ \mu$ will have come to 0.546, so in the economic conditions which prevailed in 1975, a tax increase would have opened up a dynamic sequence which produced further tax increases and consequent declines in the market sector, at repeated intervals. These subsequent tax increases would have gradually diminished in extent, by perhaps about one-half in each round.

That is where Britain might have headed in the absence of the significant policy-change in 1976 that the government would cease to act as employer of last resort, and the further policy change in 1979 that the ratio of taxation in GDP would be contained. In the 1990s these have virtually eliminated the potential destabilisation sequence. Britain's fundamental policy changes at that time can be contrasted with those in another country, Sweden, which had higher public expenditure and taxation than Britain in 1976, and which took no effective measures to contain its continuing growth.

THE DESTABILISATION OF THE SWEDISH ECONOMY

The most extreme destabilisation sequence appears to have occurred in Sweden, where the ratio of public expenditure to GDP at market prices actually reached a peak of 72 per cent in 1993. In 1979, two Swedish economists, Hans Söderström and Staffan Viotti, suggested an interpretation of the destabilisation process in Sweden which is similar to the one we are presenting. As in our argument, they suggest that workers have the power to pass a fraction of tax increases on in higher money wages in the annual wage negotiations which are a feature of Swedish wage-bargaining. The tradable sector of the Swedish economy cannot pass these wage increases on in higher prices, because Sweden is a small, open economy, Swedish goods have to compete with foreign goods, and at the time Söderström and Viotti wrote, the Krona was not regularly devalued as wages increased. Since the tradable sector had to pay higher wages without being able to charge higher prices, it had to cut employment each time taxes rose. According to Söderström and Viotti, the effect of higher social spending was to raise taxes and real wage costs and so reduce the number of workers the Swedish tradable sector could employ at a profit. According to their argument it was another feature of Swedish economic life that the government had an obligation to act as employer of last resort, so anyone the tradable sector could no longer support had to be found alternative work by the government. This forced up public expenditure, taxes and wages yet again, as in our own argument. Their Swedish model is in fact virtually identical to the one presented here and it includes the three relationships which together have the potential to produce explosive growth in the public sector.

Returning to the formulae which represent our argument and implicitly theirs, the Swedish tax ratio reached 63½ per cent in the early 1980s so an increase in taxation of 1 per cent of GNP had to be compensated with a 2¾ per cent pay increase (since $1/(1 - T) = 2\frac{3}{4}$ when $T = 0.635$). That is close to what Assar Lindbeck said in 1979: that Swedish workers required a pay increase of between 2 and 3 per cent to compensate for an increase in the ratio of taxation to the national income by 1 percentage point. If we assume the same degree of passing-on of taxation in Sweden in the late 1970s and the early 1980s as we have assumed for the UK in 1975, namely that 60 per cent of a tax increase will be passed on (so that $\varsigma = 0.6$), the same elasticity of substitution between labour and capital (so that $\tilde{\sigma} = -0.6$), the same ratio of the marginal product of labour to the average product in the market sector (so that $\beta = 0.7$) the same ratio of the cost of providing employment in the public sector to what displaced private-sector workers were formerly paid (so that $\mu = 1.3$), the combined impact of the three elasticities represented in expressions (2), (3) and (4) comes to 0.91. Thus at the height of the Swedish destabilisation sequence, each round of higher taxation was followed by another of almost the same size. Public expenditure and taxation could therefore be expected to increase relentlessly through the endogenous sequence which we and Söderström and Viotti have identified and described.

In 1965 the Swedish ratio of total government outlays to GDP at market prices was 36 per cent, a figure close to the European average at that time. In the five years from 1965 to 1970 it rose a further 7 percentage points to 43 per cent: from 1970 to 1975 it rose 6 percentage points to 49 per cent: from 1975 to 1980 it rose another 11 percentage points to 60 per cent and it reached 64 per cent in 1985. Until 1980 both public expenditure and taxation (because the budget was virtually balanced until then) increased by an average of 7 percentage points every five years. This continuing upward trend with five-year increases which varied between 4 and 11 percentage points differs from the near-constant increases depicted in the above formulae. Taxation, and therefore the multiplier $(1/(1 - T))$ which links the tax rate to the pay increases required to compensate for tax increases, rose from 1½ in the early 1960s to 2¾ by the 1980s. Other important forces were at work, but the relationships we and Söderström and Viotti have identified are a powerful element in the overall explanation of what occurred.

It is a central feature of this explanation that the ratio of public- to private-sector employment will rise relentlessly and Figure 2 illustrates the strength of this development until the mid-1980s. Sweden's ratio of public expenditure to GDP at factor cost is set out in Figure 3, which also shows how much its public expenditure ratio has exceeded the UK's and Germany's. In the 1980s and the 1990s the Swedish approach had to change. The government ceased to be able to raise taxation in line with public expenditure, so the automatic passing-on mechanism with its interconnected repercussions ceased to operate. Instead the tax impact of growing public expenditure was deferred, taxation ceased to increase and the Swedish state started to borrow at a growing rate. From 1980 to 1994 Sweden's ratio of government debt to GDP rose from 44 to 80 per cent, and in 1994 its budget deficit reached 14 per cent of GDP. Since the Swedish state was borrowing at real interest rates of 4 or 5 per cent, which were far above Sweden's real rate of growth, the extra taxation to pay interest will far exceed the taxes which have been deferred as a result of growing government borrowing. By 1994 Sweden did not have low public expenditure; this had actually risen to more than 70 per cent of GDP. It did not have low taxation, since at 58 per cent of GDP this was 10 percentage points above the European Union average, and like Italy, with unsustainable public finances the tax ratio will need to be increased as debt interest relentlessly grows, unless extraordinary public expenditure cuts can be found. But with government debt at 80 per cent of GDP and rising fast, and nominal interest rates at more than 11 per cent, debt interest is an element of public expenditure which will grow rapidly from now on. Given this, it will be difficult for Sweden to cut its public expenditure total without breaking drastically with the political assumptions which have underpinned Swedish economic policy since the Second World War. One fundamental assumption was abandoned half-way through the

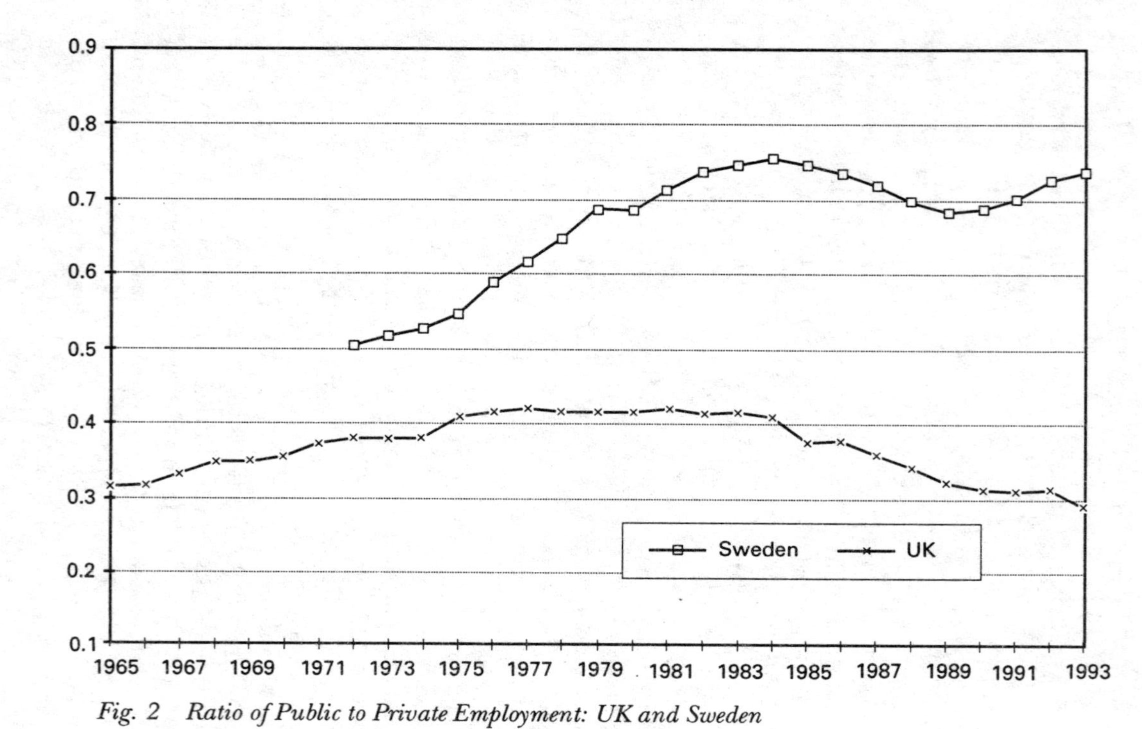

Fig. 2 *Ratio of Public to Private Employment: UK and Sweden*

Sources: *Statistical Abstract* of Sweden and UK *National Income and Expenditure*

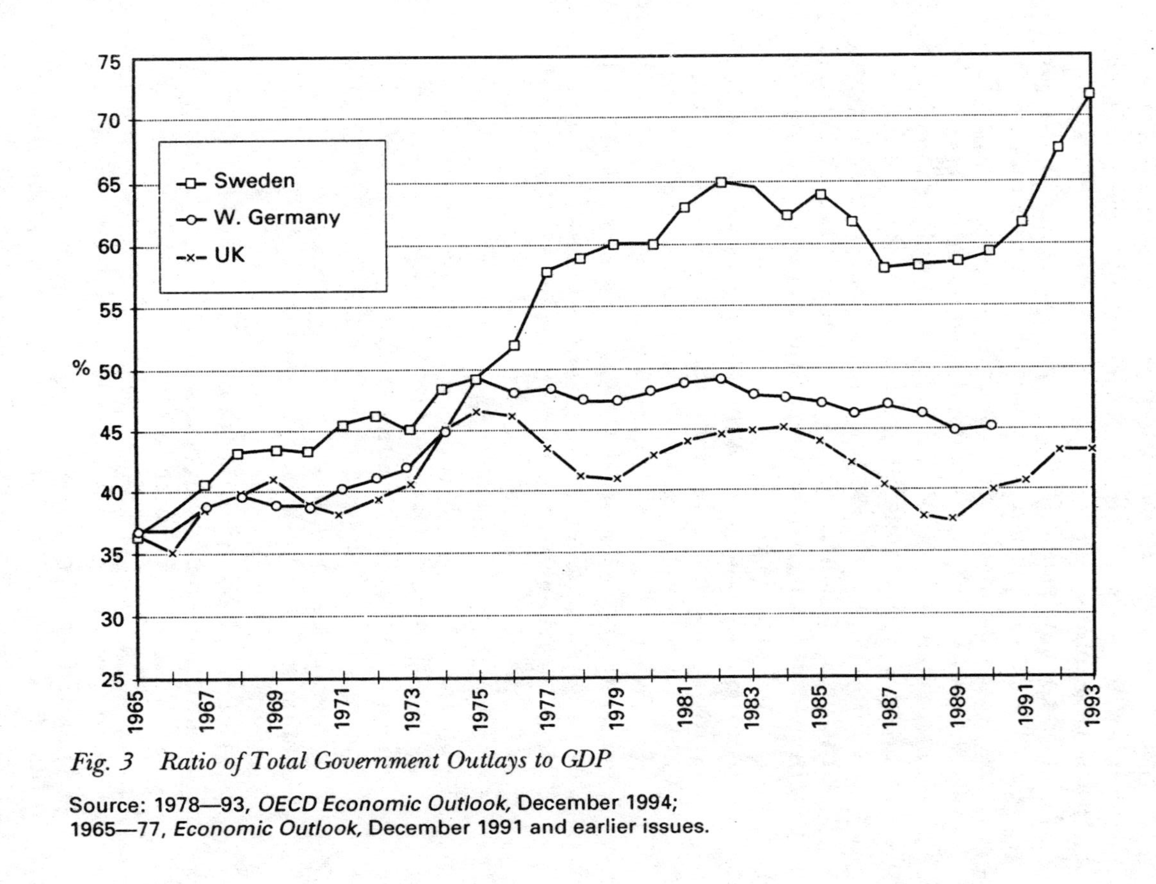

Fig. 3 *Ratio of Total Government Outlays to GDP*

Source: 1978—93, *OECD Economic Outlook,* December 1994; 1965—77, *Economic Outlook,* December 1991 and earlier issues.

1980s when the government decided that it could no longer act as employer of last resort. Swedish unemployment is now close to 10 per cent with the abandonment of that key social assumption.

The relationships we (and Söderström and Viotti) have described explain much of Sweden's progress to an unsustainable economy by the mid-1980s, where the government can now no more than shuffle between intolerable taxation, unsustainable borrowing, exploding public expenditure and growing unemployment, because its market sector can no longer provide a sufficient level of employment to sustain the standard of living in the form of public and private consumption to which the Swedish people have become accustomed.

In terms of our theory that a country should seek to arrive at a balance between the need to expand those public services which are superior goods, and the need to preserve positive-sum conditions in private industry and commerce, Sweden used its entire growth potential to expand its public services, and gave its market sector none of the fruits of growth. Because of that imbalance, it has destroyed both the effectiveness of its market sector and its macroeconomic finances.

In 1976 the Swedish economics profession discussed our 'Declining Britain' articles and their implications for Sweden. An issue of *Economisk Debatt* was devoted to a summary of our articles and analyses of their implications by Erik Dahmén, Carl Johan Aberg, Karl-Olof Faxén, Erik Lundberg, Assar Lindbeck, Johan Myhrman, Jan Bröms, Rolf Millqvist and Anders Östlind. We were not invited to contribute to that debate, and it is evident that those who believed that growing public expenditure could destabilise a modern economy had no impact on the conventional wisdom which continued to govern Swedish economic policy. One of the Swedish authors, Jan Bröms, outlined a statistical development which should have alerted his colleagues to the extent of the danger. Between 1962 and 1973, the ratio of public to private consumption grew from 26.3 to 29.6 per cent in the UK, from 22.8 to 27.2 per cent in OECD Europe and from 28.2 to 43.2 per cent in Sweden. Public consumption was growing three times as fast in Sweden as in OECD Europe and four times as fast as in the UK. Someone should have noticed that this mattered and that it would come to matter a good deal more if these trends were allowed to continue. At the time of this debate, Sweden's public expenditure ratio was 52 per cent of GDP, 20 percentage points below the level it went on to reach in 1993. It would have been easier to avert destabilisation by halting its growth in 1976 as Britain did, than it will be to restore the structure of the Swedish economy so that it can produce what its population has become accustomed to consuming.

CAN *BRITAIN'S ECONOMIC PROBLEM* RECUR?

Our analysis suggests that a return to the destabilisation sequence from which Britain began to suffer in the 1960s and the 1970s would require two significant developments. First, extra public expenditure would again need to be allowed to cream off most of the fruits of growth. In 1994 Britain's public expenditure ratio was 10 percentage-points below the European Union average, so there are many items of expenditure, and especially on infrastructure, state pensions and social benefits, where Europe spends considerably more than the UK. Those who believe that the other countries in the European Union have achieved a superior economic and social balance between public and private provision could persuade governments of either party to resume significant public expenditure growth at a rate considerably faster than the output of the economy. Conservative governments raised the public expenditure ratio from 40 to 45 per cent of GDP between 1990 and 1994 (when GDP scarcely grew on balance), while Labour governments reduced it from 48 to 44 per cent of GDP between 1976 and 1979 (during a cyclical recovery).

If the UK's public expenditure ratio is allowed to return to the sustained expansion which occurred from 1961 to 1976, the ratio of taxation in GDP and in all paypackets and salary cheques would inevitably rise. There would be powerful adverse effects if the UK private sector was again allowed to return to near-zero-sum conditions, where the real net-of-tax pay of the average worker scarcely grew. The need to limit the relative growth of the public sector so that there is room for private-sector net-of-tax incomes to grow at adequate rates must continue to be understood. Otherwise trade-union militancy and endemic strikes could return in both the private and the public sectors, whatever the colour of the government.

A second serious danger would arise if future governments returned to the former practice of acting as employer of last resort in an effort to bring unemployment back to the far lower levels of the 1950s and the 1960s. Tax and public expenditure ratios would then escalate as in Sweden in the 1960s and the 1970s. There have been voices which have begun to suggest that a situation has been reached in the UK where only the state can provide adequate employment for the uneducated and the unskilled. There are vast areas of underprovision to which the state could contribute by harnessing the energies of those who cannot find employment in private industry and commerce. If pay for new public-sector jobs is raised well above present benefit levels to encourage more of the unemployed to move into work, and if central government and local authorities created many more jobs which the unskilled could perform, unemployment could appear to fall, though not for long, as the example of Sweden illustrates.

But to restore the role of the government as employer of last resort, and to allow a disproportionately rapid rate of growth of public expenditure, would involve a return to past policies, and this would resurrect the economic conditions from which Britain suffered in the later 1960s and the 1970s. Some believe that these would not recur if, in the 1990s, renewed growth in the public sector was accompanied by sustained control over inflation through the granting of independence to the Bank of England, and possibly also the adoption of European monetary policies by joining or tracking a single currency if one is adopted. Sweden's macroeconomic policies were entirely conservative until the 1980s and the 1990s, but the channelling of the whole growth of the economy into extra public expenditure nonetheless destabilised the economy through the detailed economic interactions we describe here and those we originally set out in our book of 1976 and 1978, which we now republish.

Many in economics and politics forget previous disasters and the political and intellectual battles which had to be won to re-establish the foundations of a viable economy. Another crisis like those the UK survived in 1976 and 1979 could recur if the combination of policies which destabilized the economy in the 1970s is allowed to re-emerge.

REFERENCES

Arrow, K. J., H. B. Chenery, B. Minhas and R. M. Solow (1961) 'Capital–Labour Substitution and Economic Efficiency', *Review of Economics and Statistics*, 43, August.

Bacon, Robert and Walter Eltis (1975) The 'Declining Britain' articles: 1. 'Where We Went Wrong', 2. 'The Chances We Missed', 3. 'What We Would Do', *The Sunday Times*, 2, 9 and 16 November.

Bacon, Robert and Walter Eltis (1976) *Britain's Economic Problem: Too Few Producers*, 2nd Edition 1978 (London: Macmillan).

Bacon, Robert and Walter Eltis (1979) 'The Measurement of the Growth of the Non-Market Sector and its Influence': A Reply to Hadjimatheou and Skouras', *Economic Journal*, 89, June.

Bacon, Robert (1980) 'The Effects of Public Employment and Other Government Spending on the Rate of Wage Inflation', in *Public Finance and Public Employment*, Proceedings of the 16th Congress of the International Institute of Public Finance, Jerusalem (Detroit: Wayne State University Press).

Blake, Robert (1985) *The Conservative Party from Peel to Thatcher* (London: Fontana Paperbacks).

Brown, George (1975) 'How Near We Came to the Right Answers 10 Years Ago', *The Sunday Times*, 30 November.

Butler, David and Dennis Kavanagh (1980) *The British General Election of 1979* (London: Macmillan).

Ekonomisk Debatt (1976) Symposium on 'Offentlig Expansion – Privat Stagnation', 4, 2. With contributions by Erik Dahmén, Carl Johan Aberg, Karl-Olof Faxén, Erik Lundberg, Assar Lindbeck, Johan Myhrman, Jan Bröms, Rolf Millqvist and Anders Östlind.

Eltis, Walter (1979) 'How Rapid Public Sector Growth can Undermine the Growth of the National Product', in Wilfred Beckerman (ed.), *Slow Growth in Britain: Causes and Consequences* (Oxford: University Press).

Eltis, Walter (1982) 'Do Government Manpower Cuts Correct Deficits when the Economy is in Deep Recession?', *Political Quarterly*, January–March.

Gemmell, Norman (1993) 'Wagner's Law and Musgrave's Hypothesis', in Norman Gemmell (ed.), *The Growth of the Public Sector: Theories and International Evidence* (Aldershot: Edward Elgar).

Healey, Denis (1975) 'The Government Alone Cannot Put Britain Back on its Feet', *The Sunday Times*, 14 December.

Howe, Geoffrey (1975) 'Industrial Growth with a Diminishing Workforce', *The Sunday Times*, 30 November.

Knoester, Anthonie and Nico van der Windt (1987) 'Real Wages and Taxation in Ten OECD Countries', *Oxford Bulletin of Economics and Statistics*, 49, 1.

Lindbeck, Assar (1979) 'Imported and Structural Inflation and Aggregate Demand: The Scandinavian Model Reconstructed', in Assar Lindbeck (ed), *Inflation and Employment in Open Economies* (Amsterdam: North Holland).

OECD (1990) *OECD Employment Outlook* (Paris: OECD).

Sato, R. (1970) 'The Estimation of Biased Technical Progress and the Production Function', *International Economic Review*, 11, June.

Söderström, Hans and Staffan Viotti (1979) 'Money Wage Disturbances and the Endogeneity of the Public Sector in an Open Economy', in Assar Lindbeck (ed.), *Inflation and Employment in Open Economies* (Amsterdam: North Holland).

Wagner, Adolph (1876) *Grundlegung der Politischen Oekonomie*, Leipzig.

1 Where Britain Went Wrong

Those who seek to manage economies or advise on their management are either tinkerers or structuralists. Tinkerers believe that a country's economic ills can be cured by adjusting demand, the exchange rate or the money supply, and by persuading workers to accept periods of wage restraint. Structuralists are concerned with the underlying structure of economies, and believe that tinkering about will not suffice where this is out of line. Treasury civil servants are generally tinkerers, and they usually seek to put things right by adjusting what they actually control. Many politicians are also tinkerers, and indeed in many economies minor adjustments to this and that are all that is needed to produce highly satisfactory results. In these economies – West Germany, Japan and recently France are examples – the underlying structure has been such in the past fifteen years that government control of effective demand, the money supply and the exchange rate were really all that was needed to produce an economic environment where businessmen and workers could co-operate to increase wealth and real incomes at very rapid rates.

There are other economies with an inappropriate underlying structure where tinkering is not enough, and it is becoming increasingly recognised that Britain – like many underdeveloped countries – has an economy with serious structural problems. This is now recognised by a growing number of economists, and politicians ranging from Mr Tony Benn on the left of British politics to Sir Keith Joseph on the right. Mr Benn has drawn attention to the problems raised by Britain's declining industrial base, while Sir Keith Joseph has been concerned about the continuing fall in the proportion of the economy that is allowed to respond to

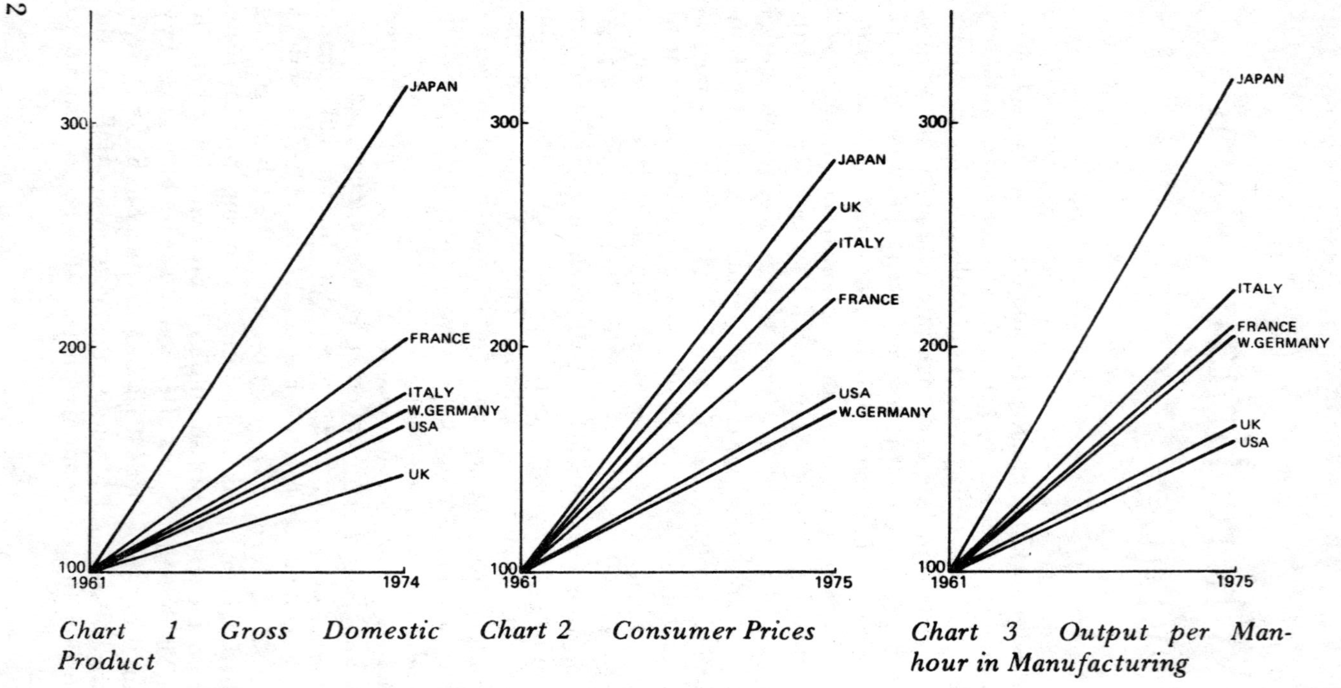

Chart 1 Gross Domestic Product

Chart 2 Consumer Prices

Chart 3 Output per Man-hour in Manufacturing

market forces, and to produce outputs that consumers are actually prepared to pay for. The account of the deterioration in the structure of the British economy which will be given in this book will support those who believe that Britain's industrial base should be strengthened and also those who think that Britain's problems would be easier to solve if a higher fraction of output was marketable. The tinkerers, in contrast, can provide no viable solution. All their remedies, tax reductions, tax increases, devaluations, incomes policies of various kinds, have been tried again and again, and they have failed to arrest the underlying deterioration of the economy that has occurred.

That there has been serious deterioration is only too obvious. Crisis has followed crisis; government packages have become increasingly drastic, and each failure has reduced the reputation of Britain's leading politicians with the people. Charts 1–5 show the well-known evidence that Britain's growth rate has been one of the slowest of any major Western economy since 1961, that Britain's share of investment has been one of the two lowest, that Britain's share of world trade has been falling while others have had rising shares, and that Britain's rate of inflation has been one of the fastest in the Western world.* Some of these trends have a very long history. Britain's share of exports in world markets has been falling fairly continuously since about 1870, and Britain's growth rate has also been low compared to those of the United States and Germany for about a century. That the British economy has performed comparatively poorly for a very long time is well known.

What is less well known is that Britain's economic performance, as measured by the usual statistical yardsticks, has become incredibly worse in the last decade than it was (even by British standards). Industrial production increased 35 per cent in the decade 1955–65, and it increased less than half as much, 17 per cent in 1965–75. This is partly, but only partly, the result of the world recession.[1] As all

* The statistical sources on which the various charts in this book are based, and their derivation, are set out in detail at the end of the book in the order in which the charts appear in the text. The derivation of Charts 1–5 is explained on pp. 208–10.

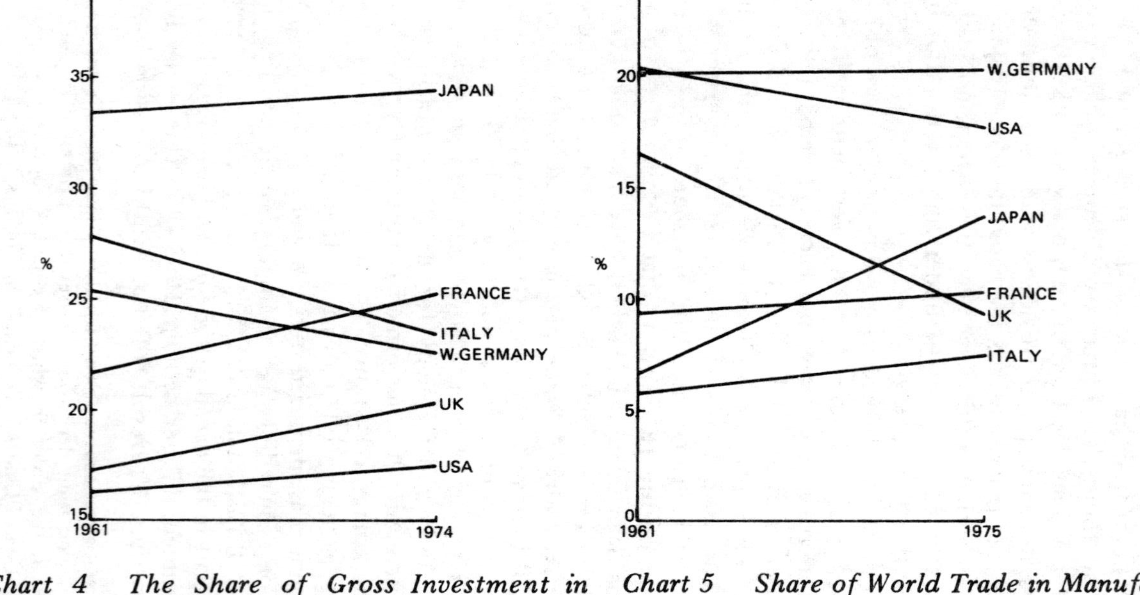

Chart 4 The Share of Gross Investment in GDP

Chart 5 Share of World Trade in Manufactures

manufactured exports, all building of houses and factories, indeed investment of all kinds in the public and private sectors, and all consumption of consumer durables like cars, not to mention clothing and even nowadays quite a lot of packaged food, must come from industry (or foreign industry), the slower growth of industrial production says much about the underlying causes of Britain's problems. Apart from growth, the economic targets are usually considered to be price stability, full employment and balance of payments equilibrium. There was substantial deterioration in each case in 1965–75. Britain's inflation rate averaged 3.1 per cent in 1955–65, and it doubled to over 7 per cent in 1965–74, and it has accelerated fairly steadily in that dreadful decade to 26 per cent in 1974–75. Unemployment was much higher in the second decade than the first. It averaged 1.9 per cent in 1955–65 and 2.7 per cent in 1965–75, and in 1975 it reached 5 per cent. In 1955–65 the pound kept its international value and its exchange rate actually rose as an average of those of France, Italy, West Germany, the USA and Japan. In 1965–75 the pound fell 38 per cent compared to these other currencies. That industrial disputes became increasingly virulent with 2.1 times as many days lost through strikes in 1965–74 as in 1955–65 scarcely needs to be said. Some of this accelerated deterioration in 1965–75 can be put down to the quadrupling in the price of oil at the end of the decade. However, the whole Western World suffered from this and Britain's difficulties have been far more acute, so something other than oil has contributed to Britain's crisis. Indeed no other major economy suffered an equal failure to achieve every economic objective. In 1965 at the beginning of the decade that was to prove so disastrous for Britain, the examination question 'Can economies have simultaneously, zero growth, rapid inflation, substantial unemployment and a balance of payments deficit?' was set in Oxford. Undergraduates answered that this combination of failures was only possible in an underdeveloped country. It has now been achieved in Britain.

It must be emphasised that this has happened, in spite of the fact that every gimmick suggested by the tinkerers has been adopted by successive governments. The great nostrum of the 1960s was devaluation, and successive British governments allowed the exchange rate of sterling to fall more often and more sharply in 1965–75 than ever before. Incomes policies, a second important and improved method of tinkering, were repeatedly used in tougher and tougher forms, and after each attempt the rate of inflation became faster than before. The tax tinkerers persuaded British governments to introduce five radically new taxes, and virtually every new tax that any economist of repute advocated in 1965–75 was actually introduced (if only to be withdrawn and replaced by another). Finally, the tools of demand management were used repeatedly, and in both directions. It must be universally agreed that the tinkerers had an innings in which they enjoyed overwhelming support from successive governments, and that results have never been more disappointing. The case for looking for a structural explanation of the deterioration of the British economy is therefore overwhelming.

The underlying factors that are most commonly blamed for the deplorable situation that has been outlined are either militancy and obstruction to progress by the trade unions, or inadequate industrial productivity. It is a little implausible that trade unions have the power and desire to destroy the British economy when they do nothing of the kind in the successful capitalist economies where communism is actually strong. Those who believe that the trade unions are responsible for Britain's troubles must therefore argue that they are able and willing to disrupt an economy in a society which has, by objective tests, less support for extremists than most others.

What has in fact happened, and this is shown in Chart 6, is that deductions from paypackets grew so much from 1963 to 1975 that the average living standard in terms of what can actually be bought in shops rose only 1.5 per cent per annum – and since 1973 it has actually fallen. The same has been broadly true for workers and salary-earners on average earnings, one-and-one-third times average earnings, and two-thirds of average earnings. Compared to 1963, about 14 per cent more of the paypackets of all three groups is now deducted for income tax and social security contributions to

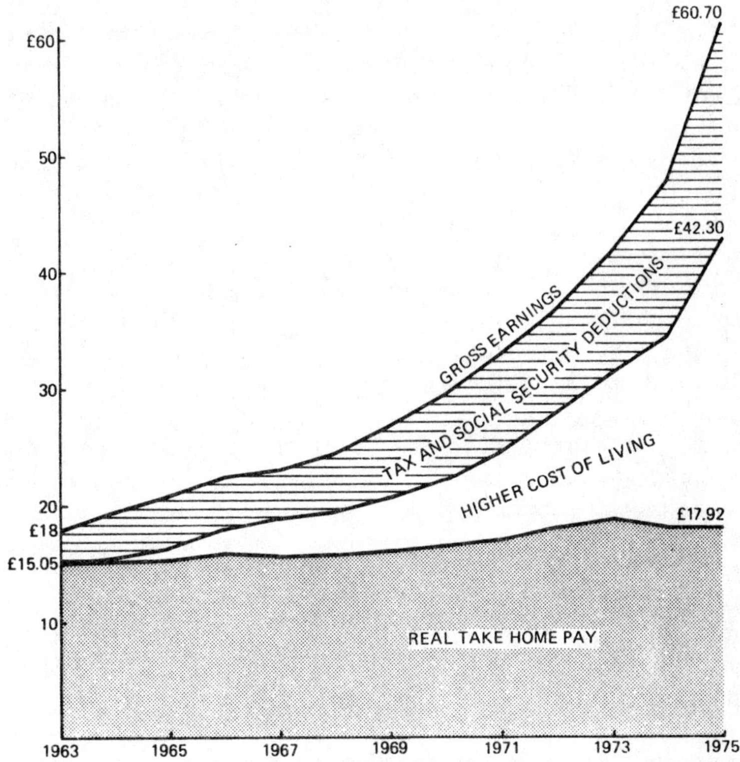

Chart 6 Gross and Net Earnings for the Average Male Worker

pay for the higher 'social wage'. Without this increase in 'deductions' what the average workers' wages could buy would have risen 43 per cent in twelve years instead of the 19 per cent they actually rose.[2] Workers and salary earners with just average earnings now suffer deduction of nearly 30 per cent from their paypackets, which is more than bank managers and university professors had to pay in tax and National Insurance contributions in 1963.

It is often argued that workers and salary earners do not notice higher taxation in their wage negotiations, and that they welcome the higher 'social wage' that greater public spending represents. The 'social wage' does not, however, enter into the money wage bargains that trade unions negotiate, and the period 1963 to 1975 when deductions from paypackets increased so sharply was one when there was growing pressure for higher money wages. Some workers have been better organised than others to achieve high increases in money earnings, and these workers with powerful trade unions have managed to increase their living standards in terms of take-home pay by much of the extra amount needed to compensate for higher taxation.

What has happened since 1963 is that all too often those who sought higher living standards, or the mere continuation of car and home ownership (which have risen in cost far more than prices in general) found that they could only obtain these by making full use of their trade union power, with the result that ordinary workers turned to aggressive union leaders to produce results. That a politically moderate population has chosen to be represented by immoderate trade unions is plausibly explained once it is appreciated that this was in many cases a response to a situation where a rising cost of living and rising taxation made the preservation of living standards increasingly difficult. With a halving of the rate of growth of industrial production, less has been available to raise living standards; so workers have had to progress at the expense of other groups rather than by accepting a roughly constant share of a rapidly growing national product. It is consequently possible to argue that the failure to achieve reasonable growth in living standards in recent years has led to the militant and obstructive trade union activity from which Britain has suffered. Hence this has been a consequence of Britain's great economic failures. It has not caused them, and things started to go wrong long before unions became militant. The underlying cause of Britain's troubles must therefore lie elsewhere.

Britain's lamentable productivity record is often seen as the root of the trouble. Certainly Britain's industrial productivity is low by international standards, and it is still falling in relation to productivity elsewhere. However, the evidence that has been outlined shows that Britain's general economic performance deteriorated sharply when the period 1965–75 is compared with the previous decade. What is not often appreciated is that in contrast industrial productivity increased very much more quickly in the second decade.

Output per man hour in manufacturing industry increased at an annual rate of only 3.0 per cent from 1955–65, but it increased 4.0 per annum from 1965 to 1974. Thus, if productivity is what matters most as many suppose, things should have gone very much better after 1965 than in the previous decade. Efficiency increased more quickly, which should have meant that all Britain's problems were easier to solve. Certainly Britain's growth rate of industrial productivity was still low by international standards after 1965, but it was not all that low. West Germany, France and Italy achieved growth at an average rate of 6.0 per cent against Britain's 4.0 per cent, but Britain's growth rate was still exceedingly high by historical standards, and it could have led to the 'economic miracle' that so many have expected for so long. That productivity rose faster is compatible with the view that many of the industrial policies of successive governments were beginning to produce results. There may have been contributions here from the tougher approach to restrictive practices from the end of the 1950s onwards, which meant that there were fewer price agreements which sheltered the inefficient. There may also have been contributions from the 'little Neddies' set up in the early 1960s which examined the particular productivity problems of a wide range of industries. There was also a great takeover movement in the early 1960s which was often assisted by the government and led to the absorption of a number of small and sometimes inefficient firms by larger and more favoured ones. There were also great increases in the numbers receiving education in virtually all the relevant age groups. Finally, successive governments gave substantial tax assistance to investment, and this must have led to the replacement of much obsolete plant. Our machine tool survey showed that by 1971 the service life and average age of British machine tools were almost exactly the same as in the USA over a very wide range of machine tool categories and user industries.[3] These helpful developments which almost certainly resulted from sensible and beneficial government industrial policies could have set the foundation for an acceleration in Britain's growth rate. This would then have provided the extra resources to satisfy the aspirations of workers for higher material living standards, and at the same time increased the capital stock in both the public and the private sectors, provided a sufficient supply of goods for overseas markets to pay for the country's import requirements, and produced in due course the kind of growth in welfare services that successful economies have achieved. In practice, the great improvement in the rate of growth of industrial productivity for which so many worked intensively in government and industry did none of these things. In the event, and only partly because of the world recession, industrial production increased less than half as fast as productivity, with the result that more than half the benefits from extra productivity resulted, not in the production of more goods but in the employment of fewer men for shorter hours. Higher productivity meant sackings, and a decline in the availability of overtime. This was not true over all industries, but it was true in the great majority.

A 40 per cent increase in productivity in ten years could have allowed the same number of men to produce 40 per cent more in the same number of hours. In the event more than half the potential increase in output was lost because the number of men employed in industry fell 14 per cent and hours of work also fell substantially. It is from this basic fact that the disastrous course the British economy followed in 1965–75 stems, and this was one result of the real structural maladjustment of the British economy that has occurred in these ten years and is still occurring. If Britain manages to cut overmanning in industry, which many regard as the economy's greatest weakness, productivity will advance still more rapidly than in the recent past, and the reduction in overmanning will produce still faster falls in industrial employment and in hours of work.* It must then be

* It is essential to distinguish *overmanning*, the use of too many men to produce a *given level of output* in a particular factory from *underproduction*. With the latter, a given number of men working in a particular factory produce *less output* than they could. The correction of *overmanning* leads to redundancies and the need to absorb surplus workers elsewhere. The correction of *underproduction* increases output and raises the rate of return on capital without any redundancies. It is therefore exactly what the British economy (or indeed any economy) always needs and unlike a reduction of overmanning, it would create no further problems.

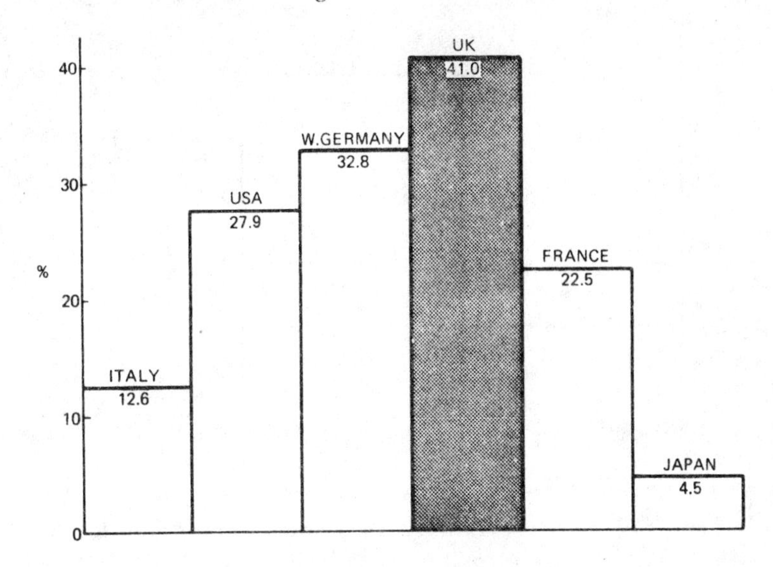

Chart 7 Ratio of Non-industrial to Industrial Employment: Percentage Change, 1961–75 (excluding agriculture)

emphasised that it is not the rate of growth of productivity that has let Britain down. What has let Britain down is that this has been allowed to produce growing numbers of redundancies instead of the increase in employment, and growth in the availability of real resources that should have resulted. It is this basic fact, and the reasons for it, which needs to be explained, and one of the purposes of this book is to show just what went wrong and why.

It is beginning to be appreciated that a very great structural shift in employment has occurred in the British economy since about 1961, and this can be looked at in several ways. Perhaps the most significant is that employment outside industry increased by over 40 per cent relative to employment in industry from 1961 to 1975 and that this increase was most rapid into the public sector. The facts, which are of crucial importance, are set out in Charts 7 and 8. These also show that the shift in employment from industry to services, and public services in particular, had no

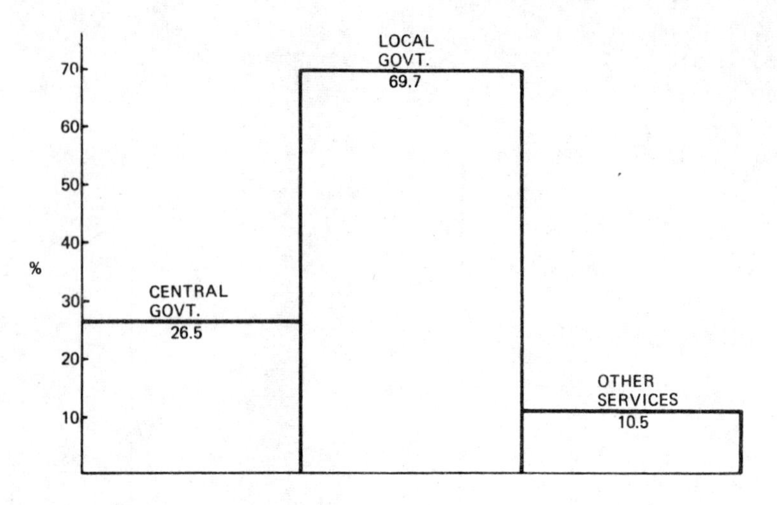

Chart 8 Percentage Change in Service Sector Employment by Category in Great Britain, 1961–75

equal in any other large Western developed economy. Virtually all modern economies gradually shift workers out of industry and into services as industrial efficiency rises, and aspirations grow for better education and welfare services, as well as for the many services provided in the private sector. They do not, however, have 41 per cent shifts in just thirteen years, and cannot without great strain.

In Britain's case the actual strain may not have been quite as great as the crude figures indicate. The employment of women (including many who work only part-time) increased 65 per cent faster in services than in industry, while the employment of men increased only 28 per cent faster. Hence, in so far as men are more important to industry (and women have become a vital part of the labour force in many firms) the strain caused by the structural shift in the labour force was less than the 41 per cent figure would indicate. But even a 28 per cent shift is a very considerable one.

The details of the shift which occurred in Britain are set out in Charts 8 and 9 which show where the extra workers in British service occupations went. It will be seen that employment by local authorities rose 70 per cent, and that

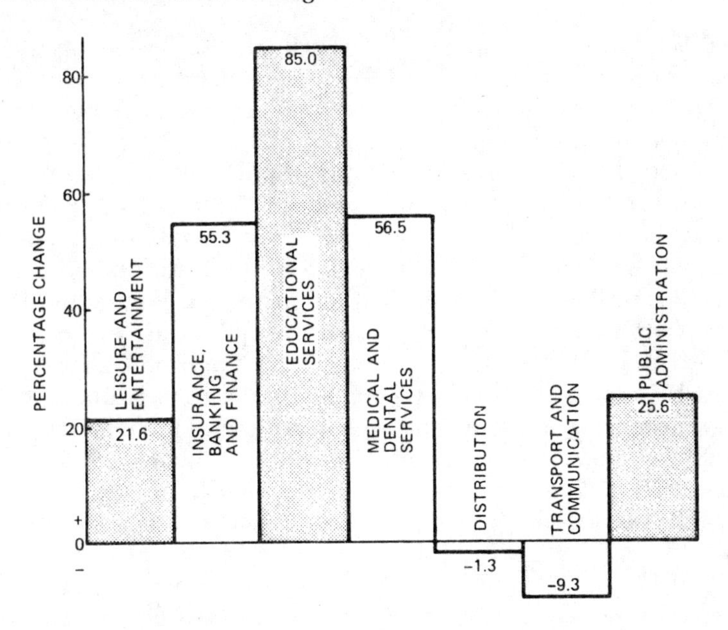

Chart 9 Percentage Increase in Service Sector Employment by Category in Great Britain, 1961–75

central government employment rose 27 per cent. By contrast, in the remaining services like retail distribution, banking, finance, insurance, entertainment, and so on, employment expanded only 11 per cent on average, so the shift from industry has been most rapid into public-employment. The Oxfordshire County Council now employs more workers in Oxfordshire than British Leyland. Within the public sector, employment in education at all levels has risen, and employment in the provision of health and welfare services has risen. All would agree that these are vital to any civilised community, and it is a realisation of this by all political parties that has done so much to bring about these very great structural shifts in the labour force. It must be emphasised that the shift has been as rapid under Conservative as under Labour governments, and employment in education increased more rapidly when Mrs Thatcher was Secretary of State for Education and Science (1970–4) than in 1964–70;

and during the same period, when Sir Keith Joseph was Secretary of State for Social Services, employment in the provision of health and welfare services grew 8.2 per cent faster than employment in general.

There is no reason in terms of population structure why resources should have been moved from industry into education and the various welfare services so extraordinarily quickly in Britain.[4] The proportion of the British population above and below the working age increased from about 35 per cent in 1962 to 37½ per cent in 1973, but it increased more than this in West Germany and Italy, and almost as much in Belgium. The proportion of the population in the age groups that need education was very similar in Britain and the major EEC economies in both 1962 and 1973, but only West Germany increased its number of teachers as rapidly as Britain. The proportion at schools or universities rose from 17 per cent to 20 per cent in Britain between 1964 and 1973, but it rose from 13 per cent to 17 per cent in West Germany in the same period, and from 15 per cent to 18 per cent in Italy. Staff to pupil ratios in primary and secondary education improved 10 per cent in Britain from 1961 to 1971, but they also improved in Italy, West Germany and Japan. This suggests that increases in employment in education need not have differed markedly from those in other countries. Turning to the health services, doctors per head of population rose 20 per cent in Britain from 1961 to 1971, but they rose 27 per cent in West Germany and 29 per cent in France; and only Italy, with a 9 per cent increase, improved this aspect of health services more slowly than Britain. The availability of hospital beds per head of the population actually fell 11 per cent in Britain from 1961 to 1971, and it increased 10 per cent in West Germany and 15 per cent in Italy, falling slightly in France. These figures only describe a small part of the vast range of social indicators, but what they suggest is interesting. There was not apparently a greater improvement in the proportion of the population that was receiving education, or in the availability of doctors or hospital beds than other economies were providing. There may therefore have been a much larger shift of labour into the public sector service occupations taken as a whole to achieve rather similar results. Britain may then have achieved a far slower increase in the real 'outputs' of public services than in the expenditures needed to produce those outputs. This might help to explain why workers apparently failed to take the increase in the 'social wage' much into account in their wage bargaining. Perhaps the social wage did not rise very significantly, measured as an increase in the *output* of social services. It rose enormously, of course, as an increase in *expenditure* on social services, which is how the great spending departments like to measure it.

The increase in employment to provide more public services continued through boom and recession, and until 1975, each increase was permanent; so the workers taken on in recession were not available to industry in subsequent booms. There was, therefore, a kind of ratchet effect, with employment in health and education rising and never falling. One reason why public sector employment could be expanded particularly rapidly was that extra jobs could be provided without an immediate need for extra capital investment. More workers can be fitted into existing offices (though new and expensive town halls and expanded office space follow an increase in civil service numbers after a few years). In industry in contrast a lot of extra workers will be taken on only if there is additional machinery with which they can work, as the high costs of present-day labour can normally be covered (and industry must cover the costs of taking on extra men through extra sales) only if workers have a considerable amount of machinery with which they can operate. The extra workers were therefore drawn into the public sector because all wanted improved social services, and because to increase public sector employment appeared a cheap and socially desirable way of achieving full employment in times of recession. The Departments of Health, Education and the Environment therefore found it easier to persuade the Treasury to approve their expansion plans at such times. The workers, often unskilled ancillary workers who were taken on by the public sector in this way, were inexpensive to employ when decisions were first taken to authorise higher public-sector employment. However, subsequent wage settlements were particularly high in the public sector; Houghton gave very large increases to teachers, administrative grade civil servants have had increases of almost 100 per cent in three years while at the other end of the scale some of the worst paid National Health Service workers have had increases of up to 70 per cent in just one year. There have been other increases which have turned what was originally cheap labour into a major element in the costs of local authorities and the central government, and this has had much to do with subsequent explosive rate and tax increases.

Much research is needed to discover whether the great increase in public-sector service employment that occurred in Britain in 1961–75 produced substantial improvements in public services of a kind that other economies which increased public-sector employment less quickly failed to achieve, or whether the improvements to services were peripheral in comparison to the extra costs involved. Whether the social benefits were minor or substantial, the shift had very great consequences for the rest of the economy, and a strong case can be made out that this very great structural change played a significant role in the deterioration in Britain's economic performance that has been recorded.

The deterioration occurred in the following way. Industrial production must supply the entire investment needs of the nation, and a very high fraction of its consumption; for durable consumer goods like cars, television sets and so on, clothing, and even quite a high proportion of what workers nowadays spend on food, have to be provided by British or foreign industry. In addition to this, a country like Britain that needs to import a high fraction of its food and raw material requirements must export more industrial products than it imports. The various private-sector service industries make a valuable contribution to the balance of payments, but this has never been sufficient, and it is never likely to be to finance the food and raw materials that Britain must buy from overseas, so a large export surplus of industrial production is always likely to be needed.

Now if non-industrial employment grows by 40 per cent in relation to industrial employment, as happened in Britain after 1961, there will be added pressures on industrial

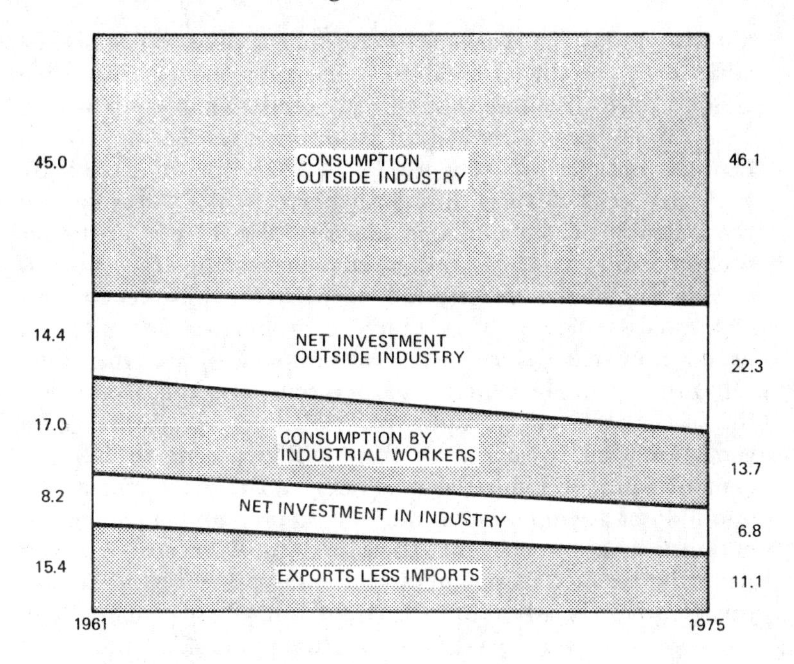

Chart 10 Where Industrial Production Went

production. With more workers employed outside industry, more industrial production will be required for the consumption of those who have played no direct part in producing it. Similarly, more investment outside industry will be needed, and the capital goods will all have to be taken from the output of the industrial sector itself. It must follow that less industrial production will be available for investment and consumption by those who actually produce it or that all the extra goods the non-industrialists require will have to be imported. All these needs can, of course, be met if industrial production can be increased rapidly, but it has already been pointed out that in Britain the rate of growth of industrial production was exceedingly slow. Hence most of the extra goods for the consumption of the vastly larger numbers of teachers, social workers and civil servants, and the extra buildings to house them (which were particularly needed as a result of local government reorganisation), could only be supplied by building fewer factories in industry itself, by allowing industrial workers to consume a smaller fraction of what they produced, and by exporting less or importing more. Chart 10 shows that this is exactly what happened. In 1961 59 per cent of industrial production was consumed and invested outside industry itself. By 1975 non-industry took 68.5 per cent, leaving just 31.5 per cent for industry and the balance of payments in place of the 41 per cent that was available in 1961. Industrial workers therefore had to consume a smaller proportion of what they produced, and what matters crucially is that the proportion of industrial production that was exported (less imports of manufactures) fell from 15½ per cent to 11 per cent; and the proportion that was invested in industry itself, net of capital consumption, fell by one-fifth from 8.2 per cent to 6.8 per cent of sales of industrial production. The great increase in non-industrial employment and the accompanying increase in non-industrial investment therefore took resources away from the balance of payments and industrial investment, and this is precisely what Britain could not afford to cut if the country was ever to escape from the trap of an industrial sector too small to provide all that was required of it. It is also obvious that the reduction in the fraction of industrial output that industrial workers were themselves allowed to consume was only achieved at a cost of the increase in industrial conflict that has been remarked upon as group after group of workers attempted to ensure that it was not they who suffered reductions in living standards to pay for the increased employment in the public services. Chart 6 showed how tax increases greatly slowed down the growth of real living standards of all but those who got sufficient increases in money wages to compensate for higher taxation. But the wage increases that the more militant obtained squeezed profits and industrial workers paid only 2 per cent of the 9 per cent extra that had to go outside industry. Hence most of the non-industrial sector's extra consumption and investment has grown at the expense of net exports and of investment in industry itself, which the government has squeezed by making deflationary periods predominate to an increasing extent in the stop-go cycle.

The squeeze on industrial investment is perhaps the most

serious effect of all, because it influences the whole future development of the economy. Net industrial investment fell, as a fraction of final sales of industrial production, to 3 per cent in 1972, 3½ per cent in 1973, 6.0 per cent in 1974 and 6.8 per cent in 1975 (about half the increase from 1973 to 1975 was investment for North Sea oil) from levels of 8 per cent to 9 per cent in the mid-1960s. This has had two devastating consequences for the economy. First, the reduction in the share of investment has greatly reduced the rate of growth of industrial capacity. Thus, while Britain was investing enough to raise industrial production 3 per cent per annum or 35 per cent in a decade until the mid-1960s the rate of growth of industrial capacity is probably only about two-thirds of this today.[5] This means that when demand is expanded as the economy recovers from depressions as in 1972–3, the plant is just not there to meet the country's requirements for goods. Hence articles which are normally produced in Britain have to be imported and the goods are just not available to exploit export opportunities. With a lower share of net investment this has become true over an increasing range of industrial products. In consequence attempts by governments to move towards full employment produce vast balance of payments deficits, which make continued expansion impossible. A prolonged share of net investment of only 3 per cent to 6 per cent in industry will gradually reduce the rate of growth, with the result that the Treasury's expansion plans which used to be based on growth rates of 2.5 per cent to 3.5 per cent will need to be revised downwards extremely drastically.[6] In addition, the deep problem that declining industrial investment is producing is unemployment which is becoming increasingly structural – the unemployment due to insufficient factories from which underdeveloped countries suffer – and this will undermine the whole fabric of society if the trend is allowed to continue. It has been pointed out that output per man-hour has been rising about 4 per cent per annum in manufacturing industry since 1965. If this continues – and it is likely to – and there is only sufficient capacity to raise industrial production 2 per cent per annum, the number of men that firms employ must fall 2 per cent every year or hours of work must fall 2 per cent each year. In practice these have both been falling sharply in recent years.

The fall in industrial employment in relation to non-industrial employment is what has caused Britain's difficulties, and this trend will continue, making the situation worse each year unless investment recovers to its pre-1965 levels. Indeed, it will need to rise above them if industrial employment is to be maintained. This is because productivity now rises more quickly than it did. Economic progress is a complicated process in which technology advances, new factories are built, and more is produced. Now the faster technology advances, the greater the number of new factories that need to be built. Advances in technology mean that the same goods can be produced by fewer men or that better goods can be produced which make others out-of-date. These advances cause a great many redundancies. The factories which adopt more efficient processes need fewer men to produce old levels of output while the better products (which will come in from abroad if Britain does not manufacture them) cause whole factories to be closed down as their products become obsolete or obsolescent. In a successful economy all the workers who are made redundant by productivity growth and technical advance get jobs producing the new and better goods or jobs that result from expanded production of old goods, but the creation of all these new jobs requires investment; and net investment in industry has fallen by one-quarter in Britain since 1965. *Hence, employment in Britain has suffered from technical progress instead of gaining from it.* The faster technical progress has produced redundancies on a growing scale but new investment has not absorbed the redundant workers. Hence, Britain has not expanded production as fast as this could have been done, and increasing numbers of workers are finding that there is just not enough work. Given this, it is hardly surprising that trade unions obstruct technical progress in so many cases. What is tragic is that all the good work that is being done to raise efficiency in factories and workshops, by the little Neddies and by the Restrictive Practices Court, work which has raised Britain's rate of productivity growth to two-thirds of the West European rate,

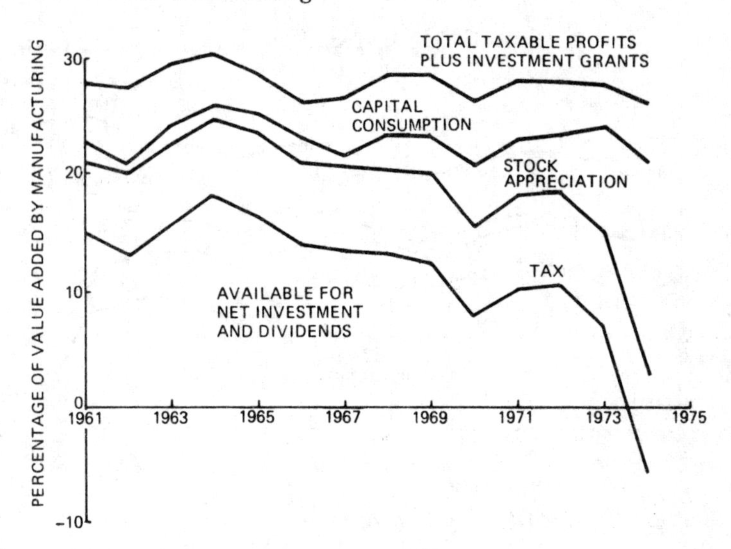

Chart 11.1 Profits of Manufacturing Companies

has reduced job opportunities instead of increasing the rate of growth of output.

How this has come about is obviously one of the most important elements in the collapse of Britain's economic performance. It is something that ought not to happen according to the theories either of Britain's Cambridge economists or of orthodox United States economists; yet it has happened. Cambridge economists, if they accept Lord Kaldor's theory of income distribution, believe that if industrialists raise investment, they will, at the same time, raise the share of profits in the National Income so that the profits from which this higher level of investment can be financed will be automatically forthcoming.[7] It will not matter how much profits are taxed. Industrialists will be able to pass any profits taxes on in higher prices and a mechanism which must raise national saving in line with national investment will ensure that business saving, net of tax, rises in line with investment. Charts 11.1 and 11.2 show how drastically company profits net of tax, capital consumption and stock appreciation have fallen as a share of output since 1964. Chart 11.2 shows that for companies as a whole,

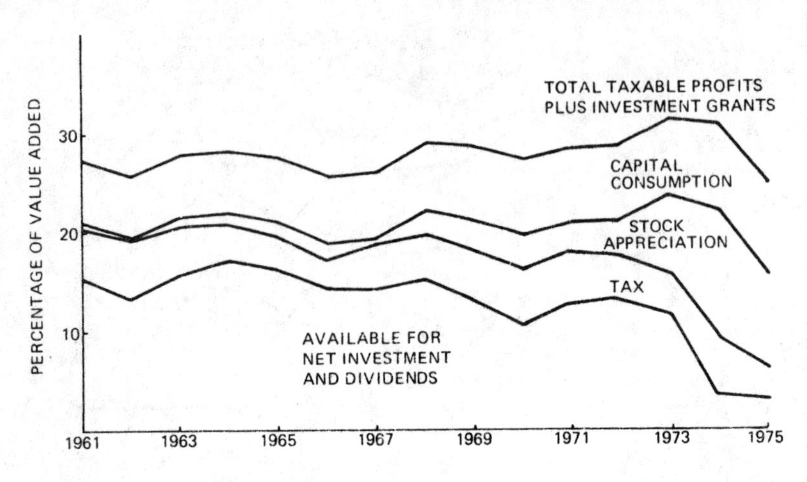

Chart 11.2 Profits of all Companies

profits were 17 per cent of value-added in 1964, 13 per cent or less from 1969 onwards, and only about 3 per cent in 1974 and 1975, out of which companies had to find dividends as well as finance for capital investment. In manufacturing industry alone (Chart 11.1) profits fell still more sharply than for companies as a whole, and this may either be attributable to the stronger international competition which manufacturing companies had to face, or to the greater strength of the trade unions in manufacturing – especially at the shop floor level. Profits were about 1 per cent higher in manufacturing than for companies as a whole in 1964 – 17.9 per cent of value added against 17.1 per cent – but they were 2 per cent lower in 1970, 1971 and 1972, 4 per cent lower in 1973 and 9 per cent lower in 1974 when manufacturing industry actually had a negative sum available for dividends and net investment. Many British industrialists must certainly have wished for enough profit to finance more investment but this extra profit could not be obtained for two reasons. First, governments (and here Mr Heath's government is particularly to blame) have not allowed companies to obtain the kind of profit margins that were needed to finance more investment. Since 1972 prices and incomes policies have forced companies to cut profit margins when they wished to increase them. Second, foreign competition sets an upper limit to profit margins in an economy where imports compete with home production over almost the entire range of output. Devaluations give domestic firms a temporary competitive edge but if devaluations are followed, as they have been, by increased wage inflation this competitive edge is soon lost; so that companies cannot maintain the higher profit margins that devaluation first makes possible. This means in practice that profit margins in Britain have been determined much more by government prices and incomes policies, trade unions and foreign competition than by the saving-investment mechanism that is crucial to the Cambridge theory. Hence, businessmen have not been able to pass higher company taxation on to the consumer through wider profit margins – the opposite has happened. This has meant that companies have just not been able to afford to invest the amount that the country has needed. In addition, the high taxes which have followed higher public spending have made trade unions more militant so that they have not been prepared to see a higher share of the National Income going to profits. Their activity forced the prices and incomes policies like Mr Heath's that so damaged profits, and they prevented companies from benefiting substantially from potentially profitable developments like devaluations and bursts of technical progress.

Orthodox United States economists would not expect companies to be able to get whatever profits they needed to finance investment, but they would expect that any level of investment would be sufficient to provide equipment for all the men who wanted work. With their approach a large reduction of investment should cause capital to be spread more thinly so that new factories were built according to designs which provided more jobs at lower cost. Any number of men could always be fitted into industry if factory designs were wholly flexible and there was equal flexibility with old plant.[8] The difficulty with this approach is that new factories which use much labour and little capital will only be built if labour is cheap and capital is very expensive. In theory structural unemployment should make labour cheap, but this has just not happened in Britain. Employment taxes have risen very steeply; the unions have succeeded in doing still more to raise the cost of labour, so companies have had no inducements at all to build new factories which use more workers than the factories they replace.[9] In consequence the 'impossible' has happened and a major developed economy is suffering from growing structural unemployment that is the result of too little modern industrial plant to provide work for more than a sharply falling fraction of the labour force. Only more industrial investment can arrest this process but the very process itself squeezes industrial profits and investment so that the economy moves into even deeper trouble.

As the unemployment figures rise, extra jobs can only be provided outside industry and only the government can provide jobs where there is no prospect of profits. Hence, governments are tempted to create still more jobs in the public services, and as they raise taxation to pay for them, in due course company profits and workers' living standards are further squeezed with the result that there is still more pressure against company profits in industry. In consequence industry invests still less, more industrial workers become redundant and still more workers need to be fitted into the public sector. This ever-accelerating spiral leads nowhere except to total economic collapse and it is so deep-rooted in structural maladjustment that it is in no way amenable to tinkering.

There is therefore a basic explanation of a structural kind of the underlying deterioration in Britain's economic performance and the succession of crises that have become increasingly severe until they threaten to undermine the repute of orthodox political parties and all that can follow from this. The explanation is that successive governments have allowed large numbers of workers to move out of industry and into various service occupations, where they still consume and invest industrial products and produce none themselves; their needs have, therefore, been met at the expense of the balance of payments, the export surplus of manufactures, and investment in industry itself, so the deterioration in the balance of payments and in Britain's rate of growth can be explained. Once the effect of taking away an increasing proportion of what workers produce is recognised, the great acceleration of wage inflation also becomes readily explicable, and the need for tougher and tougher incomes policies (which other major developed economies have not needed) to attempt to contain inflation. In monetarist terms, the unemployment rate that is compatible with stable prices (produced by a money supply that grows at the same rate as production) has risen drastically – in other words, there has been a great increase in what Professor Milton Friedman calls the *natural* rate of unemployment.[10] An economy that will not accept this exceedingly high *natural* rate of unemployment will have extraordinary inflation or draconian incomes policies instead, like Britain. Hence the whole range of economic options deteriorates sharply and societies in this terrible position must choose between very high unemployment or extra-rapid inflation, which is now undoubtedly the case in Britain, as it is in much of Latin America.

However, this explanation for Britain's decline needs to be refined. In 1776 Adam Smith said:

> The labour of some of the most respectable orders in the society is . . . unproductive of any value, and does not fix or realise itself in any permanent subject, or vendible commodity. . . . The sovereign, for example, with all the officers both of justice and war who serve under him, the whole army and navy, are unproductive labourers. They are the servants of the public and are maintained by a part of the annual produce of the industry of other people. Their service, how honourable, how useful, or how necessary soever, produces nothing for which an equal quantity of service can afterwards be procured.

He was right thus far, but he included in the same class 'men of letters of all kinds . . . opera singers, opera dancers, etc . . .'[11] and it is a mistake to assume that only physical goods represent tradable wealth. It is not only industry that exports. A British opera singer who stars at the New York

Metropolitan Opera and brings home dollars is an exporter. So, more substantially, are the bankers, insurers, shippers and other specialists for whom Britain is famous. Unlike most industrial production, Britain does these things better than a great many competitors. Britain's invisible exports, that is, exports of services, have risen massively since 1967 and there is scope for them to rise much further. The economy's private service industries also sell increasing amounts to workers, for more is spent on leisure activities as incomes grow. Moreover, all industrial production must pass through shops to reach consumers, and it must be transported, and this represents a high fraction of the total cost of turning raw materials into finished goods in the homes of those who want them. It would therefore be a great oversimplification to suppose that industry necessarily makes the predominant contribution to consumption and the balance of payments.

There are, of course, service activities that make virtually no contribution but the same is true of some industrial work. Concorde, for instance, has taken far more resources out of the economy in the form of consumer goods for the workers who make it, and plant and machinery specifically needed for it, than will ever be recovered when it starts to be sold. Other successful firms, and even some in the City of London, have therefore had to give up some of the results of their fruitful activities to make it possible for the workers who make Concorde to continue to produce something that will hardly sell enough to recover more than a small fraction of its costs. The fact that it is industrial does not mean that it relieves pressures on the remainder of the economy; it has created them instead.

This means that an argument like Mr Tony Benn's, based solely on the need to have adequate resources in industry, is incomplete; it leaves open the possibility that a government could apparently correct the imbalances of the economy by curtailing services that are essential to its functioning and substitute industrial products that people will only buy if there is no alternative. With sufficient errors by the government and the civil service, a crude pro-industry policy which increased the output of the wrong products at the expense of services that sold heavily overseas could make the balance of payments still worse (for it is British and not foreign airlines that are losing money with Concorde), curtail investments still further, and leave yet greater shortages of the goods that workers actually want. It is unlikely that an interventionist government working to expand industry on Bennish lines would do as much damage as this, but it could conceivably do so (particularly when the appalling record of mismanagement of civil service interventions in the aircraft industry is examined). This means that a crude pro-industry and anti-service approach to the deterioration of Britain's economic structure is not enough.

There is, fortunately, an alternative approach which gets round these difficulties and this has been outlined in a most interesting article on inflation by Professor J. Johnston of the University of Manchester.[12] Instead of dividing economic activities into those that are *industrial* and those that are *non-industrial* they can be divided instead between those that produce *marketed* outputs and those which do not. Almost everything that industry produces is *marketed*, that is, it is sold to someone. The private-sector services are sold, so they are *marketed*. Defence, on the other hand, is not marketed; no one now pays for the use of a regiment or frigate. What the National Health Service provides, and most schools, is also not marketed, and the services provided by policemen and civil servants are not marketed; so they must spend their incomes on the marketed products of the rest of the community.

These cases are clear-cut but others are less so; thus, the Post Office only markets a fraction of its output because it makes substantial losses. If sales revenue covered only half its total costs one could say that half its output was marketed, like that of an industrial company, while the other half would correspond to the non-marketed output of a civil service department. Concorde will cost Britain over £1000 millions but it will probably produce marketed outputs of only £100 millions, so its effect on the economy will resemble those that would be produced by a second University of Bristol located at Filton (with more money to spend than ten ordinary universities). In short, industrial production is only marketed in so far as it is sold, so all subsidies to any firm whatsoever must be subtracted from industrial production to show what industry's marketed output is. At the same time all the services that are sold contribute to the economy's total of marketed output, which is a total that matters a great deal.

All exports are marketed, so the economy's entire exports of goods and services must be drawn from the economy's total pool of marketed output. All investment is marketed so this must also come from the economy's total marketed output. Finally, all the money that workers, salary earners and pensioners spend must necessarily go to buy marketed output. *Hence the marketed output of industry and services taken together must supply the total private consumption, investment and export needs of the whole nation.*

A difficulty Britain has suffered from since 1961 is that the proportion of the nation's labour force that has been producing marketed output has been falling year by year; at the same time those who have had to rely on others to produce marketed output for them, civil servants, social workers and most teachers and medical workers, have become increasingly numerous, and they have had to satisfy their requirements by consuming goods and services that diminishing numbers of market-sector workers are producing. In addition, loss-making firms in the public and private sectors have been taking more out of the economy's pool of marketed output than they have been putting into it. Finally, pensioners and all those who receive money from the government are entitled to consume marketed output and produce none. Chart 12 shows that in 1961 the entitlement to buy marketed output by those who did not produce it directly was 41½ per cent (before tax). By 1975 the entitlement of those who did not produce marketed output had risen to 62 per cent, so on a pre-tax basis 20½ per cent less remained for those who actually produced the economy's entire marketed output. Their own consumption needs and the export requirements of the whole economy and resources for investment in the market-sector of the economy had to come almost entirely from what was left after the non-market sector had taken 20½ per cent more before tax. Put in these terms the argument is clear-cut.

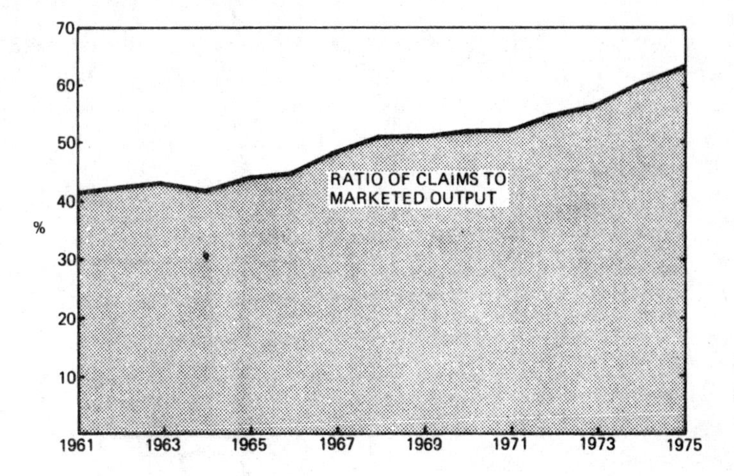

Chart 12 Pre-tax Government Claims on Marketed Output

If the entitlement to consume marketed output by people who do not produce it directly rises, and it rose from 41½ per cent to 62 per cent (before tax) in fourteen years in Britain, those who produce it may agree and think it right that they should consume less of what they produce. If taxes are raised heavily to pay for more civil servants, teachers and social workers in these circumstances, and everyone acquieseces in the higher taxation that is needed, workers will simply get a higher 'social wage' and less to spend in the shops; and all will be well. If, however, they do not acquiesce in what is happening they will try to make up for the marketed output they are losing as a result of higher taxation with higher wage demands, and these can lead to explosive wage inflation.[13] If militant workers preserve their living standards in terms of marketed output in this way the government will only be able to get its extra marketed output at the expense of investment or the balance of payments, for there is nowhere else it can come from. In Britain the growth of non-market expenditure as a ratio of marketed output from 41½ per cent to 62 per cent (before tax) has had all these effects, explosive wage inflation, a squeeze on investment in the market sector and balance of payments deterioration. This is the same argument as before but it can now be

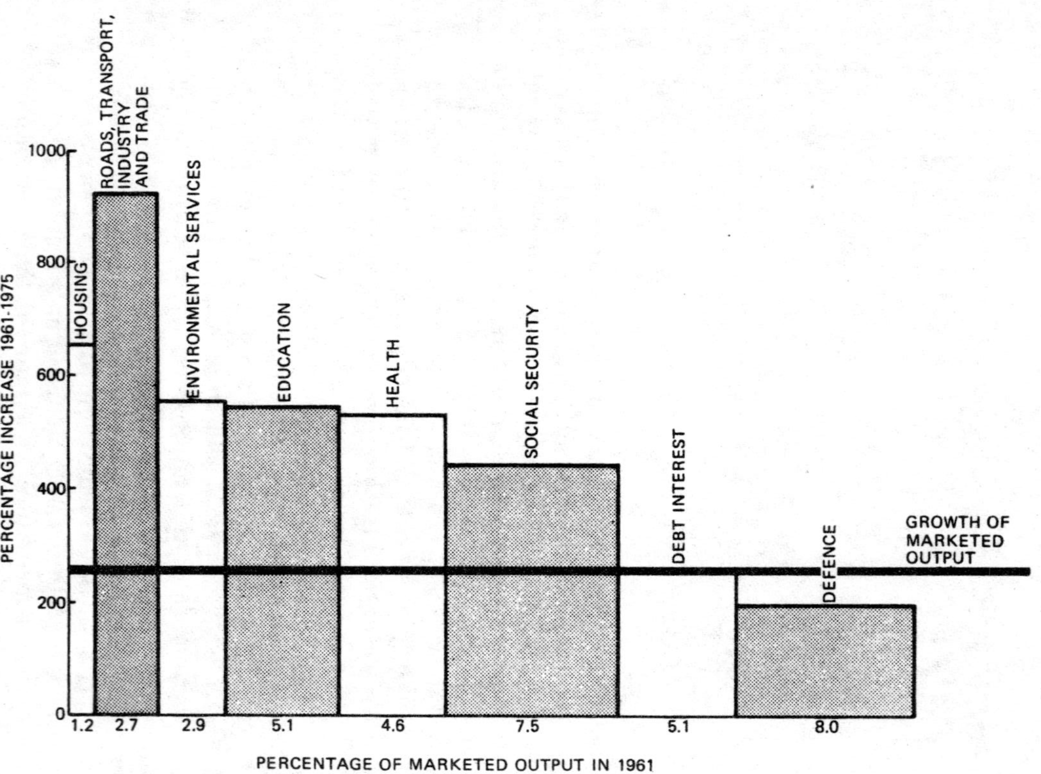

DEFENCE, THE BIGGEST SPENDER IN 1961 WITH 8% OF MARKETED OUTPUT, GREW LEAST. ROADS, ETC., AND HOUSING GREW MOST

presented without qualifications of any kind. *All* exports and everything on which money is spent must be produced by an economy's market sector. With the industry/services distinction, in contrast, industry provided *most* consumption needs and *most* exports, but not all of them; so a crude pro-industry and anti-services policy could conceivably go wrong.

It must be emphasised that the distinction between the market and non-market sectors of the economy is not the same as the distinction between the public and private sectors. A profit-making nationalised industry is in the public sector but its entire output is marketed. Council houses, if they are let at rents which cover all costs, also provide much-desired marketed output. It is only in so far as nationalised industries make losses and houses are let at rents which fail to cover costs that they are part of the non-market sector which has to draw on the market sector for its consumption and investment requirements. In reality much of nationalised industry makes a loss, and council house rents cover only a fraction of costs, so perhaps half the amount spent on them is non-market expenditure. Chart 13 shows exactly where the great increase in non-market expenditure in Britain has gone, and it shows that education, health, subsidies to industry, both private and nationalised, subsidies to housing and entitlements to buy marketed output by the old, the sick and the unemployed, have all grown sharply. These are all immensely desirable activities which most support, but they can still have adverse effects if a society will not acquiesce in a diversion of private consumption in these socially beneficial directions.

It must be emphasised that almost all the civilised activities of a modern society are wholly or largely non-marketed. Both Covent Garden and Glyndebourne cover only a fraction of their costs by selling tickets, and universities, schools, art galleries, libraries and hospitals produce outputs which are almost entirely non-marketed. Defence is also non-marketed so, in times of war, countries perforce vastly increase the non-market sector of their economies. It can almost be said that a country with a larger non-market sector than another similar country will be either militarily stronger or more civilised, but it must be able to afford to maintain its large non-market sector. If its people are prepared to give up marketed output to the government on the necessary scale it will manage this, and in all economies that manage successful transitions from peacetime to wartime conditions, people pay the taxes the government requires without causing hyper-inflation or diverting goods from investment, military production and the balance of payments; but if it is peacetime and people are not prepared to part with as much of their marketed output as the government wants the three great difficulties from which Britain suffers must occur in some combination or other. Wages and prices will be pushed up sharply; investment in the market sector will be curtailed; or the balance of payments will deteriorate.

There are two clear ways out of this difficulty and these will be the subject of Chapter 3. First, the market sector of the economy can be made larger compared to the non-market sector by cutting public spending and nationalised industry losses and subsidies. That is the solution that some members of the Labour party and government started to favour in 1975, and it is also the solution of the new leadership of the British Conservative party. As Mrs Thatcher said on 15 September 1975:

> The private sector creates the goods and services we need both to export to pay for our imports and the revenue to finance public services. So one must not overload it. Every man switched away from industry and into government will reduce the productive sector and increase the burden on it at the same time.

Alternatively, all the powers of government can be used to achieve a viable industry-based economy with a large non-market sector by financing this at the expense of private services and the better off. That is inherently the solution of the British Left, and in a still more extreme form it is the solution of the Peoples' Democracies of Eastern Europe. A Left solution along these lines is however perfectly compatible with social democracy. None of the large Western economies which are usually compared with Britain has had a shift into public services as great as Britain's, but the shift in three Scandinavian economies Sweden, Norway and Denmark, has been even faster, and these countries have only recently started to suffer from difficulties like Britain's. There are therefore examples of a viable social democratic solution involving high public expenditure which Britain has not yet found and others found for a time. There is therefore more than one viable democratic solution, and more will be said about these in Chapter 3. Before this something must be said about Britain's past, for to understand fully where one is one must first see how one got there. Britain's experience in the various attempts that were made to put things right by Mr Maudling, Mr George Brown, Mr Jenkins and Mr Barber will be set out in the next chapter. Much can be learned from their interesting and important initiatives.

NOTES

1. See n.5 below where it is argued that the rate of growth of *productive capacity* in industry fell from 3.3 per cent per annum in 1955–65 to about 2.5 per cent in 1965–73 and perhaps 2.0 per cent since then.
2. Income tax and social security contributions are actually deducted from most workers' paypackets by their employers, and Chart 6 shows the effects of this for the average worker. Many workers also pay local authority rates, and Table 6.1 (row (8)) on pp. 212–13 shows what remains after they too are deducted.
3. Bacon and Eltis, *The Age of US and UK Machinery*.
4. The evidence cited in this paragraph is derived from official EEC statistics. It is to be found in, for instance, various issues of *Basic Statistics of the Community*.
5. The rate of growth of productive capacity can be estimated by calculating the rate of growth of output between similar points in the cycle. Thus, industrial production increased 35 per cent between the cyclical peaks of 1955 (fourth quarter) and 1965 (first quarter) or at 3.3 per cent per annum. Capacity also grew at this rate if both booms peaked when there were similar margins of slack in the economy. Industrial production increased 22 per cent from 1965 (first quarter) to the cyclical peak of 1973 (first quarter), or at only 2.5 per cent per annum; and investment has been so much less since 1973 than in 1965 to 73 as a whole that the rate of growth of productive capacity is now almost certainly less than 2.5 per cent per annum, – probably as little as 2.0 per cent.
6. See David Smith, 'Public Consumption and Economic Performance', *National Westminster Bank Quarterly Review*, November 1975.

7. See N. Kaldor, 'Alternative theories of distribution', *Review of Economic Studies*, vol. XXIII (1955–6).
8. The first detailed exposition of the modern neo-classical theory of growth, where structural unemployment cannot occur, is by R. M. Solow, of MIT ('A contribution to the theory of economic growth', *Quarterly Journal of Economics*, vol. LXX, February 1956).
9. There is indeed evidence that the capital-output ratio has been rising in Britain. It certainly cost more capital investment to achieve each one per cent of growth in 1965–75 than in 1955–65 (i.e. the Incremental Capital Output Ratio or ICOR was higher in 1965–75). Britain's ICOR has also been the highest of any major developed economy. Those who regard a high ICOR as a low rate of return on investment see this as the result of British managerial weaknesses. It is also compatible with a bias towards labour-saving investment, due to high wages and employment taxes and low profitability.
10. See M. Friedman, 'The role of monetary policy', *American Economic Review*, vol. LVIII, March 1968.
11. Adam Smith, *An Inquiry into the Nature and Causes of the Wealth of Nations* (1776) II 3.
12. J. Johnston, 'A macro-model of inflation', *Economic Journal*, vol. 85, June 1975.
13. This propostion has been tested by J. Johnston and M. Timbrell ('Empirical tests of a bargaining theory of wage rate determination', *The Manchester School of Economics and Social Studies*, 41 June 1973). Cf. also, Dudley Jackson, H. A. Turner and Frank Wilkinson, *Do Trade Unions Cause Inflation?*, Cambridge University Press, 1972, Chapter 3, and S. G. B. Henry, M. C. Sawyer and P. Smith, 'Models of Inflation in the United Kingdom: An Evaluation', N.I.E.R., 1976.

2 The Lost Opportunities

An outstanding fact that emerged from Chapter 1 is that Britain could have achieved almost everything for which the most optimistic hoped. The really crucial obstacle to rapid growth in any economy is slow productivity growth. If productivity advances only 2 per cent a year and a country's labour force is fixed, no power on earth can produce long-term growth at more than 2 per cent a year. If more workers are unavailable the rate at which existing workers raise their output each year, in this case 2 per cent, sets the upper limit to growth. Now in Britain from 1962 onwards output per man-hour in manufacturing industry started to advance at an annual rate of 4.2 per cent in place of the mere 2.2 per cent per annum achieved from 1951 to 1962. The first published forecasts of the *National Economic Development Council*, Britain's first planning body, were influenced by evidence that technical progress was accelerating[1] but few appreciated that in industry it would actually all but double from 1962 onwards. If this greatly increased potential had been turned into faster actual growth, as it could and should have been, Britain would have had about one-and-a-half times as much growth from 1962 onwards as it achieved up to then. The higher growth rate in Mr George Brown's *National Plan* of 1965,[2] 3.8 per cent per annum, required almost exactly the rate of growth of labour productivity in industry, 4.1 per cent per annum, that was actually achieved throughout the period 1962–75. This was the aspect of *The National Plan* about which there was most scepticism, and there need not have been. So far as productivity was concerned, and this is the crucial factor that determines the potential growth rate of an economy, Mr George Brown's plan was spot on.

It was explained in Chapter 1 that this greatly improved potential for growth after 1962 was thrown away. Industrial production was allowed to increase at rates which averaged

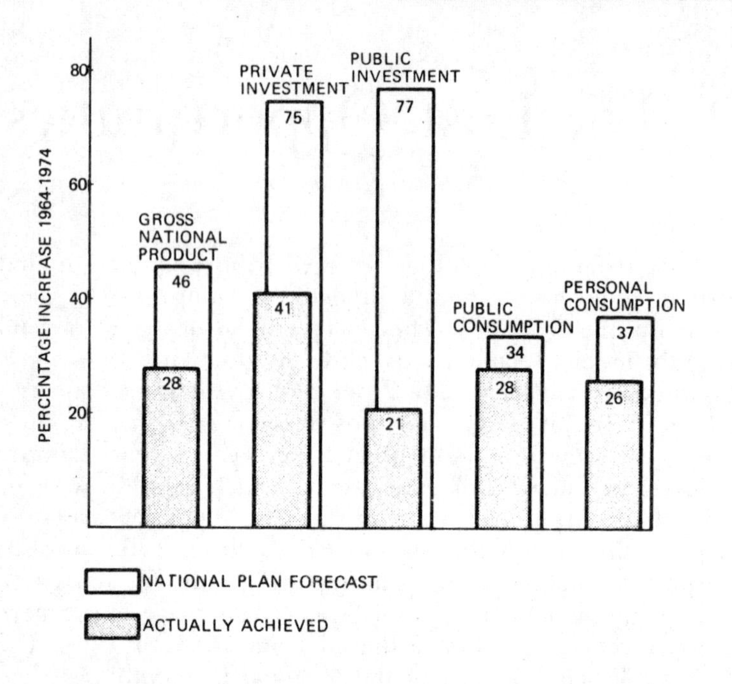

Chart 14 The National Plan and What Actually Happened

only 1.7 per cent per annum from 1965 to 1975 and this slow rate is only partly attributable to the world recession, which only began to influence output in 1974. The result has been that the 4.2 per cent growth rate in productivity produced growing redundancies and falling hours of work instead of the vast increase in capital in the public and private sectors, increased personal consumption of 25 per cent in six years and the *improved public services* that the plan promised. Chart 14 shows what would have been achieved if the annual growth targets of the Plan had been met from 1964 to 1974, as they largely could have been, and in contrast what was actually achieved. It shows that consumption and investment increased very much less than they might have done. This means that if the National Plan's target growth rates had been achieved after 1964, Britain could today have immensely more industrial production, more non-industrial production, more marketed output and more non-marketed output. It does not matter whether the economy is divided into industrial and non-industrial or market and non-market sectors – which, it was argued in the last chapter, is a distinction that goes deeper. With much more growth of both investment and consumption Britain could today have more of everything that our present society considers important. Ironically, the diversion of Britain's resources from investment and exports to social spending after 1964 has not even resulted in a faster increase in social spending. The National Plan projections in Chart 14 show how much greater public sector consumption could have been by 1974 if its expansion had been a consequence of, instead of a rival to economic growth.

In 1962–4 the Conservative Government then in power also took planning initiatives with a very similar growth target to Mr George Brown's, and what it hoped for could also have been achieved. The story of how these opportunities were thrown away is a very sad one, and in this chapter an account will be given of the various attempts that were successively made to exploit Britain's new potential for growth, and how they came to grief. The most interesting of the new initiatives were those of Mr Reginald Maudling in 1962–4, Mr George Brown in 1964–6, Mr Roy Jenkins in 1967–70 and Mr Anthony Barber in 1970–4. In this chapter their successive attempts to improve the functioning of the economy and solve Britain's fundamental economic problems will be set out together with the reasons why they failed, leaving the economy in the end in a far worse position. Before the important initiatives and the reasons for their failure are examined in detail, something must be said in general terms, making use of the argument of the previous chapter, about what needed to be done.

Britain had the opportunity from 1962 onwards almost to double the rate of growth of manufacturing production and therefore greatly to increase the extra resources available for capital investment, the balance of payments and consumer needs. However, this opportunity could only be seized if there was a greatly increased rate of capital investment in industry, which forms the predominant fraction of the market sector of the economy. The doubled rate of productivity growth after 1962 meant that in no-growth years industry had about twice as many redundancies as before. To absorb these redundant workers and turn 4.2 per cent productivity growth into 4.2 per cent real growth would have required almost twice as much *net* investment in new factory building in industry, etc., as before. It is in fact reasonable to suppose that faster output growth (when supported by productivity growth) is associated with economies in the use of capital,[3] so Britain's higher potential rate of growth of industrial production resulting from the doubling of the rate of productivity growth could have been realised with an increase in net investment (as a ratio of sales of industrial production) from 7.2 per cent in 1962 to perhaps 12 per cent. This meant that something like 5 per cent of industrial production had to be diverted from other uses to investment in industry. Now this extra 5 per cent of industrial production had to come from somewhere.

There was excess capacity in industry in 1962, probably of up to 10 per cent. If half of this 10 per cent had been diverted to industrial investment Britain's investment share could have risen to what was needed, and the most optimistic growth targets could have been quite easily achieved from that point onwards. Alternatively, the resources needed for this extra investment of 5 per cent of industrial production could have come from overseas. With a sufficient balance of payments deficit the extra investment needed to increase the economy's industrial base twice as fast as before could have been imported or diverted from exports. Once Britain's industrial base and domestic capital goods output were in line with the new opportunities for faster growth, the balance of payments could have been restored. A further way of finding the extra 5 per cent of industrial production would have been to divert this from consumption. Here workers needed to forgo an extra 5 per cent of industrial production over perhaps a five-year period in which the share of net industrial investment was almost doubled. In each of these years workers' consumption in terms of industrial products needed to grow at 1.2 per cent instead of at 2.2 per cent per annum. At the end of the transition period, as Chart 15

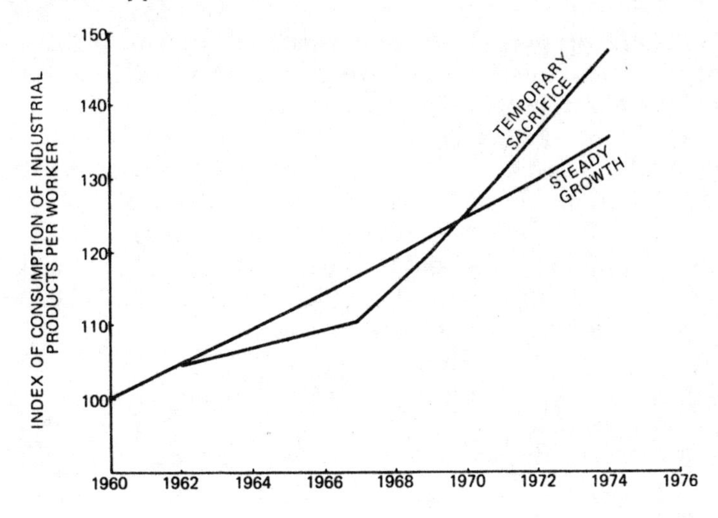

Chart 15 Sacrifice of Consumption for Growth

which illustrates a hypothetical new growth path shows, consumption per head could have risen 2 per cent faster than before at 4.2 per cent instead of 2.2 per cent per annum, with the result that workers could have overtaken the level they would otherwise have reached after a further three years. The chart shows how, if 5 per cent of industrial production had been diverted from consumption to industrial investment in 1962 to 1967, living standards could have started to rise exceptionally rapidly from 1967 onwards and reach higher levels from 1970 onwards. The fall in consumption could have been confined to private consumption, or to consumption in the public sector; but if public-sector consumption had to be exempted from any cuts, private consumption would have had to fall much more in the transition period and therefore taken longer to recover, making the switch of resources more difficult to achieve. Finally, 5 per cent of industrial production could have been diverted from non-industrial to industrial investment from 1962 onwards, which would have allowed the industrial capital stock to grow at the necessary rate. With faster growth of industrial production, non-industrial investment could then have been restored to its previous level after a few years and risen above it, like workers' consumption.

It is crucial to realise that to raise Britain's growth rate industrial investment had to rise substantially and that this required that something else be sacrificed for a time – the balance of payments, consumption by industrial workers, consumption by the public sector, or investment outside industry. One of these had to give way for a few years unless a particularly clever transition where the economy's spare capacity was used to provide the extra resources with no one paying for them could be organised; but the Treasury never came anywhere near to organising a Keynesian export and industrial investment-led boom of this kind. Nor indeed did it attempt to do this.[4] In the event, none of the temporary sacrifices that were required were made for long enough, and investment and consumption outside industry were increased so rapidly that they took growing resources away from industry with the result that the amount of sacrifice required from the remainder of the economy became quite unattainable. A failure to divert adequate resources to industrial investment because the remaining pressures on output were always too great to make this possible is, therefore, in outline what went wrong, and this will now be shown as the successive initiatives of Mr Maudling, Mr Brown, Mr Jenkins and Mr Barber are examined in detail.

MR MAUDLING'S BOOM

The foundations for a new attempt to solve Britain's economic problems were laid in 1962 when Mr Selwyn Lloyd set up the National Economic Development Office and Council with Sir Robert Shone as its first Director General. This performed the necessary groundwork for Britain's first attempt at indicative planning. The Office and the Council brought together industrialists, trade unionists, civil servants and academic economists to work out a practicable programme for growth. Documents were published which set out the evidence on how rapidly Britain's productive potential could be raised by making detailed enquiries involving a close study of seventeen of the most important industries. It was concluded that growth at an annual rate of 4 per cent was practicable, and it was decided that attempts should be made to achieve it. It fell to Mr Reginald Maudling, who became Chancellor in succession to Mr Selwyn Lloyd in 1962, to achieve 4 per cent growth, and the Maudling boom was set off in the autumn of 1962. Industrial production then was no higher than it had been in the first quarter of 1960 for there had been no growth at all for three years. This meant that there was considerable spare capacity in the economy. Net investment had continued since 1960 and the capacity it provided had not been used. Mr Maudling, as Chancellor, had the opportunity of picking up this slack and getting up to 10 per cent extra output by merely raising demand. The plant was there, the men were there, unemployment was 612,000 and there were only 197,000 vacancies in 1963; and all that was needed for substantially higher production was extra demand.

Mr Maudling created this in the first instance by increasing investment in the public sector at a most extraordinary rate. This was actually increased 25 per cent in fifteen months in real terms from the fourth quarter of 1962, so it increased at the quite exceptional annual rate of 20 per cent. This great boost to public investment sufficed to set the economy on a very rapid expansion path. Public investment was increased in every direction, and this created extra jobs for workers on the projects in question, and it increased orders to the private sector which supplied some of the plant and machinery. In addition, the workers on the projects had more money to spend in the shops. Mr Maudling took other important steps to raise demand, and he cut income tax substantially in his 1963 budget. Purchase tax rates on cars and other durable consumer goods had been almost halved in October 1962, and a consumer boom superimposed on a public investment boom sent growth beyond what the economy could be expected to achieve in the long run. In the event more cars and commercial vehicles were produced and sold in 1964, 2,332,000, than in any year since then.

There was a futher underlying trend in the economy of which many were unaware. The Neddy planning document *The Growth of the Economy*, which was published in March

1964, envisaged that from 1961 onwards industrial employment would rise at an annual rate of about 0.5 per cent and non-industrial employment at an annual rate of about 1.0 per cent, comparative growth rates which were very much in line with what happens in the long term as advanced economies develop and gradually shift workers from industry to services. Here Neddy envisaged a relative shift in favour of services of perhaps 5 per cent in a decade. But non-industrial employment actually increased 5.7 per cent (instead of 1.5 per cent) in relation to industrial employment from 1961 to 1964, so it increased 4.2 per cent or by about 450,000 workers more than the initial Neddy calculations indicated. Of the increase, 140,000 was in education, 84,000 was in medical and dental services and 45,000 was in central and local government administration, so employment in these three categories increased 269,000, or 8½ per cent in just three years. This was a small foretaste of what was to come. There must be pressure on total resources in a plan if it is assumed that particular categories of employment should increase 1 per cent per annum and they then actually increase nearly 3 per cent per annum. This leaves less labour for the rest of the economy whenever it is at full employment. The public sector pre-empts much of the available labour at the start of the boom so less is available for industry as its demands grow. Then full employment is reached sooner and growth slows down. This was to happen again and again whenever the economy was expanded in the next decade.

With this background the story of Mr Maudling's boom can move towards its climax. Nothing has been said yet about industrial investment, the linch-pin in any attempt to set the economy on a new growth path, and that is because it only started to expand very late in the boom. Industrial investment was only 1 per cent higher in 1963 than in 1962, but in 1964 it was 14 per cent higher than in 1963, and it rose a further 6.5 per cent between 1964 and 1965. The greatest increase in industrial investment therefore took place in 1964, the year in which car output reached a historical peak that has never been repeated. Manufacturing investment, the major component of industrial investment, expanded only 4 per cent in the first year of the boom and 25 per cent in the following two years. There was thus considerable lagging of industrial investment behind everything else. Public investment started to grow a year earlier, and consumption and public-sector employment also started to grow earlier.

The reasons for the late expansion of industrial investment are among the most crucial in any account of the British economy since 1961. Industrialists have generally been prepared to increase investment in new plant only when new orders that they could not meet with existing plant were actually coming in. Mr Selwyn Lloyd and Mr Maudling increased investment incentives substantially long before 1964, but it was in this expansion year that industrial investment suddenly surged upwards. This pattern of late expansion of industrial investment was to recur again and again, which is why it mattered so crucially that booms should not end too soon because most of the available labour had been pre-empted by the public sector.

Because of the late expansion of industrial investment it was only from 1964 onwards that Mr Maudling's boom could begin to make a contribution to the solution of Britain's long-term problems, but the boom was by then approaching capacity limits. The reasons for this are several. The first is that the pool of unemployment was rapidly diminishing, assisted by the rapid growth of public-sector employment. By 1964 unemployment was down to 414,000, and much of this was in the Celtic fringe, while vacancies were up to 319,000, so much of the unemployed labour had been absorbed and it was mainly absorbed outside industry. Moreover, by the second quarter of 1964 industrial production was 13 per cent above the level at the start of the boom so all the spare capacity in the economy had been absorbed. From that point onwards capacity had actually to be created through new investment, and investment in industry only started to increase in 1964. In 1964 therefore, at this crucial moment when industrial investment started to move to a new and higher bracket, the economy was quite fully stretched because public investment had already advanced 25 per cent, consumption was booming because taxes had been slashed, and public sector employment was rising rapidly.

In this situation only one thing could happen. Demand was

rising far faster than the domestic capacity to produce and every component of demand was rising fast. The goods needed to meet all these pressures could only come from abroad because there was no chance of meeting all these demands domestically. Imports of manufactured goods increased £126 million from 1962 to 1963, but they increased £453 million from 1963 to 1964. Other components of imports, particularly basic materials, increased too, with the result that total imports were £643 million higher in 1964 than in 1963. Exports only rose £200 million, so the trade gap widened by about £450 million.

Britain's overall current account deficit in 1964 was about £400 million but the gold and foreign exchange reserves were only £949 million in 1963, so a deficit of this order of magnitude appeared to matter, puny though it was by 1976 standards. If Mr Maudling had remained Chancellor he would have attempted to ignore the deficit and continue to expand, albeit at slower rates. Mr Maudling's 1964 budget was already mildly deflationary. Each year of expansion (with demand in excess of capacity over much of industry) would have persuaded industrialists to raise investment further, and a near to doubling of net investment might have been achieved by 1968 or 1969, but the balance of payments might well have remained in deficit until then. This deficit would have had to be financed through borrowing, which would have been possible, as is demonstrated by the fact that Mr Wilson's government incurred short-term foreign debts of over £3000 million by 1967. Mr Maudling could have borrowed £3000 million if Mr Wilson could, and it would have more than financed the rest of the boom.

In so far as raising industrial investment was part of Mr Maudling's strategy, this had to be achieved at the expense of the balance of payments. Certainly none of the other possible strategies that were outlined were adopted. There was no attempt to raise industrial investment by making use of the slack in the economy that there undoubtedly was in 1962 because industrial investment only started to rise when this slack had already been absorbed. There was no attempt to raise industrial investment relative to consumption, because Mr Maudling increased every element of consumption, public

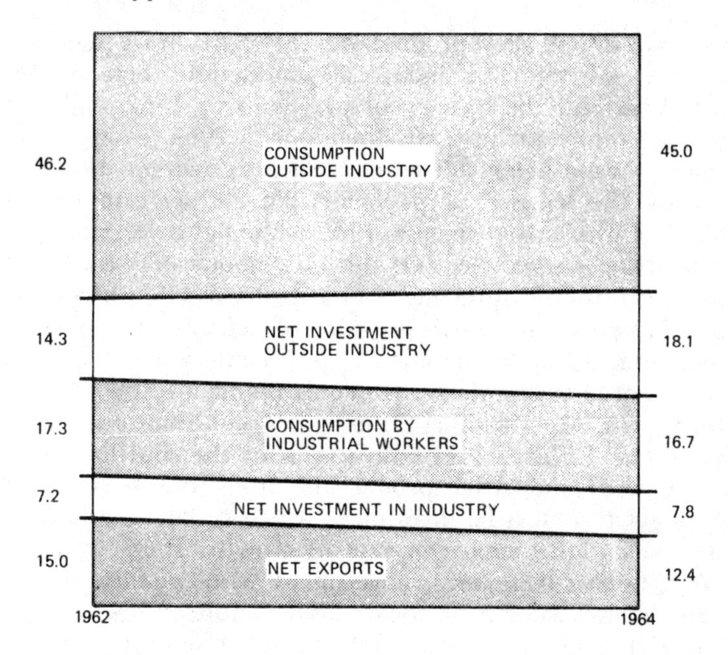

Chart 16 Where Industrial Production Went – Maudling, 1962–4

and private, at very rapid rates. There was no attempt to raise industrial investment relative to public investment or investment outside industry because Mr Maudling started the boom by raising public investment 25 per cent. Simple laws of arithmetic therefore left the sole possibility that the structure of the economy was to be improved in favour of investment at the expense of foreigners and the foreigners were to be repaid amply once Britain's growth rate had been successfully raised to 4 per cent.

Mr Maudling might have achieved what was needed if Sir Alec Douglas Home had won the election of 1964, which he very nearly did. However he did not, and Mr Maudling therefore had far too little time. What was achieved in 1962–4 can be looked at in terms of Chart 16, which is similar to Chart 10 in the last chapter (p. 17) and shows what happened to industrial production. The chart shows that 36.5 per cent of sales of industrial production went to net investment and the balance of payments in 1962, and that 38.3 per cent went in these directions in 1964, so aggregate resources were being shifted in the right direction. However in 1964 the balance of payments got 2½ per cent less of industrial production than in 1962 while net investment got about 4½ per cent more. Of this only about an extra ½ per cent went to net investment in industry itself, which rose from 7.2 per cent to 7.8 per cent of net sales of industrial production. The remaining 4 per cent went to extra investment outside industry – mainly public investment.

That was Mr Maudling's immediate contribution to the solution of Britain's long-term problem: the shuffling of ½ per cent of industrial production from the balance of payments to industrial investment which could, to a limited extent, raise the long-term rate of growth. There were, of course, further increases in investment in the pipeline which helped his successors who took over in October 1964.

In terms of the fraction of marketed output that the market sector of the economy could itself consume and invest, which is also of great importance, Mr Maudling again left the economy in a slightly stronger state than he found it. In 1962 the non-market sector had a pre-tax entitlement to invest and consume 42½ per cent of marketed output, and by 1964 its entitlement had fallen to 42 per cent.

It can be concluded that Mr Maudling left the structure of the economy slightly better placed to produce growth than it was when he took over. This is more than it will be possible to say of some of his successors.

MR GEORGE BROWN'S NATIONAL PLAN

When Labour took office in October 1964 hopes were exceptionally high that Britain's fundamental economic problems would be solved. It was widely felt that the new government would be better able to make use of the talents of both sides of industry than its predecessor. Mr Wilson's speeches had suggested that his government would do more than previous administrations to see that the technological opportunities opened up by modern science would be fully exploited and redound to the advantage of the British people. A new planning ministry, the Department of Economic Affairs, was set up to ensure that the economic policies pursued would serve the country's long-term interests, and Mr George Brown, the Deputy Leader of the Labour Party, was appointed its first Minister.

The Department of Economic Affairs continued and elaborated the work that Neddy had started, and a number of economists under Sir Donald MacDougall, the former Economics Director of Neddy, worked to produce a much more elaborate planning document than anything thus far attempted. After detailed industrial enquiries, this concluded that Britain could achieve 3.8 per cent growth per annum from 1964 to 1970, and 3.4 per cent growth in output per worker. It has already been pointed out that subsequent events have shown that the assumptions about productivity growth in the plan were wholly realistic, so there was no fundamental technical obstacle to its fulfilment. The principal obstacles were two: first, its realisation would require a 55 per cent increase in industrial investment in 1964–70, a larger increase than Britain had achieved previously in just six years; second, a Labour Government could be blown off course by the balance of payments much more easily than a Conservative one because foreigners would expect it to follow prudent financial policies before they were prepared to lend substantial sums. A Labour Government could not, therefore, make use of Mr Maudling's strategy of raising industrial investment at the expense of foreigners because it could not deliberately run deficits *and expand* until 1968 or 1969, which a Conservative Government might well have done. It had instead, since raising industrial investment at the expense of public investment or public-sector consumption could also be ruled out for a new Labour government, to pursue the strategy of raising industrial investment at the expense of private consumption. Hence, the plan envisaged that personal consumption would increase almost 1 per cent per annum less than the national product.

So far as immediate problems were concerned the new government attempted to deal with the balance of payments by introducing a 15 per cent tax on manufactured imports, and the current account deficit fell from £395 million in 1964 to £77 million in 1965 for this and other reasons. There were some increases in taxation in the first year but these were no more than those needed to make goods available for extra public spending and the improvement in the balance of payments, so there was virtually no net deflation in 1965. The Maudling boom was simply allowed to roll on with slight modifications to the pattern of demand and resource allocation.

It has been widely argued that the new government should have devalued the pound at once; the apparent failures of recent devaluations make it less clear that this was necessary. The account of Mr Maudling's boom suggested that the balance of payments was in deficit in 1964 because every component of demand had been expanded at the same time, with the result that some of the country's requirements had necessarily to be met from overseas. There is no exchange rate at which Mr Maudling could have balanced trade, given his demand expansion policies and their extent. Correspondingly, the British balance of payments could only have been improved faster after 1964 if the government had slashed investment or public or private consumption. As the first Labour government since 1951 it was committed to greater public expenditure and it needed more industrial investment for the National Plan, so a more substantial improvement in the balance of payments than was actually achieved in 1965 could only have been practicable if the new government had been prepared to increase taxation on private consumption far more drastically and immediately than it did.

As it was, the balance of payments improved in the early months of 1965, the momentum of expansion was maintained, and there appeared to be no particular reason to do more to raise exports and cut imports. Unemployment fell to less than vacancies in 1965, industrial production grew nearly 4 per cent and industrial investment grew faster than industrial production as a result of delayed benefits from Mr Maudling's rapid expansion.

In September 1965 the National Plan was published, and

this was intended to give businessmen the confidence to continue to invest. By publishing growth targets for each industry the government made it clear that it was the responsibility of firms to see to it that there would be sufficient capital to meet those targets. Investment decisions generally precede the availability of new plant by two or three years (and its efficient functioning by up to four years in some cases) and it was hoped that a knowledge of what the government intended would give businessmen the confidence to spend more than they otherwise would in the firm expectation that the government would see to it that the extra markets would be there. During 1965 all went smoothly and there was no particular cause for concern in any direction.

There were, however, underlying developments in the economy which were to make it increasingly difficult to provide the resources that were needed for productive investment without a return to Mr Maudling's balance of payments deficit. In the Plan it was assumed that Britain's total labour force would grow 789,000 in 1964–70, and that 460,000 of these extra workers would go to professional and scientific services, including health and education. A sector of the economy with just one-tenth of the labour force in 1964 was therefore to get more than half the extra workers. In fact, from 1964 to 1967, just half the planning period, education got an extra 191,000 workers, health an extra 99,000, and national and local government administration an extra 114,000 workers. Thus, these groups of mainly public-sector employees gained 404,000 workers in just three years, when total employment actually fell 15,000. There was, therefore, a diversion greater than any envisaged in the National Plan. Because the total labour force declined 15,000 between 1964 and 1967, the rest of the economy had 419,000 fewer workers to perform all of its tasks by 1967. This had several important implications.

Perhaps the most important was the effect on the overall availability of resources. In 1965 and 1966 the Plan was having its desired effects and businessmen were increasing investment at most satisfactory rates. For the reason that has just been given, public consumption was rising rapidly as the government had to pay growing numbers of teachers, doctors and civil servants. The economy's total output, however, was very close to capacity, so this could only increase rather slowly. Therefore private consumption needed to be much more severely curtailed than was envisaged in the National Plan. It has already been explained that the growth of private consumption had to be cut as part of the new government's long-term strategy, and the faster public consumption rose the more private consumption needed to be cut if the planned increase in investment was to be achieved without a recurrence of Mr Maudling's deficit.

By the summer of 1966 the overall pressure on resources appeared to be too great, for investment and consumption, mainly public, were growing rapidly at the same time. The balance of payments appeared to be in deficit (subsequent figures show that the deficit, associated with a seamen's strike, was not as great as appeared at the time) and there was a sterling crisis. Faced by this, Mr Brown and his advisers wanted to devalue. This had not been necessary in 1965, but in 1966 it was felt that devaluation was needed to provide an adequate balance of payments for the years ahead. This would have achieved the desired result of improving the balance of payments without prejudicing expansion if there had also been drastic cuts in consumption, so that extra resources could have gone to exports without damaging investment. Without cuts in consumption, a devaluation would not have made much impact on the balance of payments because the economy did not have enough excess capacity to exploit it. Something would have needed to be cut but, as public consumption was increasing faster than the projections in the Plan, cuts even in this could have been afforded. The Department of Economic Affairs therefore had a viable strategy for maintaining continuing full employment and the kind of expansion rate that would persuade businessmen to continue to raise investment in line with the Plan's projections.

Sadly, the Department of Economic Affairs failed to make out its case for the policies it wanted. There were severe expenditure cuts and no devaluation. Expansion therefore ceased, the National Plan was abandoned, and nothing was done to make it possible for the spare resources released to go to exports where they could lay a foundation for the future.

The businessmen who had co-operated with the Plan by investing ahead of demand, in the expectation that the government would fulfil its commitments, were at the same time badly let down. After the July measures of 1966 some firms had to sack workers, and Ministers actually accused them of failing to understand their own job when they took them on. They were therefore criticised for believing the government's own Plan which the government went on to abandon.

Mr George Brown left the Department of Economic Affairs over the July measures, the failure to devalue and the abandonment of the National Plan. In retrospect this was to prove the decisive turning-point after which the structure of the United Kingdom economy deteriorated almost without interruption.

From 1964 to 1966 policy had been very much a continuation of Mr Maudling's; the share of industrial investment was gradually raised. The economy was run near to capacity, and while Mr. Maudling had been able to ignore the balance of payments his successors used a series of expedients and higher taxation of private consumption until 1966 to prevent the economy from being blown too much off course by a trade deficit. Chart 17, which shows what happened to industrial production in 1964–6, confirms that this was a period when the economy was on the whole adjusting, albeit slowly, in the right direction. An extra 1 per cent of industrial production went to net industrial investment in 1966 (which was to prove the peak year for this with 8.8 per cent of industrial production invested in industry, as 1964 was to prove the peak year for the motor-car industry). The proportion of industrial production exported net also rose ½ per cent from 1964 to 1966, so this was a period in which both the industrial structure of the economy and the underlying balance of payments in industrial production improved. Non-industrial investment, on the other hand, fell slightly as a share of industrial production, to make way for the extra investment in industry and the improved export surplus. Understandably, with a Labour government in power

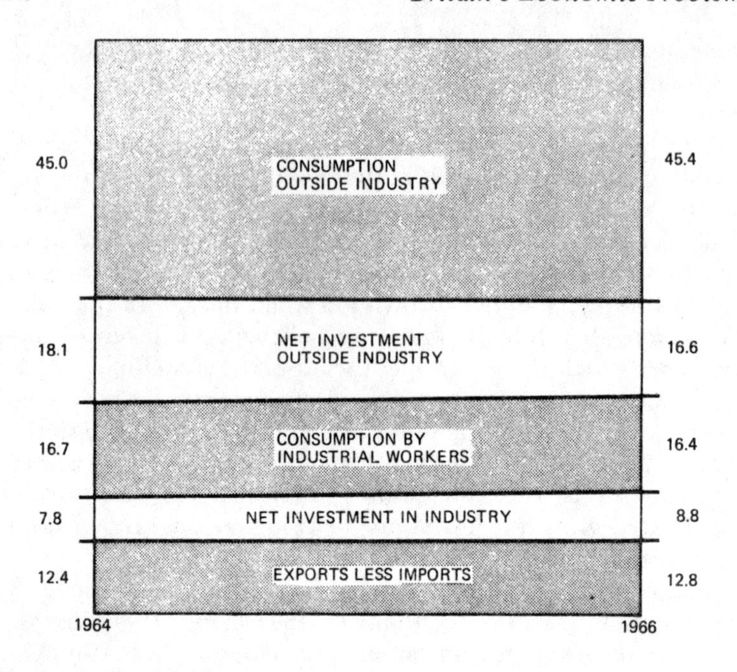

Chart 17 Where Industrial Production Went – Brown, 1964–6

the proportion of marketed output the non-market sector was entitled to buy increased – from 42 per cent to 45 per cent before tax – but, with exports and industrial investment rising, the economy's structure was in general terms moving in the right direction.

The changes in this two-year period, for which the favourable long-term effects of Mr Maudling's boom must take some of the credit, were exactly what was needed, and what believers in the merits of indicative planning had expected. A further few years of growth at near to full employment, with the share of industrial production going to investment in industry rising at around ½ per cent a year, and the share of consumption falling correspondingly, would have been enough to transform the economy and allow it to expand at unprecedented rates from about 1970 onwards; but this was not to be. Virtually all the sensible initiatives of the 1962–6 period were to be abandoned very rapidly.

MR JENKINS' CHANCELLORSHIP

Mr Brown's immediate successor at the Department of Economic Affairs was Mr Michael Stewart, but the Treasury, where Mr Callaghan was Chancellor, had clearly won the policy debate of 1966, and it held power over the country's economic affairs from that point onwards. The Treasury's policy of deflation meant that growth of industrial production ceased entirely while it was hoped that the inflationary pressures in the economy would gradually run down. The abandonment of the National Plan targets meant that businessmen had no reason to invest except to meet actual current orders, so industrial investment ceased to grow. The balance of payments should have improved with this deflation, and early in 1967 there was actually a small surplus in the trade figures in a single month, but the Middle East war of 1967 produced some very bad figures towards the end of the year, the pressure on sterling became intolerable, and the pound was at last devalued in November 1967. Mr Callaghan felt obliged to leave the Treasury, where Mr Roy Jenkins was appointed to succeed him. There followed three years in which attention was focused above all on the balance of payments.

Devaluation made Britain's exports highly competitive, and Mr Jenkins raised taxes severely enough to release resources to exploit this opportunity. The result until the end of 1968 was export-led growth. Exports increased 14 per cent in volume in the fifteen months after devaluation, and this provided the growth in demand that kept the economy expanding. Investment was also allowed to grow a little outside industry, but industrial investment failed to maintain its 1966 peak share and it gradually fell back as a proportion of industrial production until 1970. This was to have major implications. What happened was primarily that export demand ceased to grow at exceptional rates in 1969, when the favourable effects of devaluation had worked their way through, but by actually moving towards a balanced budget

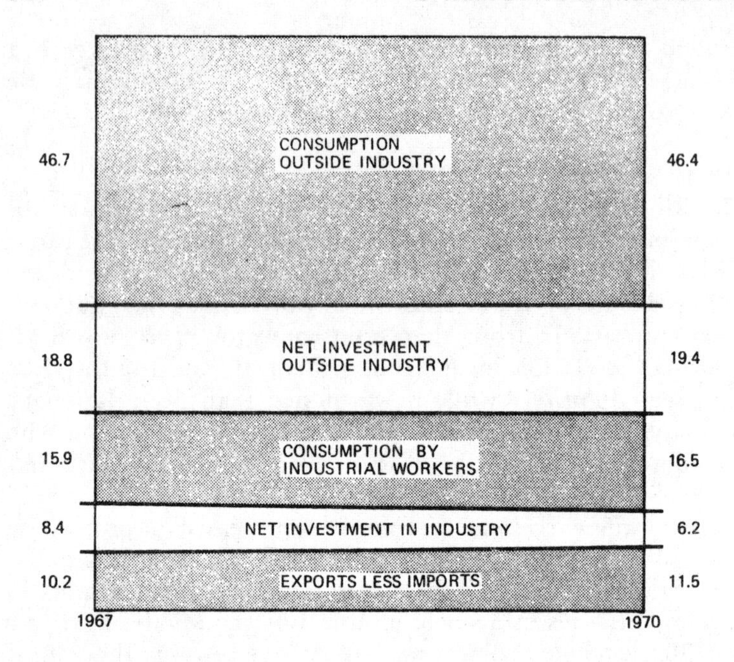

Chart 18 Where Industrial Production Went – Jenkins, 1967–70

in 1970 Mr Jenkins allowed no other component of demand to take its place. Hence there was no increase at all in industrial production during 1969 and 1970.

Chart 18 shows what happened to industrial production in the period of Mr Jenkins' Chancellorship. It shows that 1 per cent of industrial production was diverted to the balance of payments, Mr Jenkins' primary aim, but that industrial investment fell by 2 per cent of industrial production, and this was just as vital to the country's long-term interests. In fact it was the public-sector component of industrial investment that fell sharply from 1967 to 1970, while private industrial investment rose. The Treasury was sensibly asking the nationalised industries to apply more stringent criteria. The share of net investment in manufacturing industry, which is predominantly in the private sector, actually rose by about 1 per cent of sales of manufactures, while the share of net investment in the rest of industry, mining and quarrying, gas, electricity and water, and construction, fell by two-thirds.

A further development in 1967–70 was the continuing increase in public-sector employment when total employment in the economy was falling. Employment in education grew 121,000 from 1967 to 1970, employment in health increased 45,000, and employment in public administration increased 7000, so employment in these three categories increased 173,000 at a time when total employment in the economy fell by 354,000. The increase was slower than in the Maudling and Brown periods, but given the fall in total employment the shift towards the civil service and the public sector meant that there were 527,000 fewer workers available to provide resources for the consumption and investment needs of social workers, teachers, doctors and civil servants. As the 527,000 fewer non-government workers were also obliged to transform the balance of payments, it is no wonder that the resources needed for this could only be found by cutting industrial investment.

The alternative way of examining the changing structure of the economy is to see what happens to the fraction of marketed output that the non-market sector is allowed to invest and consume. On a pre-tax basis, this increased from 45 per cent in 1966 to 51 per cent in 1970, a much sharper rate of increase than in 1964–6. This meant that there was a reduction of about one-tenth in just four years in the fraction of marketed output actually available to workers and companies, so investment and consumption were bound to suffer, and with workers dissatisfied inflation accelerated. There was increased pressure for higher wages as workers appreciated that their living standards (in terms of marketed output) were rising more slowly than before. This was puny in comparison with the wage explosions of the 1970s, but universal pressure for settlements in excess of 10 per cent, at a time when the inflation rate was much less than this, put up inflation a few notches, so that prices were rising at nearly 10 per cent a year when Mr Heath won the General Election called in June 1970.

These underlying trends help to explain why the electorate was not particularly impressed by the economic achievements of Mr Wilson's two administrations. In June 1970 voters were offered the achievement of a transformed balance of payments (though maverick trade figures published in June clouded even this) but inflation had accelerated, there had been slow growth for two years, and there was no pretence that the government was planning the future course of the economy. The electorate may not have appreciated what the abandonment of the National Plan and most of Mr George Brown's policies meant. Many probably did realise, however, that the restructuring of the economy to take advantage of the new technological opportunities of the 1960s and 1970s had been abandoned in favour of Treasury fine tuning – which had succeeded in shuffling resources from industrial investment to exports when the country needed more of both of these.

MR BARBER'S BOOM

Up to June 1970 each administration achieved successes as well as failures. Mr Maudling and Mr Brown increased the ratio of industrial investment. Mr Jenkins transformed the balance of payments. It is true that Mr Maudling only managed to improve investment at the expense of the balance of payments, while Mr Jenkins only improved the balance of payments at the expense of investment, but at least there were successes as well as failures. What was unique about Mr Heath's 1970–4 administration was that failure was total. World prices are often blamed for this, but it will soon become evident that it was weaknesses in domestic policy that were fundamentally to blame.

Chart 19 outlining the shift of resources between 1970 and 1973 shows just how serious the deterioration in the underlying structure of the economy was in this three-year period. First the export surplus of manufactures fell by no less than 5½ per cent of industrial production. As this export surplus does not include oil, this had nothing directly to do with the quadrupling of its price. Deterioration at this rate was quite without precedent and under Mr Barber's Chancellorship this component of the balance of payments deteriora-

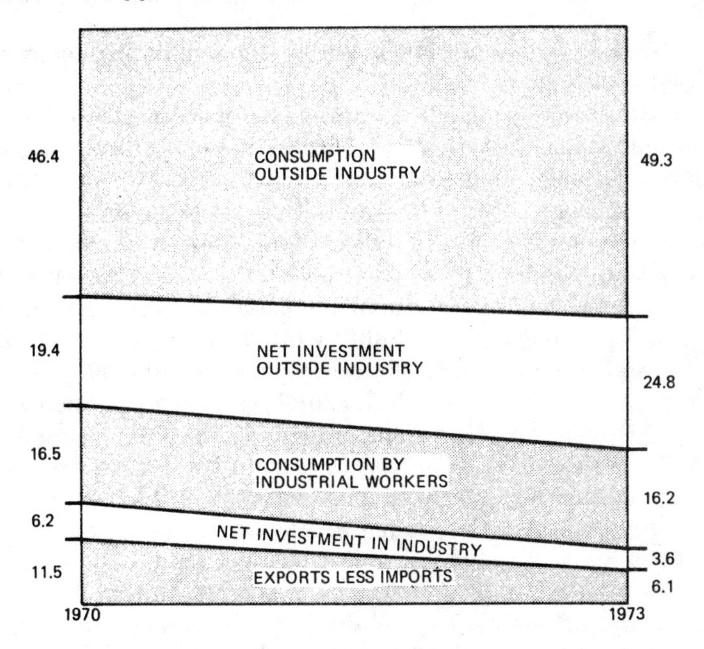

Chart 19 Where Industrial Production Went – Barber, 1970–3

ted five times as quickly as it improved under Mr Jenkins. Under Mr Maudling deterioration of the balance of payments had been the price paid for an improved ratio of industrial investment, but under Mr Barber this fell by a full 2½ per cent of industrial production. Hence, in just three years the proportion of industrial production that was invested in industry plus the proportion that contributed to the balance of payments actually fell 8 per cent.

Thus, out of every £100 of industrial production £8 less went to pay for imports or for investment in industry, and therefore £8 more was consumed and invested outside industry. Of this, roughly £4 went to extra consumption and £4 to the great increase in non-industrial investment that followed from the property boom that Mr Barber indavertently created in 1971–2.

There was another adverse trend which put pressure on the economy. In 1970 to 1973 employment in education and health actually increased more than in any previous three-year period, with the result that those employed in education increased 208,000, those employed in health increased 97,000, while the number of civil servants in national and local government increased 98,000 in just three years. This increase of 403,000 workers in these occupations was similar to the increase achieved by the previous government from 1964 to 1967. Total employment increased 189,000 in 1970–3, so there were 214,000 fewer workers in 1973 than in 1970 to provide goods for the soaring numbers of teachers, social workers, civil servants and so on, not to mention goods for the balance of payments.

Largely as a result of these changes in the pattern of employment, the proportion of marketed output that the non-market sector was allowed to consume and invest increased on a pre-tax basis from the already high 51 per cent that Mr Jenkins allowed it in 1970 to 53 per cent in 1973. Thus, in spite of the ideological-seeming steps in the other direction like charges for museums and school milk, the net effect of the decisions taken by Mr Heath's government was to make the market sector of the economy smaller and to use more of its production in government-financed activities. A consequence of this was that private consumption per worker rose very much less than public consumption. Mr Heath's government aimed to reduce taxes, but Chart 6 in Chapter 1 (p. 7) showed that workers suffered proportional deductions from their pay packets in 1973 similar to those in 1970. From 1973 onwards, the living standards of most workers fell, but those with industrial muscle managed to preserve their own position with industrial action of unprecedented militancy. The consequences of this are only too well known.

That the economic policies of Mr Heath's government should have failed in every direction requires explanation. How did Mr Barber manage to do so much damage to industrial investment and the balance of payments in so short a time? Mr Jenkins certainly left behind him a very low level of industrial investment (though investment was not low in manufacturing) but he left a balanced budget and an extremely sound balance of payments as a foundation for a return to better things. He also left 600,000 unemployed which was soon to approach 1,000,000, which meant that any boom that Mr Barber initiated could be a long one.

In the event Mr Barber expanded far faster than Mr Maudling, and industrial production was 8.4 per cent higher in 1973 than in 1972 – and imports of manufactured goods were 44 per cent higher (in volume terms) than in 1971. This makes it very clear that capacity limits were reached long before any beneficial effects from expansion upon investment could come through.

Also, by failing to appreciate the significance for the economy as a whole of expansion plans in education and health (which is the Chancellor's responsibility) he allowed a very high fraction of the economy's spare labour to be drawn into national and local government employment, mainly the latter, so that labour became scarce in the South of England and the Midlands extraordinarily quickly, with the result that the output of many products could not meet demand. Consequently imports surged upwards long before industrial investment began to increase. Public consumption increased very sharply at the start of the boom and, as taxes were also cut substantially, the budget moved rapidly to a huge deficit. This was much larger than Mr Maudling's puny deficit, and it had monetary effects of a kind which had not been seen in Britain since the war. The budget deficit pumped money into the economy, and simultaneously, as a result of the Bank of England's new 'Competition and Credit Control' regulations which were introduced in 1971, the commercial banks were allowed to raise their deposits from about four to nearly seven times their liquid assets. Money was consequently easy to borrow and portfolio holders had much higher ratios of money to real assets than they considered ideal. They therefore used their surplus money to buy into real estate and buildings (which were considered more likely to keep pace with inflation than shares) and the price of land and every kind of building and office space soared in consequence. This raised the cost of living (for the cost of housing is part of this) and led to an upsurge in investment outside the industrial sector. Some of the investment was not a response to real need. People expected to make large paper profits even on empty property (which was not then rateable). It was simply felt that land and buildings were the best potential source of profits or, at worst, the safest hedge against inflation. In 1970–3 private sector investment in buildings of all kinds (including houses) increased 83 per cent in current money terms while investment in new plant and machinery, which Britain needed vitally to solve long-term problems, increased only 25 per cent, which means that this did not increase at all when inflation is allowed for.

It was public investment that provided much of the early impetus in Mr Maudling's boom, but it was private investment outside industry which increased so explosively in Mr Barber's. This grew at unprecedented rates for the reasons which have been outlined, while industry was unable to raise the money it needed – either from profits or from financial institutions. Industrial investment was considered risky in the City, and with reason after the Rolls-Royce collapse. A stagnant industrial sector was therefore carrying both a growing educational and health superstructure as a result of Mr Barber's failure to check expansionist policies, a growing local bureaucracy, and a growing output of empty and under-utilised buildings as a result of the extraordinary expansion of the money supply.

It fell to Mr Heath to attempt to pick up the pieces with phases one, two and three of his prices and incomes policy. These were tragically constructed to cut profit margins and seriously weaken industrial liquidity and hence industry's ability to finance investment. Firms were not allowed to pass on cost increases in full, so profit margins were inevitably squeezed, and the collapse of profit margins then made industrial investment unattractive to the City of London. A handicap Conservative governments suffer from is that they must attack company profits if they need trade union goodwill. This may be one reason why Mr Heath's price code was so much more damaging to industry than Mr Healey's more recent one. Another may be that the effects of what was being done were just not understood. Whatever the reason, industrial profits collapsed after 1972 and investment with them. The City lost confidence in British industry and foreign capital inflows were also damaged. Therefore the economy's ability to increase its output of industrial products fell drastically at the very time when, because of Mr Barber's boom, unprecedented demands were being placed upon it. Exporters wanted more goods because the pound was undervalued after 1971. Property developers wanted extra resources. Teachers, doctors and civil servants wanted more goods, not particularly because they had a claim to higher living standards but because there were more of them every year. Workers of all kinds wanted more goods, and these included the miners who, unlike the others, actually had the power to get them and bring Mr Heath's administration to an end.

In an economics textbook these simultaneous pressures would have made industrial investment extremely profitable. Mr Heath's squeeze on profits (so much more devastating than trade union pressure, because wage increases can so often be passed on to the consumer while Mr Heath's burdens could not) prevented industry from emerging as an attractive place to invest money. There were therefore no self-correcting forces in the economy of the textbook kind. The industrial base of the economy just continued to fall in relation to what was required of it, while most were quite oblivious of what this meant. They noticed the symptoms of the increasing distortion of the structure of the economy, however, a total failure to meet the reasonable aspirations of a growing proportion of the population. The British people were puzzled. Most did not believe that the right decisions had been taken since 1970, and enough voted Liberal and Labour to withdraw Mr Heath's majority.

THE CRISIS IN 1974–6

The Labour governments of Mr Wilson and Mr Callaghan inherited a balance of payments deficit of nearly £4000 million, a share of net industrial investment in sales of industrial production which had fallen to less than 4 per cent in 1973, and a massive frustrated desire for improved living standards that the economy was wholly unable to meet. It scarcely needs to be said that the inflation rate exploded in consequence, leading to the most draconian prices and incomes policy that has yet been tried, here or elsewhere. Faced by a crisis of these dimensions, it is understandable that members of these Labour governments have not agreed about solutions. Policy first moved in several directions at the same time. Moreover, a world recession which raised unemployment to over 1¼ million, and increases in public expenditure of over 40 per cent in just one year, accentuating all the unfavourable trends which have been outlined, made the fundamental problems of the economy still more difficult to solve.

The fact that it was the structure of the economy and not the level of demand or the exchange rate that was wrong came increasingly to be recognised during 1974 and 1975. Industrial employment fell 1,986,000, or by 246,000 a year from 1966 to 1974. In the same period industrial production of all OECD countries increased 45 per cent, and world exports of manufactures grew 115 per cent. Britain lost out on this feast. The structure of the British economy started to deteriorate slowly after 1966 and rapidly after 1970, and it can only be put right at a rate of 1 per cent or 2 per cent per annum, the rate at which it was allowed to deteriorate. The alternative ways in which it can be put right, which have very different social implications, will be outlined in Chapter 3. The steps Mr Callaghan's government has taken in 1976 and 1977 to attempt to restore the structure of the economy will be outlined and discussed in Chapter 5.

NOTES

1. *Growth of the United Kingdom Economy to 1966*, HMSO, February 1963, paragraphs 151–3.
2. *The National Plan* (Cmnd 2764) HMSO, September 1975.
3. See for instance W. Beckerman and associates, *The British Economy in 1975* (Cambridge University Press, 1965), chapter 1.
4. The case for solving the problem of transition to a faster growth path with an export-led boom to provide the markets to encourage industrialists to invest more was set out by W. Beckerman in 'Projecting Europe's growth', *Economic Journal*, vol. LXXII, December 1962, and *The British Economy in 1975* (op. cit.), chapter 2. It was also set out by N. Kaldor in 'Conflicts in national economic objectives', *Economic Journal*, vol. 81, March 1971.

3 Alternative Solutions

Three broad groups in British politics question the economic policies which led to the impasse the country reached in 1975.

Mr Tony Benn and his associates appreciate the relevance of investment to the preservation of jobs in industry. They also know that other jobs depend on these. They understand that industry, in the absence of government intervention, will fail to undertake the investment that Britain needs. In their view the state must direct major investment decisions and the allocation of finance for investment. Accordingly they are evolving one set of policies to get industry out of the trap of insufficient investment, inadequate profits and continually declining employment which can destroy the economy. They may of course put the economy and society into a quite different trap, but they are at least trying to arrive at a set of policies that can solve the principal economic problems.

Secondly, there are members of the Labour party and of the Labour government who, though they distrust some of the policies of Mr Benn and the Left, believe that Britain's manufacturing and private service industries are no longer productive enough to support a public sector of the size reached in 1975 and 1976. They therefore favour shifting resources from the public sector and finding work for the unemployed in the economy's profit-making industries and services. Once the economy was restored they would favour expanding public services again, but they believe that building up a prosperous market sector must come first.

Thirdly, there are Mrs Thatcher and her Conservative colleagues who believe still more strongly that the market sector should be strengthened in relation to the public sector. Their initial remedies might have much in common with those that several members of the Labour government favour, but once the productive base was sufficiently strong, policies could diverge significantly. The Conservatives might be expected to give greater priority to increasing private consumption though they could also be expected to improve social services from greater resources, as do the successful fast-growing West European economies. Some of these have governments well to the right of the British Labour party, but their rapidly growing resources have enabled them to provide social services which are in many respects superior to Britain's.

Both a Left and a pro-market sector government must achieve two objectives. They must solve the problem of high unemployment which represents obvious waste – and damages the economy and society. In addition, they must do this in ways which increase the economy's long-term capacity to provide jobs. The mistake has been made repeatedly of solving short-term problems by weakening the economy's ability to produce and employ in the long term, and it could be fatal if this error was repeated once more. In contrast, policies to achieve a distant Utopia which ignore the need to solve immediate problems will not do. The British people will hardly tolerate deterioration for several years with little to show for it.

A LEFT SOLUTION

The British Left maintains, and with reason, that industry will not undertake the investment the country needs. The Left's great strength is that it is prepared to do something about this. It hardly needs to be said that Mr Benn and his associates would set up new institutions to provide industrial finance on a massive scale. Mr Benn himself is on record as saying that the investment programme that is needed 'would involve us as a nation in spending some £6 billion a year on capital investment in manufacturing, double what we have been spending . . .' (*Trade and Industry*, 4 April 1975). The National Enterprise Board and other similar new institutions would therefore have to make very large sums available to industry. Firms are already investing almost all that they can afford from historically low net-of-tax profits. Extra sums would therefore have to be made available to industry approximately equivalent to what is now spent. These are huge requirements but Mr Benn's conclusion that spending on industrial investment must be doubled is similar to the one that was arrived at in Chapter 2. Moreover, these expenditures would be helpful in both the short and the long run. They would raise employment at once and create still more jobs in the future.

The expenditure of these huge extra sums raises a number of problems. First, where will the government find the money when its 'borrowing requirement' is close to limits set by the IMF? Second and of crucial importance, by what mechanism could so much money be usefully spent in industry? Third, what would industry have to give in exchange for so much public money? Finally, how would these extra expenditures influence the balance of payments? A collapse of sterling would have vast adverse consequences including a great and immediate acceleration of inflation.

The answer to the first question, where the money would come from, is simple. Any government faced by high unemployment will be driven to reflate at some point. The only question is the form reflation will take. In the past governments have reflated by creating more jobs for teachers, social workers and civil servants. They have also encouraged consumers to buy more cars and television sets. In addition they have stimulated housebuilding. If policies like Mr Benn's were followed instead, it would be extra factories that were built instead of extra houses; extra machines and not extra cars, and the new jobs would be for industrial workers. What is at issue is therefore the direction of extra expenditure and not its amount. There are some who would not wish to reflate until the world economy allowed this to be achieved through export growth. If the world economy recovers quickly enough, growing exports will indeed provide much of the reflation the economy needs; and as industrialists see that they can sell more abroad, they will raise investment and the government will need to use its own reflationary expenditures to reinforce these helpful trends – and not divert resources into less essential directions. But if recovery from the world recession does not produce an export and investment-led boom, unemployment will gradually rise from one towards two millions in the absence of domestic reflation, and the Left would almost certainly consider the use of wartime financial expedients justifiable to reduce this.

A problem in any reflation, be it in favour of industrial investment or social spending, is that it must add to the government's already large borrowing requirement. Once the government is unable to sell enough bonds to the public to finance this, it must sell Treasury Bills (three-month IOUs) or simply print money – which would produce a return to Lord Barber's vast inflation of property values. A Left solution to this difficulty could be a return to the use of 'special deposits' on a wartime scale. In 1945 40 per cent of bank deposits were compulsorily frozen in the Bank of England, and the banks received low interest rates for this money. What was done in 1945 can be done again. It would not work indefinitely but the government would buy time.

The Left has also said that it would like to oblige life insurance and pensions funds to invest more of their money in industry, using direct intervention if necessary. It would argue that in 1971–3 a high fraction of the nation's investment finance was invested outside industry in buildings of various kinds, not basically because the economy needed them, but because office space and commercial buildings were judged to be better hedges against inflation than factories. A Left government would claim that it could prevent the diversion of the nation's investible resources to mere anti-inflation hedging of a kind that failed to develop the country's real economic potential.

If the Left could get money for industry (which would need to be spent in any case) by obliging the banking system and insurance companies to provide it, the question of how the money should be spent arises. Would not much of the money the National Enterprise Board spent be wasted or at any rate allocated less well than by the market? The market allocates investment resources to maximise prospective profits and in theory this will direct money where sales are expected to grow fastest, and where most can be saved by substituting capital for labour. However, the Left contends that the market often gets investment decisions wrong. They believe that a National Enterprise Board which could take social costs and benefits into account, avoid polluting the environment, avoid directing the nation's capital to the areas of maximum monopoly power, and think ahead, should have advantages over the market. With more money to lend than any present financial institution, it should have companies flocking to borrow, and after detailed and expert appraisal it could decide which projects should be encouraged and supported.

However, a pragmatic Left government could hardly believe that it would allocate the nation's finance better than the market in its early years. There would be neither time nor qualified personnel to make detailed cost-benefit appraisals of each project if £3000 million extra a year was to be spent by 1980. The world recession is the crucial period when extra industrial investment can be afforded because the economy must in any case be reflated, so resources can go to industrial investment without needing to be taken from somewhere else. Once the economy is back at full capacity working, this will no longer be the case. Now each proposed investment project could be appraised in detail in 1977–80, in which case £600 or £800 million extra might be spent each year which would have only a modest impact on total industrial investment. Alternatively companies could in most cases be given virtually all they asked for extra spending which they could not afford from their own resources, and very quickly too, and in this case £3000 million extra a year could perhaps be spent. If a Left government is to attempt a quick expansion of industrial investment, its main hope will therefore have to be that the spending projects industrialists themselves put forward make sense so far as the future development of the economy is concerned. The mediocre effects on the country's economic performance of poor projects approved in haste must be compared with the still more damaging long-term effects of other increases in expenditure in 1977–80. Extra industrial investment would do less long-term damage, and in most cases it would create extra jobs that were self-sustaining and in the long term self-financing because tax revenue would rise with extra production and this would provide the resources from which further jobs could be created in the 1980s. The same cannot be said if the economy is reflated by increasing consumer incomes or social spending.

If a Left government actually provided £3000 million a

year for extra industrial investment from 1977 onwards, it would certainly expect something in exchange from the companies which benefited. But it could not acquire ownership of a large slice of industry or worker control as a *quid pro quo* because only bankrupt or near-bankrupt companies would come forward to borrow on the required scale if they had to accept this. If the National Enterprise Board insisted on this, its role would be limited to the absorption of the bankrupt into the public sector. This would lead to extra spending, but it would be in precisely those places where there was a record of past failure. It would mean spending on projects where sales were falling, where the world market was weak or foreigners had an unbeatable lead. To concentrate public funds where there were most business failures would be an absurdity the pragmatic Left would wish to avoid. They might not believe in the market, but they would hardly expect it to be so wrong that the firms it condemned should have all the available money.

If this is recognised, a National Enterprise Board which wanted viable companies to come to it on a massive scale would have little bargaining power at first. It could not exact any measure of state ownership, and all it could ask for would be 'planning agreements'. Companies could agree to expand aggregate investment at particular rates (if the government paid), to co-operate with the government on location policy (where plant was financed from public funds), and to *attempt* to export particular fractions of output. Companies should co-operate with the government to this extent in any society, and industry would give up nothing it ought to preserve by entering into such agreements. They have often been made in France and Japan. If the government wanted more, industry would not borrow, and the regeneration of British industry could only go forward after massive nationalisation which would take time, and alter the economy and society in directions which few prefer.

A further point to note about a Left policy to make public money available for industrial investment in 1977–80 is that it would have to be lent at extremely low interest rates. The state would therefore lend money to the private sector and get little in exchange. This might appear un-socialist to some on the Left but it would bring substantial benefits to the workers of Britain. It would also bring benefits to the government, the nation and the political reputations of those who engineered the economy's recovery. Workers who would otherwise lose jobs would keep them. Living standards which would otherwise stagnate would rise. If profits rose, so would tax revenues. Finally, once the immediate crisis need to regenerate industry had passed when virtually all prospective projects would require approval, the Enterprise Board could afford to become more selective, and it would then acquire real power over Britain's future industrial structure. It is to be hoped that it would use this more sensibly than the power to influence the structure of the aircraft industry which British governments have possessed since the Second World War.

Some on the Left would object that the channelling of public funds to private sector investment on a vast scale would make the rich richer, but this need not follow. Dividend controls could be maintained so that those who relied on profit incomes for their consumption failed to outpace inflation. In the absence of real dividend growth equity prices would remain low (provided the government was able to control the growth of the money supply) so those who owned industry would get neither higher real dividends nor real capital gains. It is industry's workers who would benefit and of course the government, which would be feeding the geese which lay golden eggs instead of killing them off one by one.

It is interesting to note that there is a country which had Labour governments for over thirty years and chose to adopt measures quite similar to those set out here. In Sweden in 1960–70 non-industrial employment actually grew 41 per cent in relation to industrial employment, even faster than in Britain, and a welfare state was built up more quickly and successfully. At the same time and partly as a result of continuing pressure from workers to increase living standards in terms of marketed output, the undistributed profits of companies fell drastically as in Britain, from 14.9 per cent of the national income in 1950 to 4.5 per cent in 1969. But industrial investment was maintained in spite of this, and in 1966–70 over one-third of industry's external finance came from government insurance institutions, a source that provided no finance at all in 1951–5 when industry itself had ample funds.[1] The insurance companies lent to the firms judged to have the best profit prospects, so market considerations influenced the direction of investment more than they probably would in a Left British scheme. In socialist Sweden by this and other means a profits squeeze was not allowed to prejudice industrial investment. It is to be hoped that the Left in Britain would be prepared to do as much as the Left in Sweden to support workers' jobs, and a period of high unemployment is ideal for new initiatives.

But the balance of payments is likely to be an obstacle to any attempt to create a continuing investment upsurge in Britain prior to the recovery of the world economy, in spite of the receipt of growing sums from North Sea oil, for hitherto booms of any kind have always produced soaring imports. Exports might rise almost enough to pay for these if the world economy recovers strongly, but if it does not the balance of payments could easily become unmanageable. Therefore an investment boom could hardly get off the ground without special measures to protect the balance of payments, and a falling exchange rate or import restrictions are the obvious alternatives. These would have the added virtue of creating growing markets for industrial production, either at home (as a result of import controls) or overseas (if a lower exchange rate is preferred), which would help to encourage investment still further and create conditions for continuing export and investment led expansion.

The orthodox prefer to use the exchange rate, but up to now a falling exchange rate has actually made the balance of payments worse for twelve to eighteen months because Britain has had to pay higher prices for imports long before exports expanded enough to compensate. Moreover a sharply falling exchange rate causes the cost of living to rise steeply, because most raw materials and foodstuffs rise in price as fast as the exchange rate falls, and if the Left was without an exceedingly tough incomes policy, wages would explode upwards. The rise in the cost of living that followed a lower exchange rate could to some extent be mitigated with subsidies on essential foodstuffs, but these would need to be paid for, and a fraction of them would go to foreign farmers instead of domestic consumers.

If a falling exchange rate is not the answer, then import restrictions are needed and the Left appreciates this. A Left government could be expected to concentrate controls on luxury consumer goods that have little effect on the cost of living index because this measures the prices of the goods that dominate the average worker's budget. By concentrating on what the better-off buy, a Left government might aim to cut imports of manufactures by one-fifth, which would allow much extra machinery and raw materials to be imported. As the controls would be predominantly on goods bought by those with virtually no trade union bargaining power there would be little adverse effect on wages. Middle-class living standards would be reduced but this is where a Left government would prefer to place the cost of correcting the balance of payments. The import restrictions would also reduce (greatly in some cases) the efficiency of the protected industries.

Import controls are permissible under EEC rules where a country is in chronic deficit. If import controls were imposed and investment was expanded sharply at the same time, the rest of the world would sell no less to Britain. Other countries would earn less in Britain from sales of consumer goods, but they would earn more to compensate from sales of machinery and raw materials, so total earnings in Britain would show little change. Most should appreciate Britain's problem and not object to a change in the *pattern of imports* of this kind. The Left would consider it hard if foreigners retaliated when they were earning as many dollars, francs, deutschmarks, lira and yen in Britain as before. Most countries might well allow Britain time to progress towards the solution of fundamental problems before they retaliated on a significant scale.

With the steps that have been outlined, a Left government could start to alter the structure of the economy in favour of industry. It is however only for a time that extra investment could be obtained easily by making use of the economy's spare capacity. Once full employment was reached the

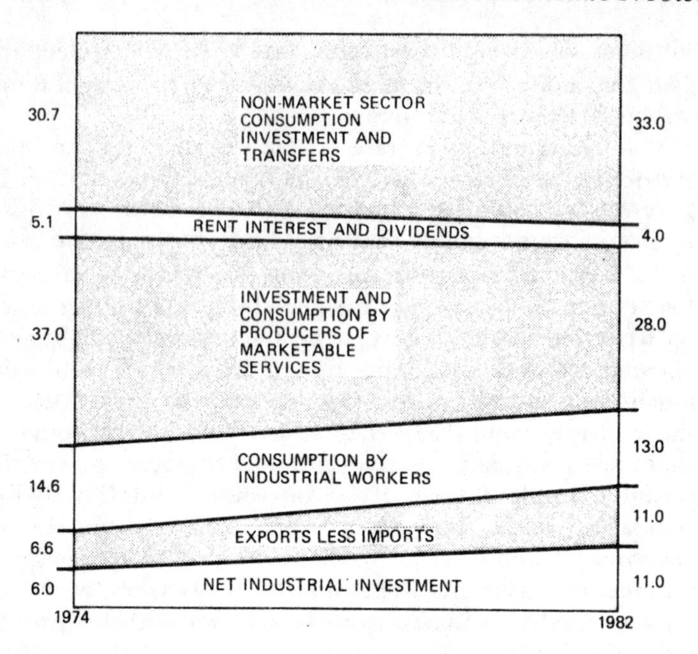

Chart 20 A Left Solution: Shares of Sales of Industrial Products

pattern of resource use would need to be planned so that the improvement in industrial investment could be sustained. With full capacity working, a higher *fraction* of output would be able to go to industrial investment and the balance of payments only if permanently lower fractions were invested outside industry and consumed. The pattern of resource use that a Left government might aim for once the economy reached a new full employment growth path is outlined in Chart 20. This shows an increase in industrial investment from the 6.0 per cent of industrial production of 1974 to 11 per cent, and an increase in net exports from 6.6 per cent to 11 per cent which was the industrial export surplus in 1970. A markedly smaller export surplus than this in terms of industrial production will be needed if North Sea oil has the impact on the balance of payments by 1982 that many expect. The chart is drawn on the conservative assumption that as large an industrial export surplus as Mr Jenkins achieved will be needed. But this means that more industrial production will be available for other uses than Chart 20 indicates, to the extent that North Sea oil contributes substantially to the balance of payments.

The chart shows an increase in non-market sector investment and consumption from 30.7 per cent to 33 per cent of sales of industrial production. A Left government can be expected to increase public spending faster than the national product because of its concern to improve public services, and to help those whose needs are greatest. The rest of the economy – the private service sector, industrial workers, and those who receive rent, interest and dividends – would therefore have to make do with 45 per cent of industrial production in place of the 56.7 per cent they invested and consumed in 1974. Their share of industrial production would therefore need to be cut by 11.7 per cent less such contributions as are made by North Sea oil. Rent, interest and dividends, at 5 per cent in 1974, could sensibly provide no more than 1.1 per cent of the extra 11.7 per cent that may be needed, for a considerable fraction of non-state pensions must be found from these, and about half the 5 per cent is interest on the national debt which can be expected to rise with Left policies. Then at least 10.6 per cent of the 11.7 per cent may need to be taken from the private service industries, and the consumption of industrial workers themselves. In Chart 20 it is assumed that 9.0 per cent is found from the consumption and investment of the profit-making services. Sweden has a 25 per cent tax on non-industrial investment, but the British Left might prefer something more drastic like a return to the building licences and controls of the early post-war years. The 9.0 per cent cut would reduce the resources available to the profit-making services by almost one-quarter and they are not widely regarded as inefficient. A greater cut than this would threaten to destroy the viability of the whole economy, which needs shops, transport, communications and banks. A smaller cut in private services will, of course, suffice if North Sea oil makes a major contribution. The remaining 1.6 per cent cut which may be needed for higher industrial investment, exports and public expenditure can only come from the consumption of industrial workers themselves, and in Chart 20 this is assumed to fall from 14.6 per cent to 13 per cent of industrial production. These are proportions of industrial production, so the fall in consumption by industrial workers does not necessarily represent an absolute fall. If industrial production is raised significantly, using the economy's spare capacity, the 13 per cent of industrial production workers could consume in say 1982 should be rather more than the 14.6 per cent consumed in 1974. However, the chart shows that private consumption and investment outside industry will certainly have to fall as a proportion of industrial production if higher fractions are to be invested in industry, spent by the government and used to support the balance of payments, and where there should be cuts is a problem that a Left government would soon have to face.

The Left knows that resources must be shifted to net exports (until North Sea oil makes a major contribution) and to industrial investment on the scale indicated in the chart, but they have not, at any rate publicly, explained where they should be taken from. They do not believe that the public sector should get a smaller fraction of industrial production. On the contrary, they argue widely that it should get more, so the assumption that this would increase from 30.7 per cent to 33 per cent is in the right direction.

If investment and consumption outside industry can be cut by not quite one-quarter as is realistically supposed, and extra resources must be found for industrial investment, exports, and the public sector, more will have to be taken from the the consumption of industrial workers themselves. That is the point on which the British Left has been unconvincing because they promise immediate increases in living standards for the manual workers of industry at the expense of profits – which are no longer significant enough in net terms (with consumption from rent, interest and dividends, including the interest on the national debt, a mere 5 per cent of industrial production) to provide the extra that workers want. With insufficient scope for squeezing profits, the Left's sums will only add up when North Sea oil makes a large positive contribution. Industrial investment and net exports are to get more. Social spending will rise. Investment in the public sector will rise and, it is promised, workers' consumption will rise too. In fact, without a major contribution from oil, what is needed to raise the share of industrial investment and net exports can only be found if more is taken from the consumption of those who work in industry. They consumed 17 per cent of their output in 1961, 14.6 per cent by 1974, and a further 1.6 per cent cut would reduce their consumption to 13 per cent of what they produce.

There are two ways in which the share of consumption of industrial workers could be cut to this extent. Profit margins could widen and the share of wages fall, but that is not the way a Left government would reduce workers' consumption. It would reduce it through the tax system, and that is how the share of workers' private consumption has always been cut since 1961. In almost every year, deductions from workers' pay packets have grown and under a Left government they would continue to grow. Certainly the better-off would lose more, but in 1961–74 deductions from the pay packets of workers receiving *one-third less than average earnings* increased by about ten-pence in the pound. Taxes on consumer goods, and especially those bought by workers, increased massively at the same time. The ordinary workers of Britain have been expected to pay for much of the country's increased social spending and this would continue.

How then would a Left government prevent a wages explosion as it became clear that the living standards of ordinary workers were still rising more slowly than output, in spite of higher industrial investment and faster growth – and they would certainly need to rise more slowly than output until North Sea oil made a really substantial balance of payments contribution. It could be hoped that a faster absolute increase in living standards as growth speeded up would contain the pressure. With 11 per cent of industrial production invested, industrial output should grow 4 per cent instead of 2 per cent per annum, so over ten years workers' purchasing power could rise over 40 per cent with unchanged taxation. Higher taxes diverting more to the public sector would still leave them with an extra 20 per cent or 30 per cent. If the productivity of the economy's capital stock could be raised through a more effective use of existing resources, industrial production could rise much more than 40 per cent in ten years, because this has been achieved in several West European economies. With 11 per cent of industrial production invested in industry, there *could* be faster growth than before, *both* because plant was being expanded faster, *and* because workers and managements were getting more output from the economy's capital stock. If this could be achieved (and governments could do no more than ensure that there was enough plant – getting more output from it must be mainly the responsibility of workers and managements), industrial production could grow 6 per cent a year as in much of Western Europe if all co-operated to achieve this. Workers' living standards could then grow at unprecedented rates *and* resources could be shifted more rapidly into the public sector, provided that, as in Western Europe, enough was also found for investment and net exports.

Even without a West European rate of increase in productivity, a gradual increase in real living standards in terms of both the social wage and goods in the shops could be achieved, and there should then be a gradual abatement of pressure for higher wages that threaten to disrupt the economy. But there would not be higher living standards in the early years, before North Sea oil provided really significant help, and it is overwhelmingly probable that a Left government would need prices and incomes controls like others that have presided over great increases in social spending. In Sweden there is strong trade union leadership at the national level, and there are regular meetings with employers' associations and the government to allocate the nation's resources. Britain does not yet have a TUC central committee with the power to commit member unions, but a Left government which might need to allow workers as little as 13 per cent of the industrial products that they produced for their own personal consumption, would need Swedish negotiating machinery if it did not wish to preside over hyperinflation, or seek dictatorial powers of an East European kind.

A Left government placed in power with trade union support should be able to co-operate closely with the unions.

The Left believes in greater participation by workers in decision taking, so it is to be expected that trade union leaders would sit on the boards of companies and nationalised industries. As trade unions became part of the 'establishment' that ran the country, union leaders would also play a direct role in the decisions to allocate resources between investment, personal consumption and social spending. If they acquired so much power, the Left would expect that they would not prevent the economy from functioning. Their role would be what it was in 1940–51 when workers' leaders behaved with great responsibility. There might of course be irresponsible splinter unions with leaders who were not part of the new power structure of Britain. The Left would perhaps optimistically expect such maverick behaviour with consequent unofficial strikes to be slight, for it would expect the official leaders to represent the economic, political and social aspirations of the great majority of workers. There might however be more unofficial strikes in favour of extra private consumption than optimists expect.

But if the economy could achieve an export and investment-led transition to a larger industrial sector so that the situation depicted in Chart 20 (or the still better one assisted by North Sea oil) could be achieved without significant absolute falls in consumption, discontent might be containable. The Left might then be able to satisfy the economic aspirations of most manual workers and of those in the middle classes who prefer greater equality to high individual consumption. The society that resulted might not be the preferred choice of the majority in Britain, and there is a viable alternative.

A PRO-MARKET SECTOR SOLUTION

All British Conservatives, most Liberals, and many members of the Labour party will be deeply suspicious of certain elements in the solution that has been outlined. Some will have obvious political and social reservations, but in addition to these many will have serious doubts about whether the proposed measures would improve economic efficiency and the living standards of the people. In particular it is not clear that giving private industry priority over private services for labour and investment funds makes economic sense. Britain is among the world's leaders in internationally marketed services, and an industrial laggard. To bias resources away from marketable services which provided exports of £7325 million in 1975 could therefore harm the balance of payments and reduce living standards. It would take workers away from the production of high marketed outputs and place them somewhere new where they would produce less. Many would also expect deterioration from the use of government agencies to allocate an increasing proportion of the nation's investable resources, for civil servants and politicians subject to local pressures have made many recent errors. The market also made mistakes in 1971–3 but many would attribute these to Mr Barber's errors. Some would fear that Government agencies might well create a whole range of new and unviable industries which would then be protected from foreign competition through import controls.

Some of those with doubts about the Left solution would give greater weight to the role of managers, the salaried and the self-employed. They would expect an economy with ample factory space in giant firms to be extremely inefficient if managements could not take initiatives, salaried workers were alienated, and there was no scope for small businesses with new ideas – the Plesseys and IBMs of the future. They would not expect a bureaucrat-dominated industry with frozen market shares for each firm to produce growing prosperity.

The essential feature of a pro-market sector solution, applied by a Labour or Conservative government, is that scope should be given to firms in the private sector to solve Britain's fundamental problem of inadequate exports and investment and too few productive jobs. In terms of the argument presented in Chapter 1, an increase in the size of the *market* sector of the economy is needed, that is in the industries and services which sell what they produce (which includes the nationalised industries) in relation to the *non-market* sector. It is the *market sector* that produces exports, investment and private consumer goods for the whole nation. In 1961 the non-market sector's pre-tax entitlement to buy market sector output was 41½ per cent, and this rose to 62 per cent by 1975. Many believe that the extra taxes needed to take these vast extra resources away from those who produce marketed goods and services must hit incentives however they are levied, curtail private consumption and so increase the pressure for higher money incomes. They must also cut the country's productive investment. The frustration from this great weight of taxation must also hit enterprise and initiative which matter particularly in a world where technical change is both continuous and rapid.

The most fundamental way of reducing the size of the non-market sector is to use the price mechanism to allocate resources which are now given away. A reduction in the range of functions of the state would automatically make the market sector larger, and the non-market sector smaller. Some Conservatives would wish to adopt this fundamental solution, but the members of the Labour party who believed that the cost of the public sector was rising too rapidly in 1974 and 1975 would not wish to return any of its functions to the market sector. However, even without fundamental changes in the role of government in society, much can be done to make the non-market sector smaller so that more can go to those who produce directly. Control of employment in health and education would reduce the marketed output that must be transferred from industrial workers to teachers and social workers, and at the same time increase the labour available to provide marketed goods and services. Cuts in the size of the civil service, or in the relative salaries of civil servants, would have the same effect. Cuts in subsidies to both private and nationalised firms would reduce the marketed output that profitable firms must give up. Council house rents which covered a higher fraction of costs would bring similar benefits, as would cuts in subsidies in favour of the consumption of particular goods. Finally any reduction in the transfers that have to be made from those who produce to those who do not would allow the productive to keep more of what they earn. Hence any reduction in public expenditure of any kind would help to ease the adverse pressures on the economy provided that the output of the market sector did not fall at the same time.

This is the crucial element in a pro-market sector solution, and anything else is tinkering. A Conservative government like Mr Heath's which failed to cut the ratio of public expenditure to marketed output, and actually increased the number of civil servants by 98,000 in three years, failed to ease any of the economy's real adverse pressures because it failed to improve the underlying structure in which businesses and workers have to operate. His government managed to cut some taxes like surtax, but because public expenditure rose faster than marketed output, others like local authority rates had to be increased. This failed to give most of those who had voted Conservative in 1970 an increase in the proportion of their incomes that they could spend themselves, and it undermined any attempt to improve the functioning of the economy. It meant that there was still bound to be too little marketed output to give both manual workers and the better-off the consumer goods they wanted without depriving industry of resources for investment and putting pressure on the balance of payments. A new Conservative government would avoid these particular errors. It would know that the market sector will only have enough to satisfy workers, managers and the investment needs of the nation if the government takes less. But any government, Labour or Conservative, which sought to shift resources into the market sector on a substantial scale by cutting public expenditure would need to solve several problems. The number of workers the market sector could provide work for was falling, even before the onset of the world recession in 1974. There has been low investment since then, so the likelihood is that the number of jobs it can provide has fallen further. Therefore extra workers made redundant in the public sector will only find jobs in the market sector when its capital stock starts to grow far more rapidly than in 1970–4. Jobs can be found for some without extra investment by merely raising demand while there is excess capacity throughout the economy as a result of the world recession, but as soon as the economy moves towards full capacity working, it will emerge that there are fewer productive jobs than in 1974.

More investment in the private industries and services will

therefore need to *precede* any large switch of labour from the public sector. A government that sought to cut public expenditure would therefore need an investment boom no less than a Left government before it could start to alter the structure of the economy as it wished. Also like a Left government it would have the opportunity to raise investment sharply without having to give up other resources if the country could recover from the world recession with an export and investment-led boom. This opportunity must be seized if public sector employment is to be cut without causing mass unemployment at the same time.

The period of recovery from the world recession when export growth will provide markets for extra sales of industrial production will be one when there will already be some stimulus to investment in the market sector, but it will almost certainly be less than that required. The likelihood is that strong incentives to greatly inrease investment in new plant and office space will be needed in addition.

Strong investment incentives will also directly assist recovery from the recession, as these will create employment in the machinery-producing and building industries, and then raise incomes elsewhere through the Keynesian multiplier. A new Conservative government would expect private sector businesses themselves to decide where the investment in an export and investment-led boom should go. It could do this by creating new incentives all firms could take advantage of, which made investment in new plant and office space in the period of recovery from the recession a bargain that would not be repeated. Thus for tax purposes the whole United Kingdom could be regarded as a development area in those years alone. Investors in London and the Midlands would then get the tax benefits that are now obtainable only in areas of exceptional unemployment. With net-of-tax profits down to low levels in manufacturing, even this might not be enough and the government could offer to lend all companies money at 5 per cent, 6 per cent or 7 per cent for investment they could not finance internally. Companies would then be able to borrow at rates far lower than the expected rate of inflation if they did so in the years when investment would help the economy most. Companies could be allowed to borrow one pound for investment on these terms for each pound of their own money that they spent on investment in new plant and machinery. Alternatively they could be allowed to borrow one pound for every pound by which investment exceeded the level achieved in the low investment years of 1971–6, due allowance being made for inflation. With bargains like these available from the government for a limited period only, companies could be expected to snap them up. Moreover they would have incentives to spend the extra money in the most profitable directions – and it would at no point be in their interests to borrow for loss-making investments (in current money terms). Concorde would not have attracted the British Aircraft Corporation on these terms, for it would have bankrupted the company even at 5 per cent. The principal market sector criterion that investment should go where it is expected to earn the greatest profits would therefore be at least partly fulfilled. Each company would direct the resources available to it in the most profitable directions without outside interference. Particular companies might get too much and others too little, but any state-engineered investment boom in 1977–80 must involve some distortion of market forces.

As with Left policies, the investment boom would have balance of payments consequences that would need to be dealt with unless the recovery of the world economy was exceptionally strong. It would also have implications for the government's 'borrowing requirement'. The orthodox solution here is to use a lower exchange rate to produce export demand to aid recovery from the recession and provide sufficient foreign exchange earnings to finance the import boom that would undoubtedly accompany economic recovery. Taxes would need to be raised or expenditure reduced to ensure that exports and investment, not consumption, grew most. These policies would in theory raise employment, improve the balance of payments and reduce the 'borrowing requirement' at the same time, so this is what a government with widespread support, including trade union co-operation, could do to put matters right. It is therefore what a Labour government pursuing policies to strengthen the economy's productive sector might be able to put across for so long as it retained union support. Mr Callaghan's government attempted it in 1976–7. However, a lower exchange rate raises prices at once, and exports a year or more later. Without a really tough incomes policy which a Conservative government lacking union goodwill could hardly negotiate, this sets off much faster inflation. A Conservative government pursuing these policies could therefore only lower the exchange rate to the extent that workers could be convinced of the need to divert resources from personal consumption to the balance of payments. It might well attempt to ride out a deficit as in 1964 and 1973, devaluing slightly to prevent excessive deterioration in the balance of payments in the long term, and expanding more slowly than in the past to prevent massive deterioration. It should be able to live with a moderate deficit much longer than a Left government. There would be greater capital inflows into Britain for there would be confidence that profits could be repatriated, that firms would not be nationalised with inadequate compensation, and that the Conservatives were not hostile to multinational companies. A Conservative government would of course have every confidence that once the market sector of the economy was large enough in relation to the non-market sector, balance of payments problems would be far easier to solve, so there would be less objection to a continuing deficit (which foreigners were prepared to finance) if the structure of the economy was being altered in favour of productive employment.

A new Conservative government would probably be as concerned about the government's own 'borrowing requirement' as the foreign balance. This would remain high until economies in public expenditure could begin, and really large economies could only start when work could be found for former public sector workers in the private sector. There would of course be slight immediate economies as nationalisation plans were cancelled or reversed, and expansion plans that the previous Labour government failed to cancel were stopped, but there could not be significant expenditure reductions without reduced employment in the public sector, or gratuitous increases in the cost of living as subsidies were removed. Indeed pro-market sector investment policies would raise the borrowing requirement at first, for new investment incentives would cost public money. But this is the only form of public expenditure which can bring in more tax revenue than the government's initial expenditures in the long term, for new plant raises the potential output of the market sector (provided that decisions on where to invest are moderately competent) and therefore the economy's taxpaying capacity.

The long-term strategy of a new Conservative government could be that tax revenue would be expected to rise gradually with the increased size of the market sector, while the curtailment of increases in public expenditure would slowly reduce the proportion of output taken by the government. At the same time most fundamental improvements would have to wait until the market sector could provide jobs for those the public sector released, for that is when real structural changes in favour of the market sector could begin.

It is in many ways fortunate that a government which sought to shift resources towards jobs that were directly productive would have to wait several years before it could sensibly make substantial economies in public expenditure. It is unlikely that more than a small minority in Britain would wish to see much of the welfare state dismantled. However many are prepared to believe that there is great waste of resources in the public sector. The non-market sector took a pre-tax 62 per cent of marketed output in 1975 in place of 41½ per cent in 1961, but many doubt whether the public services are significantly better where it matters most. Few believe that the sick or the old are better looked after in Britain than in West Germany, or that children are better educated in Britain than in France; but Britain spends far more in the public sector. There were much longer waiting lists to get into hospitals in 1975 than in 1961 and complaints about almost every aspect of the Health Service have grown. There are doubts whether the 85 per cent increase in employment in education has improved even elementary literacy and numeracy. These doubts may be unjustified but they are not confined to the Right. The housing situation has deteriorated sharply since the days of Mr Macmillan and the public services provided by the post office, railways and buses have contracted, in spite of immense increases in losses and subsidies. There is therefore a widespread belief that there have been great inefficiencies in the management of the public sector, and this is supported by many reports of the House of Commons Public Accounts and Expenditure Committees. Overmanning is clear in the case of steel, where direct comparisons with other countries can easily be made. If it is true that the Health Service provided better treatment for the sick in 1961 and used fewer workers to do so, what are the extra workers doing today? In 1965–73, the administrative staff in National Health Service Hospitals increased 51 per cent while the number of beds occupied daily fell from 451,000 to 400,000. There was one administrator or clerk to every 9.5 occupied beds in 1965 and one to every 5.6 occupied beds in 1973.[2] Only 51 per cent of the 1,453,000 that local authorities employ in education are actually teachers and only 70 per cent of those who work full time teach.[3] Are so many non-teachers needed in a service that overwhelmingly runs day and not boarding schools? Do other countries have them, and how many are highly paid administrators? How does employment in the post office and public transport compare with other countries? Where does Britain employ more people and get little for it?

These are all questions which need to be answered before it can be discovered where public sector employment can safely be slimmed, but they cannot be answered in haste. If attempts were made to cut employment quickly, the wrong economies might be made and services would certainly suffer. The objective should be to provide the indispensable public services, teachers for children, doctors, nurses and hospital beds for the sick, railwaymen and trains for pasengers, and to make no economies at this level. At the same time, expert committees assisted by firms of business consultants could be set up to examine each public sector activity thoroughly, comparing what happens in Britain with the same services in the world's most successful economies. In some cases the expert committees of inquiry might find that Britain was as efficient as the best, that there was no significant overmanning, and that fewer workers could not be used without a genuine loss of quality in the services provided. In other cases it might be found that Britain employs larger numbers to little purpose. Economies could then be made by cutting employment in these areas without loss to the public. There should indeed be gain, because excessive employment in administration slows down decisions, leads to confused areas of responsibility and provides the public with inferior service in all kinds of ways.

If the committees of inquiry found that no significant economies could be made without serious reductions in the quality of services an economising government would face a real dilemma. If the public sector is indeed as efficiently run as it reasonably can be, public expenditure cannot be cut very far without adopting the more controversial policies of returning certain activities to the market sector, i.e. charging for public services that are now free. Some Conservatives would support this, and it would make the public sector smaller and the market sector larger and more viable, but there would also be considerable opposition. There would on the other hand be virtually no opposition to policies to make the public sector efficient.

If the committees of inquiry found substantial inefficiencies, thought would have to be given to the present administrative machinery for controlling public expenditure. The responsibility for this is now divided between the Treasury which controls expenditures, and the new Civil Service Department which controls personnel. It may be that this has meant that there has been no proper check of the old-fashioned kind on *how* money is spent. A series of detailed reports by expert committees of inquiry to examine every institution in the public sector and the efficiency of its functioning is set down here as a pro-market sector policy but the Left could adopt it too. Better public services for the same expenditures would increase support for its policies.

If it proved possible to make economies in public-sector employment as the detailed reports started to come through, this could be done humanely provided that previous investment policies in the market sector had created enough jobs. Some established civil servants would be prepared to move to private-sector work if gratuities for early retirement from the public sector were adequate, and it would be possible to make quite rapid changes in the structure of employment by simply not replacing the 5 per cent to 10 per cent of non-established workers who change their jobs each year.

By methods like these, resources could gradually be shifted from the non-market to the market sector. A Conservative government might hope to move towards the pre-tax 41½ per cent of market-sector output that non-producers were entitled to buy in 1961 from the 62 per cent of 1975. A 50 per cent ratio might however be all that could be achieved without serious deterioration in services, and an economising Labour government would presumably aim for a smaller shift. Any movement of resources would allow more for private consumption, home ownership, investment and the balance of payments.

A Conservative pro-market sector government would not be particularly concerned about what happened to industrial production as such but its allocation might change as in Chart 21, where, as in Chart 20, possible future benefits from North Sea oil are not taken into account. With possible benefits from this disregarded, investment and exports might need to rise from 12.6 per cent to 20 per cent, less than in the Left solution because private services would make a greater contribution to employment and the balance of payments. Consumption or investment would therefore need to be cut elsewhere by 7.4 per cent of industrial production and the necessary cuts will be less than this to the extent that North Sea oil makes a major contribution to the balance of payments. It is assumed in Chart 21 that all the cuts needed are achieved by reducing the share of non-market sector investment and consumption as a result of public-sector economies, for which there is considerable scope. If the economy achieved rapid growth, public expenditure might need to fall little *in absolute terms* to achieve the results indicated in Chart 21 by say 1982. Thus if workers and managements could achieve a rate of productivity growth comparable to the rest of Western Europe's, public expenditure might merely need to be held stable in real terms for five or six years to reduce the proportion of industrial production consumed in the non-market sector from 30.7 per cent to 23.3 per cent, and much

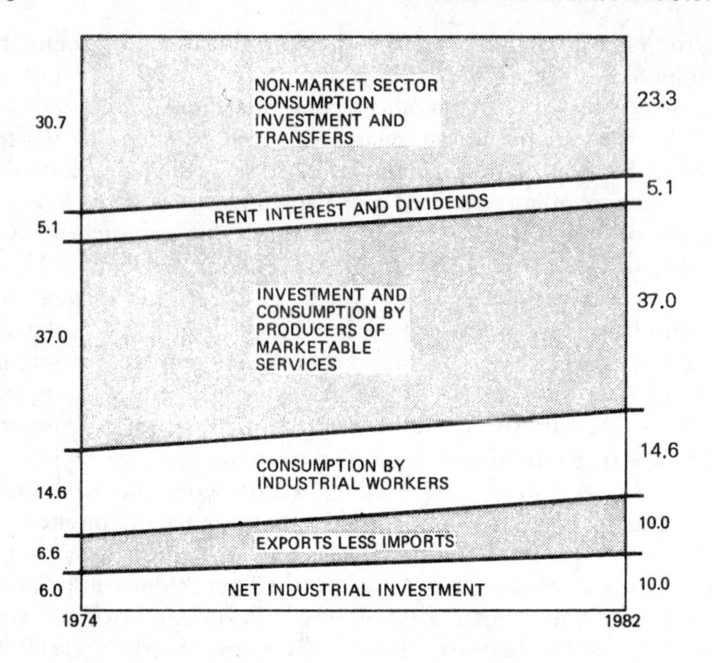

Chart 21 A Pro-Market Sector Solution: Shares of Sales of Industrial Products

smaller cuts than this will be needed once North Sea oil provides really significant help. After whatever cuts are needed in the adjustment period, non-market expenditure could be allowed to increase at the new and faster rate at which the economy was growing. In Chart 21, the shares of industrial production available to the private profit-making services and workers' consumption are left intact. This means that the private consumption of industrial workers can rise at the same rate as industrial production. This would rise faster with a near to doubling of investment, and faster still with more productivity growth, so workers would do well once the benefits for private consumption from public sector economies started to come through. Far less would be heard of the need for incomes policies by the time that stage was reached.

A Labour government pursuing these policies might well be unwilling to cut the share of public expenditure as much as Chart 21 indicates. It would have to cut the consumption of industrial workers and the private services, as in the Left solution, to the extent that it cut non-market expenditure by less than the necessary fraction. Its solution could then have many of the characteristics and disadvantages of the Left solution.

The early years would be the dangerous ones in the pro-market sector strategy that has been set out. At the beginning there would be few economies in public expenditure and all the extra pressures from an investment boom superimposed on a vulnerable balance of payments and a budget already in deficit. There are obvious risks here, but there would be the certainty of disaster if a Conservative pro-market sector government came to power and just sat back, balanced the budget, and let unemployment mount waiting for the market to solve its problems. That is not how France, West Germany and Japan recovered from the war, and it is not how Sir Winston Churchill and Mr R. A. Butler reacted to the opportunities and responsibilities of 1951. They slowly moved the economy in the right direction until, six years later when living standards had risen for all, their successors felt able to reduce rates of surtax and equalise rates of taxation on dividends and incomes from work. Britain has come to resemble a post-war economy, not nearly as damaged as in 1951 but nevertheless with proportions that are out of line. Some of the tools of post-war reconstruction are therefore needed. A Right government would need to use these tools (which it would not think of using in prosperity) to bring the economy slowly to the point where they could be dispensed with.

Once the risky phase was over and profit-making industries and services were selling enough to support the non-market sector at full employment, a new economy could emerge with growth in industry and in private and public services at rates which actually exploited the country's technical potential.

THE PROBLEM FOR BRITAIN

Britain's problem can be solved if one of the viable solutions that have been outlined is chosen and implemented. These can be no more than suggestions of a most general kind. There are fortunately many in British politics with administrative experience who are now aware of the problem and the need for solutions, and it is they who will come forward with alternative sets of policies that are complete and practicable.

The danger is that the British people will prefer to avoid a solution of either kind. A choice to drift and tinker could be disastrous. The world's viable economies are those which have solved the problem of providing adequate resources from their productive sectors for *both non-market expenditure and investment*. The successful Left economies have high non-market expenditure (for defence or welfare or both) and the state uses its powers to ensure that the productive investment needed to provide jobs is also undertaken. The successful market economies have low public expenditure as a fraction of output, and resources can then be found for both public expenditure and investment without much government intervention.

The economically unviable countries of the world are those with high non-market expenditure and low investment. They have chosen to spend on welfare or defence and failed to ensure that there will also be sufficient productive investment. In consequence their productive sectors have become too small for what is required of them. The result is chronic inflation, structural unemployment, and perpetual balance of payments crises and requests for aid and loans from the rest of the world as people try to get what their own economies are incapable of supplying. This all too often leads to 'strong' governments which either preside over chaos or use their powers to repress the living standards of all but those who keep them in power.

Since 1961 Britain has unwittingly started to become one of the world's high non-market expenditure and low investment economies, and since 1970 the ill-effects have begun. What has gone wrong since then is only a foretaste of the chaos to come if the country fails to accept the need for new policies.

The argument by which this conclusion has been reached has been presented in general terms so far, but there are a number of precise propositions on which it is based. These will be outlined in the next chapter so that readers will see that it was not a mere accident that rapid growth in non-market expenditure caused such difficulties for Britain. It could cause similar problems for any country, for reasons which will now be set out.

NOTES

1. See Assar Lindbeck, *Swedish Economic Policy*, Macmillan, 1975.
2. Dr Max Gammon, *Manpower and Numbers of Beds Occupied Daily 1965–73 UK NHS Hospital Service* (St Michael's Organization) 1975.
3. *Department of Employment Gazette*, December 1974, p. 1141.

4 The Fundamental Problem

The fundamental ways in which extra-rapid growth of non-market expenditure cause difficulties for an economy will be explained in this chapter. The full implications of the argument, which applies to Britain particularly sharply, will then be set out.

It is not obvious to all that non-market expenditure has grown particularly rapidly in Britain. Some confuse this with public expenditure and believe that this has grown at quite modest rates. Such a view can be based, for instance, on official statistics like those which state that the current spending of central and local government increased only from 17.5 per cent of the gross domestic product at constant market prices in 1961 to 21.9 per cent in 1974. Their capital spending merely increased from 4.0 per cent to 4.9 per cent of the gross domestic product in the same period, so it can appear that the current and capital spending of the public authorities in Britain increased only from 21.5 per cent to 26.8 per cent of the gross domestic product.[1] Spread over thirteen years, an increase of this order of magnitude should hardly squeeze the remainder of the economy to any significant degree, and OECD data show that public spending increased as mueh as this in many developed economies.[2]

There are three reasons why such conclusions cannot be drawn from official figures like these. First, they are expressed in constant prices, so they exclude much of the relative price effect – teachers' and civil servants' salaries rising faster than the general price level – which has increased public spending so much more than private spending in Britain in current money terms. Second, figures like the above exclude transfers from those who produce to those like pensioners who do not, so they underrate the extent to which producers have had to finance the increased spending of others. Third, they are based on a division of the economy into public and private sectors rather than market and non-market sectors. The latter division is more relevant to the problems that really matter – inflation, growth and the balance of payments – for marketed output has to provide for the full private consumption, investment and export needs of the nation.

How much difference the first two qualifications make is brought out as soon as figures like those quoted above are contrasted with those of Professor Cedric Sandford and Dr Ann Robinson, who published a survey of public expenditure in Britain which showed that the combined spending of the central government and local authorities, with pensions and other transfers included, increased from 40.6 per cent to 52.5 per cent of the gross national product in just ten years – 1964 to 1974. With expenditure on financial assets excluded, it still increased from 38.0 per cent to 49.3 per cent.[3] It is far more plausible that increases like these, which show a reduction of about one-fifth in the share of the money national income available to the remainder of the economy, had significant effects.

It was argued in previous chapters that it is the public sector activities which do not provide marketed outputs that put particular pressure on the resources of the remainder of the economy, and these increased still faster than the ratio of public expenditure to the gross national product. The claims on marketed output from outside the market sector increased from 41.4 per cent of marketed output in 1961 to 60.3 per cent in 1974, thus apparently reducing the proportion of output that market-sector producers could themselves invest and consume by nearly one-third. This increase in government claims is expressed on a pre-tax basis. Civil servants, doctors and teachers pay taxes with the result that they cannot buy as much marketed output as their incomes indicate, so the non-market sector workers and pensioners could not actually have claimed 60.3 per cent of marketed output in 1974 – they could only have done so if they had paid no taxes. But the same qualification applies to the other measure, public expenditure as a share of the gross national product, where again the central government and local authorities could not actually claim 52.5 per cent of the gross national product in 1974, since some of this represented incomes from which taxes were paid. The qualification applies to both measures, and the claims of non-producers on marketed output which grew from 41.4 per cent to 60.3 per cent of marketed output from 1961 to 1974 (and from 42.1 per cent to 60.3 per cent in 1964–74) increased massively more than the ratio of public expenditure to the gross national product.

This much greater increase in the ratio of government claims on marketed output is due to the fact that the transfer of workers from the production of marketed output to the provision of unmarketed public services like administration, teaching and health has two distinct effects. It reduces the economy's marketed output and, at the same time, it increases what producers must give up out of a diminished total to supply the needs of non-producers. Thus if workers earning £2000 million are transferred from the market sector to the provision of unmarketed public services, marketed output will fall by £2000 million and the claims of the non-market sector on what remains will rise by £2000 million on a pre-tax basis.[4] With the change in public expenditure shown as a share of the national income, the increased claims of £2000 million would be shown, but not the fact that £2000 million less purchasable output was available to meet them, for civil servants' salaries are included in the national income, like those of market-sector workers. The marketed output measure of increased government spending shows such a great increase in Britain's case because it brings out this dual effect.* Not all public spending raises claims and

* This can be illustrated with an example. Suppose the national income is initially £8000 million consisting wholly of marketed output. Suppose workers earning £2000 million are then transferred to the provision of public services. With conventional definitions their work still contributes to the national income with the result that this remains at £8000 million. The increase in public expenditure of £2000 million then raises the ratio of public expenditure to the national income from zero to 25 per cent. But

reduces the resources available to meet them at the same time, and an increase in old age pensions of £2000 million would not have this dual effect. It would increase claims on market-sector output by £2000 million like the extra paid to civil servants transferred from the market sector, but it would not reduce marketed output.† An increase in food or housing subsidies of £2000 million would increase claims by £2000 million and *increase* real incomes within the market sector by a fraction of this, so the pressure on resources would be still less. Different types of public spending therefore have very different effects on the ratio of government claims to marketed output.

The marketed output measure that is favoured in this book shows the largest increase in the *ratio* of government claims where resources are actually transferred from the market sector, and the prime reason why it has shown non-market sector claims taking so much extra marketed output in Britain on a pre-tax basis is that the actual transfer of resources from the market sector to the non-market sector has been exceptionally great. Much of the increase in spending therefore had the dual effect of increasing claims on resources by non-producers and reducing their supply at the same time. There was more shift of the labour force into services – mainly public – in Britain than in most other comparable economies according to the evidence quoted in Chapter 1, so it is likely that Britain's increase in non-market sector claims as a ratio of marketed output will prove to be one of the world's larger ones as soon as comparable data for several countries become available.

The increase in government claims on marketed output certainly had powerful effects in Britain, and it required a

---

the economy's marketed output falls from £8000 million to £6000 million, so the ratio of non-market expenditure to marketed output rises from zero to 33¹/₃ per cent.

† Suppose the national income, all marketed, is initially £8000 million, and that there is no initial public expenditure. A decision to pay pensions of £2000 million would increase both the ratio of public expenditure to the national income and the ratio of non-market expenditure to marketed output from zero to 25 per cent.

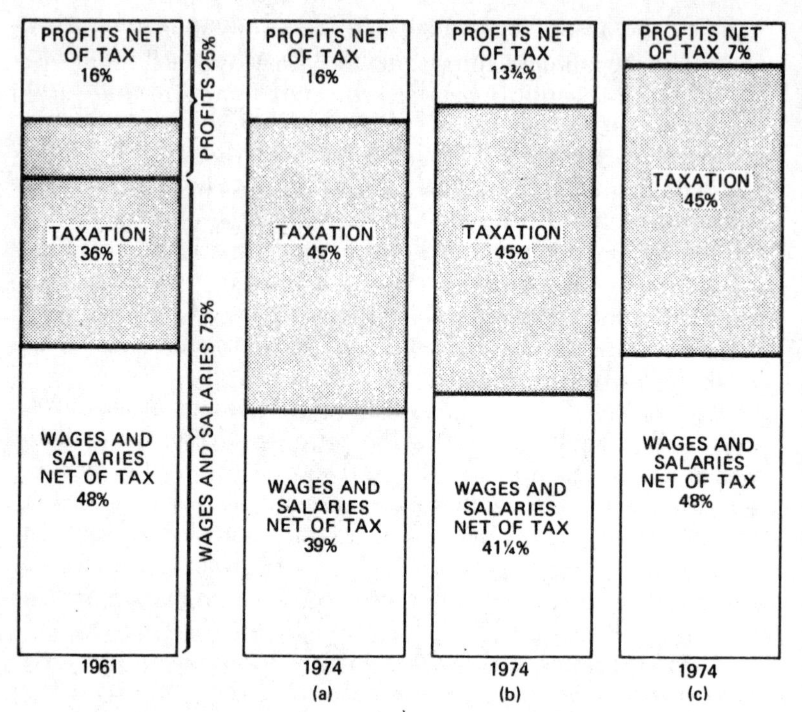

Chart 22 Three Possible Effects of Higher Taxation in 1961–74

great increase in overall taxation. In what follows it will be assumed conservatively that overall taxation in the market sector had to be increased by 9 per cent of marketed output from 1961 to 1974 to finance the increase in non-market sector claims of 18.9 per cent. The increase assumed is much less than 18.9 per cent for two reasons. First, non-market sector workers and pensioners pay some taxes themselves so it is not necessary to finance the whole cost of the non-market sector by taxing the market sector.[5] Second, the British budget was in substantial deficit in 1974 (partly because the world recession was beginning to have adverse effects on tax revenue in that year), so taxes were not increased as much as expenditure. The actual increase in taxation in the market sector was a little less than 9 per cent in 1961–74, but it will need to be more than 9 per cent when the economy approaches full employment, so a 9 per cent figure is sensibly between the actual one and the normal capacity one.

Increased taxation of 9 per cent of marketed output must have strong effects on the economy of the kind that chart 22 illustrates. The left-hand block shows the assumed division of marketed output between profits, wages and salaries, and the government in 1961. It is assumed that 25 per cent of marketed output went to profits before tax (net of capital consumption) while 75 per cent went to wages and salaries. Total taxation is assumed to be 36 per cent, and it is assumed that this was charged on profits and wages and salaries at equal rates, so one-quarter of the 36 per cent of total taxation was taken from profits and three-quarters from wages and salaries. After tax, profit-receivers therefore kept 16 per cent of marketed output (in place of 25 per cent before tax), workers kept 48 per cent (in place of 75 per cent) and the government obtained the remaining 36 per cent of marketed output. This simplified example can obviously be no more than an approximation to the situation in 1961, but it gives the broad orders of magnitude of the division of marketed output between workers, profit-receivers and the government.

The three blocks on the right give three possible examples of what could happen when an extra 9 per cent of marketed output has to be taken from those who produce it to increase the government's share of marketed output to 45 per cent. In (a), the first possible result, profit-receivers keep 16 per cent of marketed output as in 1961, and the extra 9 per cent the government takes comes wholly from workers and salary-earners. They therefore receive 39 per cent of marketed output after all taxes in place of 48 per cent. There are two ways in which this could come about. First, the government could levy the entire extra taxation of 9 per cent on workers and salary-earners while the distribution of incomes before tax remained as it was. Alternatively the government could raise taxes equally on wages and profits, but businessmen could pass profits taxes on to the consumer with the result that profits net of all taxes were the same as before and the entire extra cost of the non-market sector was paid by workers and salary earners, partly through higher taxes and partly because they received a lower share of total incomes in the market sector.*

In block (b) another possible outcome of the extra taxation is illustrated. Here profits and wages lose equal shares to pay the extra 9 per cent, so profits pay for one-quarter of this, and wages and salaries the other three-quarters. Net-of-tax profits therefore fall from 16 per cent of marketed output in 1961 to 13¾ per cent in 1974, while wages and salaries fall from a net-of-tax 48 per cent to a net-of-tax 41¼ per cent. This could come about through equal tax increases on wages and profits, or through different tax increases and compensating changes in the distribution of incomes.

Block (c) shows the third possibility, and the one that corresponds most closely to what actually happened in Britain in 1961 to 1974. Here the whole of the government's extra 9 per cent to raise its share of marketed output to 45 per cent is taken from net-of-tax profits, which therefore fall from 16 per cent of marketed output in 1961 to 7 per cent in 1974. With profits paying the whole extra cost of the larger non-market sector, workers and salary-earners continue to receive 48 per cent of this after all taxes. Again, this situation where the whole extra cost of the non-market sector is financed from profits could come about in two broad ways. First, the government could levy all the extra taxes it needed on profits or incomes derived from them while the distribution of incomes remained unchanged. Alternatively much of the extra taxation could be levied on wages and salaries in the first instance, but if workers had the power to pass these taxes on, profits could end up losing the whole 9 per cent. Workers can pass taxes on by causing exceptional wage inflation that leads to a squeeze on profit margins, either because prices and incomes policies are introduced to control inflation which impose lower profit margins on companies, or because the exchange rate is not lowered in line with domestic

* How this can come about is explained in detail in Chapter 7, pp. 178–9.

inflation, with the result that international competition squeezes profit margins.

It is thus in principle possible that the extra 9 per cent taxation of marketed output could cut net-of-tax wages and salaries by 9 per cent of marketed output as in (a), or net-of-tax profits by 9 per cent as in (c), or both together as in (b). These may all have significant effects, and something corresponding quite closely to one of these must happen, for an extra 9 per cent of marketed output must be taken from either profits or wages and salaries or both together. This is inescapable.

Suppose first that it is predominantly wages and salaries that are squeezed. Then workers' consumption has to fall from 48 per cent to 39 per cent of marketed output during the thirteen-year transition period. If marketed output rose rapidly at the same time, workers' private net-of-tax incomes could fall from 48 per cent to 39 per cent of this and still grow very fast indeed in absolute terms. Thus if marketed output per head rose at a West European rate of 5 per cent a year during the thirteen years, the *private* consumption of workers and salary-earners could rise 53.2 per cent or 3.3 per cent per annum during this period. A reduction in the rate of increase of living standards in terms of private consumption from 5 per cent to 3.3 per cent a year for thirteen years would be enough to divert the necessary extra resources to the non-market sector. It is because they have had growth rates in marketed output like these that some economies have been able to achieve a rapid transfer of resources into the non-market sector and a high rate of increase of private consumption per head at the same time. Consider in contrast a similar transfer of resources to the non-market sector with the British rate of growth of marketed output per head of about 2½ per cent per annum.[6] Here private net-of-tax incomes can grow only 12 per cent in the thirteen-year transition period, or at 0.9 per cent per annum.* Workers can be expected to accept much more readily a reduction in the rate of growth of private consumption from 5.0 per cent

* This thirteen-year transition is set out formally in Chapter 7, pp. 192–4.

to 3.3 per cent for thirteen years to divert resources to higher social spending, than one from 2.5 per cent to 0.9 per cent per annum. The latter could lead to markedly more frustration and union militancy.

There would, of course, be no adverse response to a diversion of resources of this kind if the increased social spending was a direct and exact response to workers' preferences for this. There are two conceivable ways in which this could come about. Social spending decisions could be taken through parliament, and the policies the government of the day implemented could in theory reflect the preferences of the great majority of the electorate, and therefore of most workers and salary-earners. If they were actually aware of the costs of policies when they voted for them, the increased taxation when those policies were implemented would be part of what they voted for. The electorate should then expect a much slower rate of growth of private net-of-tax incomes than of aggregate output, and there should then be no attempt to get extra wage and salary increases to compensate for higher taxation. Alternatively, a decision to increase social spending relative to private spending could be taken rationally as part of an incomes policy negotiated at the national level. A central trade union leadership with the power to commit member unions and the rank and file could agree to exercise wage restraint if the government increased social spending much faster than the national product. If either of these conditions could be met, even a slow-growing economy could divert resources rapidly into the non-market sector without a wages explosion, and achieve an orderly thirteen-year transition to the situation illustrated in block (a) where the government takes 45 per cent of marketed output in place of 36 per cent, and workers bear the entire costs of this.

But if neither set of conditions can be met, workers will not necessarily acquiesce in a reduction in the rate of increase of private consumption per head from 2.5 per cent to 0.9 per cent for thirteen years. Only the Scandinavian countries have the machinery to bargain about the social wage at the national level and trade union leadership that can commit the rank and file. Other countries must therefore rely on their parliaments to allocate resources between private and social spending, and for this mechanism to give a result that reflects the true wishes of the people the costs of social policies must be made absolutely clear at election time. If parties pretend then that they can increase both private and public consumption at rapid rates, they may be voted into office and then surprise the electorate when the bills have to be paid. The electorate as workers and members of trade unions may then all too easily respond by refusing to accept the bills which were not at all what they voted for. To refuse to pay legal taxes is impractical, because this can rapidly result in the sequestration of property and imprisonment, but obtaining wage and salary increases which make up for extra taxation is often perfectly possible – at least for a time. It was argued in earlier chapters that this is almost precisely what happened in Britain in 1961 to 1974, and lack of knowledge by the people at election time of the extra costs of higher social spending that *they themselves* would have to pay, or disappointment at the failure of the social wage to rise significantly in *output* terms, or inconsistency between votes in favour of the social wage and industrial action in favour of private consumption could all help to explain this. The likeliest explanation is that the full taxation costs of social spending programmes, local government reorganisation (which has led to soaring local authority rates) and so on were never made clear enough. The British people therefore voted for higher social spending, and then set off rapid wage inflation when they realised to their surprise that they were expected to pay for it.

Monetarists would not allow that frustrated workers can set off rapid inflation without government co-operation, for they believe that workers could only push up wages rapidly if governments increased the money supply at similar rates. They would expect prices to be stable if the government only increased the money supply in line with the economy's long-term growth rate, whether taxation on workers' consumption rose or fell. But they would concede that frustrated workers could raise money wages rapidly at first until lack of growth of the money supply began to bite. With money wages rising and the money supply held back, unemployment

would mount, and it is therefore extra unemployment that workers' frustration due to rising taxation would cause. This is surely correct, and it means that the argument can be set out more generally. If workers are frustrated by rising taxation, *either* inflation will accelerate (if the money supply is allowed to expand), *or* unemployment will rise (if the money supply is controlled).* The range of options open to a society in this situation will therefore deteriorate, and governments will be faced with the choice of *either* more inflation than in the past, *or* more unemployment, *or* as a third alternative, tougher incomes policies with stronger sanctions to enforce them if they are to be effective. Such countries are only too likely to end up with the stagflation from which so many have recently suffered.

In Britain's case, the workers certainly did manage to raise money wages more rapidly when taxation increased. This means that the increased cost of non-market expenditure was not met, as in principle it could have been, through a 9 per cent reduction in the share of marketed output going to wages and salaries. On the figures used in this chapter, which roughly correspond to the costs of transition in Britain, if workers had paid the full costs of higher, non-market expenditure, they could only have enjoyed an increase in real take-home pay of about 0.9 per cent per annum from 1961 to 1974. But in chart 6 on page 7 above it was shown that this increased 1.6 per cent per annum from 1963 to 1974, and it actually increased 2.2 per cent per annum from 1963 to 1973 when there were not significant overall effects on workers' living standards from changes in the terms of trade.[7] This suggests that workers' net-of-tax incomes increased at almost the same rate as marketed output per

* In technical terms monetarists would describe this deterioration of options as an increase in the 'natural' rate of unemployment, i.e. in the unemployment rate at which the rate of inflation is stable. It would be a prediction of the theory in this book that the increase in the 'natural' rate of unemployment (or rightward movement of the Phillips curve) throughout the world since 1960 would be partly explained by the inverse of 'the increase in marketed output per worker *less* the rate of diversion of marketed output per worker to the non-market sector', in the various countries.

worker in 1963–73, which indicates that in this period they made virtually no net contribution to the increased cost of the non-market sector. Then the case where net-of-tax profits bear the entire cost of this probably comes closest to what happened, and the collapse of net-of-tax profits in Britain from 1963 to 1973 shown in Chart 11 on page 21 above makes it very clear that this *is* what happened. Hence the case where profits net of all taxes fall by 9 per cent of marketed output appears to correspond most closely to what happened in Britain, and the full implications of this will now be considered.

If the entire extra 9 per cent of marketed output that the government needs in 1974 must be found from net-of-tax profits, these need to fall by over one-half, from 16 per cent to 7 per cent of marketed output. It is well known that businesses finance much of their investment by ploughing back profits, and if these fall by over one-half after tax, investment will be severely threatened. Companies have two possible additional sources of finance (apart from the government). They can issue equity shares on the stock exchange, and they can borrow on fixed interest terms. But equity shares cannot be sold on reasonable terms where profits are falling in relation to marketed output and profit expectations are depressed, as they will be if net-of-tax earnings fall by one-half (as a share of marketed output) in thirteen years. In such a situation, firms will only be able to invest much more than their retained earnings if they are prepared to borrow heavily on fixed interest terms.

The difficulty with fixed interest borrowing on a large scale is that this increases the risk of bankruptcy, or at any rate takeover by creditors who generally change managements that cannot pay the interest they have contracted. A firm which finances investment wholly from its own profits can continue to produce so long as it continues to earn profits. A company in contrast which has to pay interest to outsiders equivalent to half its profits in normal times will be unable to meet its interest costs from profits if these fall 60 per cent or 70 per cent. If the company also lacks reserves so that it finds the payment of interest an embarrassment, the banks and insurance companies which lent the money might well decide to put in other managers and those who borrowed imprudently will then become unemployed with a record of recent failure. Bankruptcy would follow a prolonged inability to meet interest commitments. In contrast, a fall in profits of 60 per cent or 70 per cent in a recession would leave managements relatively safe from outside interference if all the money they had used to finance investment came from their own companies' ploughed-back profits.

Because of the risks involved in borrowing on fixed interest terms, companies prefer to finance a high proportion of their investment from retained earnings. A company that considered it sound financial policy to finance at least two-thirds of its investment in this way would be able to borrow 50p on fixed interest terms for each £1 of its own profits that it reinvested, so its investment would be *at most* one-and-a-half times its retained earnings. A second company, prepared to take greater risks, might willingly borrow £1 for each £1 of retained earnings ploughed back, while a third might borrow only up to 25p for each £1 it reinvested. While the actual ratios differ, investment is limited to some multiple of the retained earnings that these companies plough back in all three cases.*

If net-of-tax profits fall from 16 per cent to 7 per cent of marketed output, the investment firms can finance by reinvesting their profits will fall drastically, and companies will also find it prudent to borrow less because their safe borrowing levels are multiples of the money they can themselves plough back. Now if most companies are well below their prudent borrowing limits, this will hardly affect aggregate investment, for companies will be able to borrow the money to finance investment that they can no longer reinvest from profits. But if in contrast most companies are at their limits or close to them, the reduction in internal finance for investment will also cut the amount it is safe to

* In technical terms, it is being suggested that there are upper limits to the gearing ratios that firms are prepared to use. The gearing ratio limit will then set a ceiling to the amount of fixed interest debt firms are prepared to incur, and investment will be at most retained earnings times a multiple which depends on the maximum tolerable gearing ratio. The argument is set out formally in Chapter 7, pp. 187–9.

borrow on fixed interest terms, so investment will be doubly reduced.

In the economy as a whole there will be some companies in the first situation, and these will be able sensibly and safely to make up through borrowing the finance they no longer obtain from profits. But there will also be many companies already borrowing as much as they think sound, and these will not be able to make good the shortfall in retained earnings by borrowing more. Indeed they will have to borrow less than in the past if they put less of their own profits into their businesses each year.

There are always likely to be some companies in the latter situation, and these will have to invest less where net-of-tax profits fall. If most companes are rather close to their safe borrowing limits, the great majority will invest less. The result will be a large fall in investment in the market sector as a share of marketed output. A fall in retained earnings of one-half would reduce investment by about one-half if all the companies in the economy were close to their debt limits. Because many companies are likely to be below their debt limits in any given year, the fall in investment could generally be expected to be markedly less than one-half where undistributed profits fall one-half after tax – but there is no doubt that aggregate investment would fall as a share of marketed output.

This raises the question of why companies tolerate a situation where net-of-tax profits are squeezed. It was argued above that workers are liable to resist strongly where they are squeezed, with the result that they can often make good, through higher money wages, any reduction in their standard of living due to higher taxation and higher prices. Why cannot companies do the same? In theory they can, and there is much evidence that profits taxes often are passed on.[8] But there is also evidence since 1960 (and this has certainly been the case in Britain) that the main effect of higher public spending has been to squeeze net-of-tax profits and therefore investment rather than net-of-tax wages and salaries. Fundamentally this must be because, in some countries, companies now lack the power of trade unions to pass taxes on, for reasons that have been outlined in earlier chapters.

It is interesting that a recent statistical study has arrived at precisely the result that increases in public expenditure and therefore taxation have had strong adverse effects on private sector investment. Mr David Smith, formerly of the Bank of England, has published a cross-section study of investment, public spending (measured conventionally), inflation and growth for nineteen countries in the period 1961–72; and his conclusions included the following proposition:

> Until further, and better, estimates can be provided by others the author would like to suggest that, as a simple rule of thumb to concentrate the mind, it be assumed that each 5 per cent increase in the share of national disposable income absorbed by direct state consumption (on the narrow definition excluding transfer payments) implies a 1.0 per cent drop in the growth rate.

And this falls primarily because '. . . each increase in the narrow definition of state consumption of 1.0 per cent of NDI [net domestic incomes] produces a 0.94 per cent drop in the ratio of investment to NDI'.[9] Smith's statistical results are completely in line with the analysis that has just been presented. Higher state consumption must squeeze net-of-tax profits or wages and salaries as a share of marketed output. In so far as it squeezes profits, and this is perhaps what it is now most likely to squeeze in many countries, it will also squeeze investment, because many companies will consider it imprudent to borrow on fixed interest terms the finance that they can no longer find from their own profits. This will especially be the case if net-of-tax profits are falling, as they are in the example in this chapter, when many will be particularly pessimistic about future profitability.

There is one further direction from which private-sector finance for investment could come. Domestic producers will invest less for the reasons outlined when net-of-tax profits are squeezed, but foreign companies could come in and provide the investment that the home country's firms cannot or will not finance. This possibility can be dismissed at once as a way out. A climate of falling net-of-tax profits with workers pushing up wages rapidly to preserve their own net-of-tax position is precisely one where foreign capital would be discouraged from coming in. If things got bad enough, money might come in from foreign governments for charitable reasons, but multinational companies will seek to withdraw as much capital as they can from a country with sharply falling net-of-tax profits and rampant wage inflation, and all the social and industrial conflict that this must produce.

It is therefore overwhelmingly likely that if net-of-tax profits are squeezed as a result of an increase in the proportion of marketed output taken by the government, investment will fall too. The implications of this are of great importance, for inadequate investment can all too easily lead to structural unemployment. It is a well-known principle of economic theory that if output can be raised 5 per cent a year and £2 of capital is needed to produce £1 worth of output per annum, 10 per cent of output must be invested each year.* This proposition is illustrated in the table.

The relationship between growth of marketed output and investment requirements where £2 of Capital is needed to produce £1 of output per annum

	Possible output	*Capital required*	*Investment needed*
Economy A: 5 per cent growth			
Year 1	100	200	10
Year 2	105	210	10.5
Year 3	110.25	220.5	11.02
Economy B: 2 per cent growth			
Year 1	100	200	4
Year 2	102	204	4.08
Year 3	104.04	208.08	4.16

In Economy A where there is 5 per cent growth, capital has to be raised from 200 to 210 between Years 1 and 2 if output is to be raised from 100 to 105, and this can only be achieved by investing 10 per cent of the first year's output. All *net* investment is an addition to the capital stock, so

* This is an application of the Harrod-Domar formula which states that a country's long-term share of investment must equal *the rate of growth* times *the capital needed to produce a unit of output.*

investment of 10 raises the capital stock by the necessary 10 from 200 to 210.

Now suppose an economy in these conditions has the technological potential to raise its market sector output 5 per cent a year because it can raise output per worker 4 per cent a year and employment 1 per cent a year. If it needs £2 of capital to produce £1 of output, it will have to invest 10 per cent of market-sector output like Economy A. Imagine that because of a profits squeeze it invests only 4 per cent of its output like Economy B. Its capital stock will then grow only 2 per cent a year from 200 to 204 in one year and 208 in two, and so on, like Economy B's. With this slow growth of capital, output will be able to advance only from 100 to 102 to 104, instead of from 100 to 105 and 110 like Economy A's. But if output grows just 2 per cent a year and output per worker rises 4 per cent a year, employment must fall 2 per cent a year. Hence if an economy with the growth potential of A limits itself to B's investment, it will only have B's 2 per cent rate of growth, so its 4 per cent productivity growth rate will lead to a 2 per cent loss of jobs each year. Thus in this simplified example, A can have a 5 per cent rate of growth and a 1 per cent increase in jobs if it invests 10 per cent, and it will only enjoy a 2 per cent rate of growth, and it will lose 2 per cent of its jobs each year if it invests just 4 per cent.

There are two true ways out of this trap and one false way. The false way out for the unfortunate country is to raise its rate of growth of productivity from 4 per cent to 6 per cent without investing more or cutting the capital costs required to produce a unit of output. With 6 per cent growth in output per worker, the country's potential rate of growth of marketed output will be 7 per cent, but with only 4 per cent of output invested its actual rate of growth will still be B's 2 per cent. Therefore with 2 per cent output growth and 6 per cent growth of output per worker, 4 per cent of its labour force will become redundant each year instead of 2 per cent. These workers will either languish in idleness, or be absorbed into the non-market sector, which would then require still higher taxation and squeeze profits yet again so that even the 4 per cent investment rate of Economy B would be difficult to sustain.

In contrast, a true way out of the trap is for the country to raise its investment to 10 per cent of marketed output. It could then grow at 5 per cent like Economy A. If this must be financed largely from profits, the non-market sector may need to be reduced in size relative to the market sector to allow taxes to be cut, and the share of profits net of tax to rise. Another true way out of the trap would be to drop the rule that £2 of capital is needed to produce £1 of output a year. If rising output from the existing capital stock could be achieved the case shown below would be a possibility.

	Possible output	*Capital required*	*Investment needed*
Economy C: 5 per cent growth with falling capital requirements			
Year 1	100	200	4
Year 2	105	204	4.20
Year 3	110.25	208.20	4.41

Economy C which solves all the problems, has A's 5 per cent rate of growth and B's 4 per cent share of investment. It accomplishes this by steadily cutting the capital needed to produce a unit of output, and the capital needed to equip a worker.

Any economy would find it marvellous if it could obtain what C achieves – extra growth without having to pay for it. In principle, with rapid technical progress, the capital cost of growth could rise (economists call this *capital-using* technical progress) or fall (*capital-saving* technical progress) or stay the same (*neutral* technical progress). C is an example of capital-saving technical progress. It can happen, but historically technical progress has been capital-using as often as it has been capital-saving. Marx based his predictions on the belief that technical progress would always be capital-using, which he assumed because of what happened in the first century after the industrial revolution, so he predicted that capital-output ratios would continuously rise and cause growing technological unemployment. There will also be growing technological unemployment if technical progress is neutral (i.e. the amount of capital needed to produce a unit of output neither rises nor falls) and the share of investment falls because profits are squeezed. If profits have to be squeezed and investment falls continuously, capitalism will only be saved if technical progress is capital-saving, the precise opposite of Marx's, so that as with Economy C, 5 per cent growth can be attained with only 4 per cent investment.* This is a great deal to hope for and an economy will be extremely fortunate if it happens. Britain has not managed to achieve it for reasons which will be discussed when the relevance of the argument to Britain's particular problems is considered in detail below.

The argument of this chapter has shown that an economy can in principle suffer from two kinds of problem if the ratio of non-market expenditure is raised significantly. First, if the share of output received by workers and salary-earners is reduced to provide the extra resources the government needs, wage inflation may accelerate, or alternatively if the money supply is controlled, more unemployment will be needed to check it. If net-of-tax profits become lower instead of wages, investment will suffer to an extent depending on how near companies are to their borrowing limits, and if investment falls, the economy's rate of growth of productive capacity is likely to fall with the result that technical progress will produce growing redundancies instead of rapid output growth. The only way of avoiding this is to achieve capital-saving technical change – and this will not happen easily.

The increase in non-market expenditure in Britain has produced both kinds of adverse effect. Attempts were made to finance extra non-market spending at the expense of workers' consumption, and deductions from paypackets rose by about the 9 per cent of marketed output needed for this, so the economy could in principle have achieved a transition where workers bore the entire cost. But workers did not acquiesce in this, so wage inflation accelerated, unemployment rose and incomes policies had to be made increasingly strict. Through the extra inflation they caused, workers managed to pass the bulk of extra taxation on to companies, so these ended up having to pay for the larger non-market sector. Companies have responded by investing less (and with its faster productivity growth rate, the country has needed more investment, not less, to maintain employment in the

* The argument in pp. 107–10 is set out formally in Chapter 7, pp. 198–200.

market sector) so the economy has also suffered from declining market sector employment, and this started to decline rapidly long before the onset of the world recession. Britain is therefore suffering from both growing structural unemployment, and a situation where incomes policies have to be tougher or unemployment higher than before to contain inflation. And the adverse trends, if left unchecked, will continue so that structural unemployment will become still higher and workers still more discontented.

That is how Britain's crisis has come about, and it has now been explained more technically than before. The one question that still requires an answer is why the country has failed to achieve the capital-saving technical progress that would have allowed it to grow faster and invest less at the same time. It can be supposed that industrialists base their choice of plant on the relative costs of labour and capital. The cost of employing labour has risen sharply in Britain since 1961. Taxes on employment to finance improved social security benefits have risen greatly, and money wages have also risen considerably relative to product prices. But the cost of capital has risen too, for when firms approach their borrowing limits it is to be expected that they will attach a high notional cost to the use of extra capital. Hence the costs of capital and labour have both risen sharply, but it may well be that the cost of labour has risen more. If it has, firms may have biased their investment in the capital-using and labour-saving direction – thus accentuating the problem.

But the problem would still have been solved if Britain had been able to achieve rapid capital-saving productivity growth. This is the solution of those who see Britain's weaknesses as the result of failures by workers and managements to achieve adequate productivity growth. It will be evident from what has been said that merely to have raised productivity faster would not have solved Britain's problem. Higher labour productivity with *the same capital requirements to produce a unit of output* would have actually increased the investment needed to prevent growing structural unemployment in the market sector, and what was needed was higher productivity and *a fall in the investment required to produce a unit of output* at the same time. In Chapter 1 and the Preface the first of these was called curing *overmanning*, and the second curing *underproduction.*[10] Britain suffers from both, given the evidence on machine tool use and the Think Tank's study of the motor car industry, but *underproduction* is the fault that is crucially relevant to the country's problems.

The Think Tank lists several reasons why the British motor car industry obtains less output from the same plant than firms on the continent of Europe, and they cite examples of similarly equipped assembly lines producing 75 per cent and 120 per cent more on the continent. They say that British assembly lines move more slowly which reduces output per unit of capital. They also suffer more interruptions from stoppages. Of the total production lost from these, manufacturers are said to attribute 40 per cent to shortages of materials due to external disputes, or poor stock control where necessary materials and components are not ordered in time. Finally, British plants lost twice as many hours through mechanical breakdowns even though the British industry employs 80 per cent more workers on maintenance.[11] If these faults apply to many British industries as they probably do – it is unlikely that the car industry is unique – it will be evident that much underproduction is due to failures by management and labour on the shop floor. There is relatively little that governments can do to put such matters right. But there is one aspect of underproduction where governments may be able to give a little assistance. The utilisation of plant can obviously be improved if output grows more rapidly, for this will allow items of equipment in particular firms that are only used for a few hours a week to be used for longer. Moreover with faster growth of demand, workers can raise productivity without losing their jobs. Therefore if Britain could achieve a faster rate of growth by other means, such as investing more and allocating more resources to activities that are directly productive, the output of existing plant should rise where it is not inefficiency due to labour and managements that is holding it back, so there could be a double benefit in some industries. The world's fast-growing economies have the lowest capital costs of growth, which makes their growth easier to sustain. If Britain could once get out of the vicious circle of slow growth, low demand for the output of particular items of plant and an industrial environment where efficiency all too often causes redundancies so that incentives to improve productivity are minimal, much might be achieved. In sum, much progress might be made to cure Britain's problem of underproduction if governments can start to solve some of the economy's other problems.

Governments will therefore need to tackle the profits squeeze, and the investment squeeze that this has caused. Here the Left's position is absolutely clear-cut. It accepts that there has been a profits squeeze and welcomes it. This is what it has always fought for. But it recognises that the consequent squeeze on investment matters. With capitalism unviable as it is in Britain in the middle 1970s, the Left knows that the state will have to ensure that there is enough capital in the country to provide the jobs that are needed, for without profits companies simply cannot ensure this. The Left thus has a wholly consistent approach to this problem. Moreover, many on the Left appreciate that the extra investment that is needed must be financed mainly at the expense of the private sector services, as indicated in Chapter 3. There is no other sector where it would willingly cut consumption and investment to the necessary extent, and it is widely believed that private-sector services are consumed more by the better-off than the poor – though many private services export a great deal and are indispensable to productive processes, so what should be squeezed (obviously office building and property development, the Left would say) would require much research and good judgement.

A pro-market sector government, in contrast, must set about reversing the sequence of events which led to the profits and investment squeeze of 1961–75. If the government's requirements fell back from 45 per cent to 36 per cent of marketed output, 9 per cent extra could go to net-of-tax wages or profits, and in all probability both would gain. This should lessen the pressure for money wage increases, and at the same time the temptation to moderate workers to elect militants to represent their interests. In so far as companies benefited from lower taxation, there would be more internal finance for investment and more willingness to borrow; and with rising profits the stock exchange should become more buoyant, enabling fast-growing companies to obtain equity finance on reasonable terms. In addition, with all these favourable trends for profitability, international investment should again be attracted to Britain to supplement the country's domestic resources.

There is an important new point to note about pro-market sector solutions that has emerged in this chapter. Equal increases in public expenditure can have very different effects on the ratio of non-market expenditure to marketed output, and therefore on the necessary increase in taxation. Extra spending which takes resources out of the market sector and thus reduces marketed output causes the maximum pressure on resources and requires the largest increases in taxation per £1000 million of extra public expenditure. Government expenditures which transfer purchasing power from market-sector producers to non-producers but leave output intact, like higher old age pensions, cause less adverse pressure. Finally, expenditures to transfer purchasing power in ways from which some market-sector producers benefit financially, such as food and housing subsidies and family allowances, put still less pressure on resources per £1000 million of extra public expenditure. It follows that the particular ways in which pro-market sector governments cut public spending are extremely important. Mere cuts in food and housing subsidies would do relatively little to relieve the situation even if total spending was cut by quite large sums. The really substantial benefits can only come from cutting employment in the non-market sector, and axing projects which have a high capital and raw material content (like Maplin or Concorde) and low sales on the market. Of course, in all these cases, the full benefits can only be obtained if the resources that the government ceases to use are fully employed in the market sector. It is this that can allow the overall taxation of market-sector workers and companies to be cut substantially, and so relieve the adverse pressures on the economy.

The Left and pro-market sector policies are distinct, but in practice it is likely that governments will not consistently pursue either. Governments which have pro-market sector intentions may fail to cut public expenditure significantly through inefficiency or concessions to pressure groups. They will then have to pursue Left policies if they want a viable economy, even if they are nominally Conservative. They will have to choose import controls, draconian incomes policies and the control of property development, or face a collapse of productive investment and the balance of payments. In times of crisis the Left and Right positions can become so mixed up that it is difficult to tell which is which.[12]

Some economists have failed to observe the disintegration of the economy because in their theoretical approach aggregate saving is what determines investment. They do not believe that collapsing company saving will cause difficulties provided that personal saving rises to take its place. But if all the saving is done in the personal sector, and the investment has to be undertaken by companies which have no profits, trouble must result. The companies will not invest without profits, and the personal saving will have to be lent to the government (for who would wish to lend directly to unprofitable companies?), which will then have to find a way of passing it on to the company sector.* This would again involve Left policies, so these are inevitable if saving is predominantly personal, and companies are unprofitable.

Other economists believe that the government should continue to take extra resources from the market sector and raise taxation to finance this, because that is the direction in which a civilised community should progress. At the same time, many who hold these views also believe that the government should avoid *dirigiste* Left policies like import controls and direct state intervention in investment decisions because such interference is inefficient. They consider the market more efficient and believe that this should take private-sector investment decisions. But with growing public expenditure and taxation, profits can become so low that the market sector will generate insufficient investment. The market will not then be able to allocate the nation's investment resources efficiently because there will be insufficient profits to allow it to function as it should.

Moreover, with workers discontented, devaluations will produce accelerating inflation instead of balance of payments equilibrium. If growing public expenditure and accompanying taxation are allowed to reduce profits to the point where a market economy cannot function effectively, only

* The implications of this line of argument are explained in detail in Chapter 7, pp. 183–4.

Left policies can prevent chaos. So these economists, and they are numerous, must choose. They can support the allocation of investment resources through the market, or they can support Left policies of higher public spending, but they cannot have both.

And the British people must decide, either to strengthen the market sector so that it can function effectively, or to support the Left. Once the choice is made, it is crucial that the policies chosen be continued long enough to allow the balance of the economy to be restored.

NOTES

1. *National Income and Expenditure*, 1964–74, Tables 14 and 59, and 1972, Tables 14 and 50. The totals are expressed as fractions of the gross domestic product at constant factor cost.
2. See, for instance, OECD, *National Accounts, 1962–73.*
3. Cedric Sandford and Ann Robinson, 'Public Spending – a feature', *The Banker*, November 1975, pp. 1241–55.
4. That Mrs Thatcher has understood this for some time is evident from the passage quoted in Chapter 1 from her speech of 15 September 1975. See p. 32 above.
5. The relationship between a higher ratio of non-market expenditure and the extra rate of taxation required if the budget is to be balanced is set out formally in Chapter 7, pp. 174 and 176.
6. The gross domestic product at constant factor cost increased at a rate of 2.64 per cent per annum from 1961 to 1974 while employment grew by 0.18 per cent per annum, so the real GDP produced per worker increased 2.46 per cent per annum. Marketed output per worker grew at about the same rate, because the proportion of the labour force which produced marketed output and the proportion of GDP that was marketed fell similarly.
7. Britain's terms of trade deteriorated 5 per cent, or at 0.5 per cent per annum from 1963 to 1973.
8. See Peter Mieszkowski, 'Tax Incidence Theory: the Effects of Taxes on the Distribution of Income', *Journal of Economic Literature*, vol. VII, December 1969, for a survey of the evidence.
9. David Smith, 'Public Consumption and Economic Performance', *National Westminster Bank Quarterly Review*, November 1975.
10. See pp. 10 and vii above.
11. *The Future of the British Car Industry*, Central Policy Review Staff, HMSO, 1975.
12. Cf. Joan Robinson, 'Ricardo existed at a particular point when English history was going round a corner so sharply that the progressive and the reactionary positions changed places in a generation.' *Collected Economic Papers*, vol. IV, Blackwell, 1973, p. 267.

5 First Steps Towards a Solution

In the winter of 1975 and the spring of 1976 it became clear that several members of the British Labour government saw Britain's economic predicament in terms very similar to those set out in this book and the previously published 'Declining Britain' articles. On 20 November 1975 Mr Harold Wilson made his celebrated Eastbourne speech where he said that British local government had seen a considerable increase in the number of chiefs working for it at the expense of the Indians, 'the people who are doing the work on the spot'.[1] On 25 February 1976, the Chancellor Mr Healey said in a major speech that:

> The TUC and Labour party are united in believing that the steady contraction in our manufacturing industry is the main reason for our disappointing economic performance since the war. This contraction must be halted and reversed. But we cannot reverse the trend if we plan to take more resources into the public services.
>
> It is not just the question of material resources. In recent years our competitors have increased the manpower in their manufacturing industry; we have seen a massive shift of manpower out of manufacturing into the public services. Local authority manpower alone rose from 1,250,000 in 1960 to nearly 3,000,000 in 1975. We cannot afford to continue eroding the foundation of our prosperity in this way.[2]

This speech was preceded by the public expenditure white paper of 19 February 1976, where plans were officially announced for the first time since the Second World War to cut public expenditure during a major business recession, and the government's reasoning was presented as follows:

> When world demand picks up, more resources – capital as well as manpower – will be needed for exports and investment. We must ensure that they are available for that purpose. Unless we are prepared to see rising taxation reduce take-home pay, these resources can be made available only if we keep public expenditure at roughly the same level for several years. Changing the structural distribution of resources in this way is the only means of restoring and maintaining full employment.[3]

The government was thus aiming to restructure the economy so that a larger proportion of output would consist of goods and services which could be exported and invested, and a smaller fraction consisted of unmarketed public services.

In March 1976 Mr Callaghan succeeded Mr Wilson as Prime Minister, and he made it even clearer that the strengthening of the economy's market sector was the means by which the government hoped to restore full employment. On 27 April Mr Norman Atkinson, a leading left-wing Labour member of parliament, said that the trade unions, which were willing to discuss a voluntary pay agreement with the government, also desired discussions on an early return to full employment, which meant that:

Mr Atkinson '. . . the public sector now has the responsibility of providing no less than one million jobs in the next four years? Will he [the Prime Minister] now give a pledge that provision will be made for that objective to be reached?'

Mr Callaghan 'He is right in saying that hand in hand with the aim of overcoming inflation is the provision of more employment. However I do not agree with his analysis that this must fall upon the public sector.

It is important that productive jobs should be created and that we should rely on investments on which a successful return can be expected. That is the way to achieve more employment rather than by transferring more and more jobs to the public sector.'[4]

Table 5.1 Employment in the United Kingdom: 1966–75

	Labour force	Employed: Market sector	Employed: Non-market sector	Unemployed	Market-sector ÷ remainder
			thousands		
1966	25 711	21 273	4 078	360	4.79
1967	25 546	20 751	4 236	559	4.33
1968	25 422	20 507	4 329	586	4.17
1969	25 433	20 483	4 369	581	4.14
1970	25 363	20 281	4 464	618	3.99
1971	25 198	19 819	4 580	799	3.68
1972	25 245	19 658	4 732	855	3.52
1973	25 600	20 099	4 871	630	3.65
1974	25 691	20 129	4 931	631	3.62
1975	25 897	19 698	5 270	929	3.18

The fact that Conservative members of parliament cheered this answer underlines how closely the senior members of the government who were determining economic policy and the Conservative opposition agreed about what needed to be done. Naturally, they did not agree so significantly about the details of policy.

The government's problem is summarised in Table 5.1 above. This shows that in 1966 21,273,000 market-sector workers had to produce enough marketed output to support 4,078,000 workers in the non-market sector, mainly in the public services, and about 360,000 unemployed workers.[5] Therefore 4.79 market-sector workers were available to produce investment and consumer goods for each worker who was producing no marketed output.

In 1974, the year in which the world recession began, 20,129,000 market-sector workers had to produce enough marketed output to support 5,562,000 workers who were producing no marketed output, so only 3.62 market-sector workers were available to support each non-producer of marketed output. In 1975, the situation deteriorated further and only 3.18 market-sector workers were available to support each non-producer of marketed output, but the trend from 1966 to 1974 is the appropriate one on which to

Table 5.2 1966–74 trends continue unchecked

	Labour force	Employed: Market sector	Employed: Non-market sector	Unemployed	Market-sector ÷ remainder
	thousands				
1966	25 711	21 273	4 078	354	4.79
1974	25 691	20 129	4 931	606	3.62
1975	25 897	19 698	5 270	929	3.18
1982	26 817	18 697	6 019	2 101	2.30

focus attention because 1975 was significantly influenced by the world recession.

From 1966 to 1974 the total British labour force was approximately constant, and market-sector employment fell by 143,000 a year while employment in the non-market sector increased by 107,000 a year, and unemployment by 34,000 a year. These slow trends were sufficient to reduce the ratio of market sector workers to the remainder of the labour force from 4.79 to 3.62 in a mere eight years. If there had been no change of policy by the government and the same trends in the market and non-market sectors were allowed to continue for another seven years while the labour force increased by the 0.5 per cent per annum from 1975 onwards that is now expected,[6] the situation in 1982 would resemble that shown in Table 5.2. Here there are just 2.30 market-sector workers to support each non-producer of marketed output in 1982, against 4.79 in 1966 and 3.62 in 1974. The reduction in the market-sector workers available to support each non-producer of marketed output from 4.79 in 1966 to 3.62 in 1974 involved ever-rising taxation. The workers outside the market sector depend on the taxes paid in the market sector for all their private consumption and capital equipment, for taxes are the principal device which has to be used to take marketed output from those who produce it and make it available to those who do not. This ever-rising taxation produced accelerating inflation in 1966–74, and the still greater tax increases which would be necessary in 1974–82 if past trends were allowed to continue could easily produce a hyper-inflation. Moreover, further tax increases would squeeze profits even more than they were squeezed in 1966–74 with the result that the rate of job loss in the market sector could be still greater than the steady rate assumed in the table, and even this produced rapidly growing unemployment. The continuation of past trends clearly produces an unacceptable outcome, so the government were right to take the decision in the spring of 1976 that a continuing growth in public-service employment and decline in market-sector employment was to be avoided if at all possible. Mr Callaghan therefore found Mr Atkinson's suggestion that unemployment should be reduced through the creation of a million extra public-sector jobs unacceptable apart from temporary job creation schemes, as this would be a permanent increase of the very kind which has produced so much strain.

The government's public expenditure white paper of February 1976 proposed a reduction of the rate of growth of real public expenditure, and the subsequent white paper of January 1977 actually forecast a real decline of 2 per cent between expenditure in 1976–7 and 1977–8.[7] At the same time, the government started to build effective machinery to control expenditure so that there was a genuine connection between its plans and what subsequently occurred. In previous years there had been overshooting of real expenditure growth of between 1 and 2 per cent per annum because of inadequate control mechanisms. In 1976 the government went over to 'cash limits' to cover a wide range of expenditures, which meant that spending departments had to cut real spending, and often employment itself, wherever pay increased at a faster than budgeted rate since this was the only way in which the cash expenditure targets could be met. The limits were not applicable to local authority expenditure, which was determined by the decisions of particular councils. Some imposed limits in their counties or districts and others did not, but employment was cut wherever limits were imposed, because inflation exceeded the rate on which the limits were based. It is too early to know the full effects of all the expenditure-reducing decisions which were taken during 1976, but there are two indications that there was an appreciable overall effect. First, while government current spending increased 2.7 per cent more than prices in 1975–6, it increased 2.0 per cent less in 1976–7.[8] Hence there was a real fall in government spending on current account in 1976, so it may well emerge that government employment also fell. The first available figures indicate that this is indeed a possibility, for growth in employment ceased in education, health and public administration which forms a very high fraction of non-market employment. In the nine-month period, June 1975 to March 1976, before any government change of policy had a chance to influence the outcome, employment in education increased by 34,000, in health by 48,000 and in public administration by 31,000. There was thus an increase in public-service employment of at least 113,000 in nine months, which is about the rate of increase which had become customary in the 1960s and early 1970s. But in March 1976 there was a change of gear and in the six months to September 1976 employment in education *fell* by 65,000 while it increased in health by only 8000. There was an increase in employment in public administration of 27,000, a faster rate of increase than before. Total employment in these three public-service categories fell by 30,000 in six months. This is to be contrasted with the increase of 113,000 in the previous nine months, and it is evident that from March 1976 onwards growth in public-service employment ceased.[9] The actual detailed breakdown of the figures is disturbing. In crude terms, those most directly concerned with producing the social wage – those employed in health and education – were starting to be cut back, while employment in administration was increasing faster than before. It is to be hoped that subsequent figures will show that employment in administration is being held down more and not less than the employment of those who actually provide social services.

The statistics make it evident that there was a change of policy from March 1976 onwards, and that this began to achieve results. The growth of employment in the public services which averaged 2.8 per cent per annum from 1961 to 1975 was halted for the first time. Table 5.3 shows what would happen by 1982 if government employment in the non-market sector was successfully held at the 1975 level of

Table 5.3 Growth in public service employment ceases but other trends continue

		Employed			
	Labour force	*Market sector*	*Non-market sector*	*Unemployed*	*Market-sector ÷ remainder*
			thousands		
1966	25 711	21 273	4 078	360	4.79
1974	25 691	20 129	4 931	631	3.62
1975	25 897	19 698	5 270	929	3.18
1982	26 817	18 697	5 270	2 850	2.30

5,270,000, while the other major trend, falling market-sector employment, continued unchecked. It will be evident from Table 5.3 that the commitments of the workers in the market sector would not be significantly less by 1982 than those where past trends continue unchecked. In each case, the number of market-sector workers available to support each worker who produces no marketed output falls from 3.62 in 1974 to 2.30 in 1982. The sole difference is that where past trends continue unchecked, 18,697,000 market-sector workers must support 6,019,000 who work but produce no marketed output and 2,101,000 who are unemployed. With public-sector employment held constant from 1975 onwards, but no favourable effects on market-sector employment, the same 18,697,000 market-sector workers must support 5,270,000 public-service employees which is 749,000 fewer, but they must also support 2,850,000 unemployed workers which is 749,000 more. The cost of supporting 749,000 extra unemployed workers is less than that of supporting 749,000 extra public employees, but it is not that much less. Therefore the outcome in the Table 5.3, where public-service employment is successfully curtailed but market-sector employment is not helped is no more satisfactory (most would call it far less satisfactory for there is greater waste of resources) than the continuation of past trends. Both outcomes will place growing strains on the resources of the market sector.

It therefore had to be an essential element of the government's strategy for the economy's recovery that the

Table 5.4 An acceptable outcome

		Employed			
	Labour force	*Market sector*	*Non-market sector thousands*	*Unemployed*	*Market-sector ÷ remainder*
1966	25 711	21 273	4 078	360	4.79
1974	25 691	20 129	4 931	631	3.62
1975	25 897	19 698	5 270	929	3.18
1982	26 817	20 747	5 270	800	3.57

market sector – industry and commerce together – increase its employment. From 1966 to 1974 market-sector employment was declining, and the government had to reverse this trend so that the unfavourable outcomes outlined in the previous tables could be avoided. The government had to aim for a result resembling that outlined in Table 5.4, where unemployment is reduced to 800,000, a long-term rate compatible with an absence of labour scarcities, by 1982, while employment in the non-market public services is held at the 1975 peak level of 5,270,000.

The table shows that a reduction of unemployment to 800,000 by 1982 and zero growth in the public services can be simultaneously achieved if market-sector employment can be raised from 19,698,000 in 1975 to 20,747,000 in 1982, a rate of increase of 0.7 per cent per annum or of 150,000 a year. If this is achieved, 3.57 market-sector workers will be available to support each worker outside the market sector in 1982 – approximately the 1974 proportion.

The task of raising market-sector employment from 19,698,000 in 1975 to 20,747,000 in 1982, a rate of increase of 150,000 a year appears a difficult one, but 1975 was a year when the world was in deep recession and the market-sector employment level of 20,129,000 in 1974 may be a closer reflection of long-term employment in the British market sector and if this is so, the required rate of increase of employment will be easier to achieve than these figures suggest.

It has been argued in previous chapters that the decline in market-sector employment in 1966–74 was associated with falling investment trends and a continuing decline in profitability, especially in industry. The government therefore had to raise investment and profitability in industry and commerce – in industry especially. Leading ministers were very well aware of the need for this.

It might be thought that what they needed to do was primarily to cut the cost of investment to companies by, for instance, reintroducing investment grants at a high rate, or subsidizing interest payments where money is borrowed for industrial investment, but this would only have amounted to a partial solution of the problem. This is because capital equipment has many dimensions of which two of the most significant are the labour productivity levels which can be achieved with it, and its output capacity. Investment in modernisation may increase labour productivity immensely without raising output capacity. The intention of the investment may be to allow the firm to produce the same output with substantially fewer workers. Here profits would rise, but employment would fall. In effect a few profitable jobs would be substituted for a larger number of less profitable ones. This would increase the economy's long-term potential for growth but not its immediate capacity to invest, consume or export. Only investment in the creation of new capacity will achieve this. Capacity-creating investment will also tend to raise average labour productivity because new plant will be the most up-to-date available. Thus investment to raise productive capacity will almost always act favourably on the productivity dimension of the capital stock, but investment to raise productivity might have no favourable effect at all on the capacity dimension. It will of course have a slight favourable effect if lower production costs lead to higher expected sales, but this effect will often be a minor one, especially if the product is one where demand is not very price-sensitive, which is often the case where components of final products are produced.

To reverse the economy's unfavourable employment trends, the government had to convert an annual rate of market-sector job loss of about 143,000 into a rate of growth of employment of about 150,000 which meant that investment to extend the economy's productive capacity was needed. Investment which raised productivity without extending capacity would be useful in itself, especially to the companies which modernised, but it would make it no easier than before for a declining market sector to support growing non-market employment. So how was the government to raise the economy's productive capacity?

Investment subsidies, whether they reduce the rate of interest or the cost of equipment, merely cut the cost of capital relative to that of labour. They therefore encourage companies to substitute capital for labour – to automate more – but they present no direct incentive to increase capacity. Such incentives would therefore primarily raise the productivity rather than the capacity dimension of the capital stock. To raise output capacity and with it the provision of profitable employment opportunities the government needed to do something more.

Economists are widely agreed that a relationship which is most important in predicting business capacity-creating investment is the 'capital stock adjustment principle' which states something like the following. Investment in any 'year' will vary strongly and positively with the level of National Income in the previous 'year', and in addition it will vary negatively with the amount of capital already in the economy in the previous 'year'.[10] In other words, industrialists will respond to a great increase in the National Income by investing substantially more a year or so later. They will react to a long period of stagnation (where the capital stock rises while the National Income does not) by cutting investment drastically. This principle has fitted British investment trends reasonably well, and the tendency for industrial investment to rise a year to eighteen months after the start of a cyclical boom is obviously what the theory predicts. Again, stagnation has clearly produced the falling investment after a time which the theory predicts. The rationale for the capital stock adjustment principle is that industrialists order the capital equipment they need for expansion when they actually see their order books lengthening. When Mr Heath's government pressed industrialists to invest more before the Barber boom, telling them that they would have marvellous markets soon, a characteristic response was: 'We'll wait till we see the orders'.

A high rate of growth of final demand is not all that is needed to produce a sustained investment boom. The boom must be financed, and since increases in productivity are as important in the long term as increases in productive capacity, it is desirable that new plant should raise both the productivity and the capacity dimensions of the capital stock, so the cost of capital to companies should not be excessive. A rate of growth of final demand and an adequate supply of finance (with a sufficient proportion from retained earnings) are each necessary (but not sufficient) conditions for a sustained investment boom. In the spring of 1976 the government allowed companies to continue to defer any tax liability on profits that resulted from stock appreciation, and it started to apply the price code more generously to assist the supply of internal finance. It also set up a series of committees with civil servants and industrialists to assist the 'new industrial strategy' by identifying future bottleneck areas with a view to giving selective financial help to ensure that these would be eliminated before the next boom. But profits were extremely low in relation to the profit levels of the mid-1960s and therefore the government had to keep in mind both the need to provide an adequate supply of cheap finance to companies, and the necessity for a resumption of economic growth so that companies would have adequate incentives to raise the capacity dimension of the capital stock.

If a substantial rise in market-sector investment of the capacity-creating kind can only be expected to follow a rise in production, and a year or more later at that, then the British government had the clear problem in the spring of 1976 of raising the economy's output level. In the days of Keynesian orthodoxy this would have appeared simple. The government would have increased its own spending substantially, and cut taxes at the same time, and output would have risen fast and capacity-creating investment would have followed it upwards a year or more later. But in 1976 the government was attempting to restructure the economy by cutting the relative size of the non-market government sector so it could not raise its own expenditures in the traditional way – and previous chapters have set out how much long-term damage has been due to these Keynesian government-led-booms. It might be thought that by cutting taxes substantially the government could have produced higher output levels without raising its own expenditures. The difficulty with this was that the government's overall 'borrowing requirement' was around 10 per cent of the National Product in the spring of 1976 and few of even the most expansion-minded Keynesians were willing to allow it to become larger still. There are also sound reasons why expanding the budget deficit through substantial tax cuts will raise output only at a cost of massive balance of payments deterioration.

The reason for this can be explained quite simply.[11] It is a truism that total injections into a country's expenditure stream from *Exports, Government Expenditure* and *Private Investment* must always equal withdrawals for *Imports, Taxation* and *Private Saving*. Hence *Exports* plus *Government Expenditure* plus *Private Investment* must always equal *Imports* plus *Taxation* plus *Private Saving*. This basic relationship can be written as:

$$(\textit{Exports} - \textit{Imports}) \equiv \left(\textit{Taxation} - \begin{matrix}\textit{Government}\\ \textit{Expenditure}\end{matrix}\right) + \left(\begin{matrix}\textit{Private}\\ \textit{Saving}\end{matrix} - \begin{matrix}\textit{Private}\\ \textit{Investment}\end{matrix}\right)$$

It will be seen that a large reduction in *Taxation* relative to *Government Expenditure* must destroy the balance of payments unless there is a large increase in *Private Saving* relative to *Private Investment*, but the whole object of a reduction in taxation would be to produce an increase in *Private Investment*, albeit one year later. Hence *Private Saving* would only get ahead of *Private Investment* for a year or so. After that they would tend to rise together – though not exactly together, of course. The essential point is that there would not be a significantly greater rise of saving. That is what has happened in recent British government-induced booms.[12]

In consequence, any boom produced by a large reduction in *Taxation* or one produced by a large increase in *Government Expenditure* will destroy the balance of payments a year or so later. It therefore contains the time-bomb of inevitable built-in balance of payments collapse, and this will be so, whether the government accompanies its tax cuts with devaluation, import quotas, tariffs or whatever. If *Private Investment* and *Private Saving* both rise substantially after the government cuts taxes, imports must rise far faster than exports. By the spring of 1976 this was quite well understood, and the disastrous balance of payments' effects of successive government-induced booms underlined the futility of attempting to achieve higher income levels by running a budget that was even more unsound than the British one of 1975–6.

The government therefore faced a very real problem. Its new economic strategy required growing market-sector investment and capacity- and employment-creating investment required growing output levels as an inducement, but the government apparently possessed no tools to raise demand and output, for it could neither cut taxes, nor raise its own expenditure.

This left it with just one line of policy with which to attempt to move in the direction it wished. It had to expand the economy through growing exports or falling imports, so that the balance of payments would not be destroyed as output rose. This was extremely well understood in Whitehall in the spring of 1976. There were two approaches to the achievement of balance-of-payments-led growth. Imports could be restricted to encourage the growth of domestic industry to supply markets that foreign goods were no longer permitted to fill. The Cambridge economic policy group had favoured this for some time.[13] It must be noted that import restriction will achieve the desired results only if it is accompanied by a sound budgetary policy. Import restriction and an unsound budgetary policy will rapidly produce banana republic conditions for the unsound budget will destroy the balance of payments while import restrictions at the same time destroy quality control in the manufacturing sector. The Cambridge proposals should have been a combination of import restrictions to expand domestic demand and sound budgetary policies to ensure that the balance of payments did not deteriorate. In practice the Cambridge group has often recommended import controls and an unsound budget, so the economy would have been destroyed or at any rate seriously destabilised if their advice had been accepted.[14] In practice their line of argument was rejected because it was judged that import restrictions by Britain would rapidly lead to significant foreign retaliation. Moreover, part of Britain's problem is lack of competitiveness in quality, design and the reliability of products, and the reductions in competition which would follow import controls would do nothing to encourage British industry to remedy these basic faults. On the contrary, quality control would almost certainly deteriorate further, which could create a situation where controls, once imposed, could only be removed at great sacrifice.

The rejection of import controls as an option left the British government with one remaining policy. It could only expand the economy by expanding exports. These would grow in any case once world trade expanded again, but this was now expected to be far too slow to produce real output growth leading to substantial encouragement to investment and a restructuring of the economy in favour of the market sector. Much more than ordinary export growth rates were needed for this, and these could only be achieved by providing massive new encouragements to British firms to sell abroad. The classical way in which such encouragement is provided (and the only way compatible with Britain's international agreements) is through a reduction in wage costs per unit of output measured in foreign currency. If wage costs can be cut, British firms can either cut their overseas prices and sell more because their products are more competitive – or they can leave their prices unchanged and earn substantially higher sterling profits on their overseas sales which will reinforce their cash flow and help to produce one of the necessary conditions for an investment boom, adequate internal finance. Higher sterling profits from exporting also provide strong extra inducements to sell abroad. A third option that is open to companies is to leave their overseas prices unchanged, earn the same sterling profits as before, and use the benefit from lower wage costs to increase overseas marketing expenditures and the provision for servicing and spare-part facilities for foreign customers. British companies might use a reduction in wage costs per unit to cut prices, to raise their own profits overseas, or to increase foreign marketing and service expenditures. In each of these cases, exports would benefit substantially, though in the second case slowly.

Wage costs per unit of output can be reduced 10 per cent in foreign currency by lowering the exchange rate of sterling 10 per cent, by cutting wages 10 per cent, or by raising labour productivity 10 per cent. Of these, lowering the exchange rate of sterling was the only option open to the British government in the spring of 1976. Money wage cuts could not possibly have been negotiated, and vast productivity gains could be dreamed of but hardly achieved as the result of a deliberate act of government policy. Indications are that the British authorities therefore deliberately engineered the substantial collapse of the sterling exchange rate which occurred from 4 March 1976 onwards.

An unconfirmed account suggests that Nigeria asked the Bank of England to sell part of its sterling holdings and convert these into dollars. Ordinarily a sale of this kind would be made as a simple book-keeping transaction. The Bank of England would credit some of its own dollar reserves to Nigeria at the ruling exchange rate. This was £1 = $2.02 on 3 March 1976, so the Bank of England could have credited Nigeria with $202 millions of its own dollar holdings in exchange for a reduction of £100 million in Nigeria's sterling credits. The market would have known nothing of the transaction and the price of sterling could have been held comfortably at £1 = $2.02 where it had been for some time, with no public sale of pounds or purchase of dollars. But the Bank of England did not handle the transaction in this quiet and unobtrusive way. Instead it offered Nigeria's sterling for sale on the market, and when the world saw that the Bank of England was appearing on the market to sell pounds in quantity, sterling collapsed because the world read the Bank of England's signal correctly.[15] The British government, far from wishing to defend the exchange rate of sterling, could be seen to be selling pounds on a large scale to push down the rate. Everyone at once joined the Bank of England in its efforts to push sterling down, and the Bank of England found this assistance so overwhelming that it had to change sides rapidly, and use a high fraction of the country's remaining reserves to prevent a complete collapse of the exchange rate. The pound in fact fell from $2.02 in March 1976 to $1.57 in September before it was stabilised at $1.71 early in 1977. It therefore fell 15 per cent in relation to the dollar in about nine months, and by more than this in relation to several European currencies including the Deutschmark. As British wages only rose about 12 per cent in the year from March 1976 until March 1977, while wages in other leading industrial countries rose at an annual rate of near to 10 per cent, the objective of cutting wage costs per unit of output in relation to those of Britain's leading competitors by 10 per cent or more was certainly achieved.

It must be emphasised that the government's economic strategy required that the reduction in wage costs be maintained. Cutting the dollar value of British wages by 15 per cent through a 15 per cent devaluation would be wholly ineffective if this was followed by an equivalent relative increase in money wages in Britain. That would have done nothing to make British goods more competitive overseas. The exchange rate had to be cut substantially and wage increases restrained at the same time. Otherwise no net competitive advantage would be attained. The government's successive phases of incomes policy were therefore as much a part of the strategy as the deliberate reduction in the exchange rate. The key objective was that the exchange rate should fall substantially faster than Britain's relative wages rose.

By March 1977 it was evident that the government had succeeded in this double objective – for one year at any rate. The incomes policy restraints were officially adhered to by all. There were no significant strikes in breach of Phase 2 of the policy (which permitted increases of no more than £4 a week) and such unofficial strikes as occurred were settled within the policy guidelines. The government and the unions therefore gave British exporters a competitive advantage of 10 per cent in the spring of 1977 that they did not possess in March 1976.

In March 1977 the hoped-for export upsurge was still relatively modest, at least so far as manufacturing was concerned. Export volume was 6 per cent higher in December 1976 and January – February 1977 than in the first quarter of 1976 and total manufacturing output was about 2.5 per cent higher. Manufacturing output was growing far more slowly than exports because with government expenditure under firm control, exports were the sole component of aggregate demand that was rising significantly. But profits earned from exporting were far higher in sterling terms, and even British Leyland published accounts in March 1977 which showed a profit of £70 million: other firms were benefiting still more. Industry's ability to finance investment was therefore being assisted by the 10 per cent relative reduction in dollar wage costs per unit of output. But given the slow growth of sales, the incentive to make large extensions to productive capacity were not yet present.

It is well known that devaluation takes considerable time to produce its full effects. There are long time lags between a rise in potential profitability overseas, going there to get extra orders, raising production to meet those orders and being paid for extra export sales. If lowering the exchange rate raises expenditures by British firms on overseas marketing and after-sales facilities, the volume of exports will be influenced still more slowly. Economists are widely agreed that the relevant time lag for an adequate export response to devaluation used to be about eighteen months, and it may be becoming longer still, so major effects are not to be expected within the first year of a competitive gain. The main upsurge of British exports of manufactures will therefore occur in the latter half of 1977 and in 1978. In August 1977 there are hopeful indications such as lengthening export order books and monthly trade figures for June and July showing export volume up more than 12 per cent in twelve months. British exports of manufactures might be 15 to 20 per cent higher in 1978 than in the spring of 1977. If these expectations are fulfilled, the government's strategy stands an excellent chance of success. A 15 per cent rise in exports of manufactures would raise industrial production 5 to 6 per cent in eighteen months. Private consumption should eventually rise rapidly also as a result of higher incomes derived from better export sales, and the expectation of higher 'permanent incomes' which would accompany export successes and encourage consumers to borrow more and save less. Production would then rise still more. Export growth produced no growth in consumption up to June 1977 because there was no confidence that future incomes would grow. There are indications that June marked the low point of consumer confidence, and that consumption is now rising as well as exports to produce real growth in output and demand. An export upsurge would also start to raise industrial investment in 1978, and profitability also as the margin of spare capacity fell. This would produce a gradual expansion of plant without balance of payments weaknesses. Britain's fundamental problems would not be solved all at once for structural readjustments cannot be achieved quickly. Improvements of 1 to 2 per cent per annum in the underlying proportions of the economy are generally all that can be achieved, but if the industrial production growth rate can be gradually raised to 4 or 5 per cent per annum while the growth of government expenditure is restrained and the balance of payments remains sound so that growth can continue, Britain's problems will be gradually solved.

They will be solved more quickly than calculations would otherwise suggest if the early stages of recovery produce a significant inflow of capital from multinational companies. There is much capital in the world capable of producing advanced products which have benefited from substantial foreign research development and design expenditures. These highly marketable products will be produced in Britain on a growing scale once it is clear that adequate profits can be earned, and that production schedules can be met. The difficulties of the economy have deflected direct investment of this kind from Britain in recent years, but it will come back to make any recovery far less costly in terms of consumption foregone if Britain manages to achieve the first stages of recovery. The pace of recovery could thus be far more rapid than many believe, once international confidence is restored.

If exports rise rapidly in 1977 and in 1978 Britain can move towards a solution of some of the fundamental problems with which this book has been concerned. But exports may expand rapidly for too short a time to produce a significant recovery in output or industrial investment. That is what will happen if past trends are repeated. On the basis of what has happened before, Britain's dearly bought competitive advantages will be destroyed by another wages explosion. It is worrying here that an official United States survey of the response of British exporters with spare capacity to the opportunities of devaluation made in late 1976 found that the typical response was to sit back and take the extra sterling profits without seeking to export more, because firms did not expect their competitive advantage to last. Exporters must invest heavily in increased overseas sales networks and other facilities if they are to sell more, and this will only prove worthwhile if it is still profitable to export two or three years after the first expenditures are made. In the past wage restraint for two years has been followed by a wages explosion so that any competitive advantage of British exporters has been transitory. Those who sought to extend their overseas sales networks were caught wrong-footed as soon as wages exploded upwards to make exporting less profitable than sales at home. A sustained recovery of British exports in 1977 and 1978 requires confidence on the part of British companies that wages will not explode upwards once again. Indications are in August 1977 that many trade unionists are unaware of the critical need for restraint until output starts to rise rapidly with exports leading so that growth can be sustained. Once this point is reached, private consumption can be increased at acceptable rates, but it cannot be increased before this without prejudicing the chances of recovery.

Much is being asked of the unions here. By allowing Britain to retain the competitive advantages of devaluation, they are being asked to accept a cut in living standards in terms of foreign currency to last well into 1978. They are therefore being asked to accept lower living standards in terms of almost everything that is imported. Wages rose 8 per cent and prices 16 per cent from August 1976 to August 1977, and this is just one reflection of this cut in living standards. Workers will need to exercise restraint until 1978 if the recovery of the economy is to be sustained. If they seek large and immediate increases in living standards in 1977 and get them, the government's strategy will fail. Export-led growth will commence in the autumn of 1977 and falter in the spring of 1978.

There are other important factors in the equation. The previous pages have focused on exports of manufactures because it is generally agreed that the de-industrialisation of Britain must be reversed if there is to be sustained growth in the economy's market sector. The 4 to 5 per cent of growth of manufacturing output which can be achieved from 1977 onwards if devaluation succeeds will suffice to set manufacturing employment on an upward path to reverse past trends. But the depreciation of the exchange rate has produced great and immediate successes in the private service industries which are also part of the market sector. Exports of tourism increased 45 per cent in 1975–6, while other exports of services and especially those of the City of London increased almost as fast. There was thus rapid export-led-growth leading to growing employment in the economy's private service sector. But there is relatively little long-term productivity growth and technical progress in this sector in comparison with manufacturing, so an economy which is unduly reliant on trade in the private services will tend to be a slow-growing one with living standards which rise more slowly than those in most of Western Europe. A switch from government into the commercial services will solve some of Britain's immediate problems and permit reductions in taxation, but it will not solve the long-term problem of slow growth. Britain needs a growing manufacturing sector also.

The final item in the equation is North Sea Oil. If manufacturing grows as a result of export growth in 1977–8, extra oil exports will be a bonus which will permit a faster rate of increase in living standards than the expansion of production would otherwise permit. There will thus be less inflationary pressure as the economy recovers. But if manufacturing exports fail to grow at the rate required, oil will give the country a further and perhaps a final opportunity. If the strategy of export-led growth through devaluation fails, a future strategy of using oil revenues to finance market-sector expansion could still succeed. Britain therefore has two chances of achieving a restructuring of the economy in favour of the market sector. The present strategy of export-led growth stands a good chance of success, but if it fails, Britain will still have the opportunity to adopt a new strategy based on the use of oil revenues to finance re-industrialisation.

NOTES

1. *The Times*, 21 November 1975.
2. *The Times*, 26 February 1976.
3. *Public Expenditure to 1979–80*, (Cmnd 6393) HMSO, February 1976, paragraph 4.
4. *Hansard*, 27 April 1976.
5. The employment statistics are derived from *National Income and Expenditure, 1965–75*, Table 1.10. Market-sector employment is the sum of employment in the private sector and the nationalised industries, while non-market employment is the sum of employment in central and local government. The unemployment statistics are the 'wholly unemployed' in the United Kingdom published in the *Monthly Digest of Statistics*.
6. See the Cambridge Economic Policy Group's *Economic Policy Review*, University of Cambridge Department of Applied Economics, No. 3, March 1977.
7. *The Government's Expenditure Plans*, (Cmnd 6721-1) HMSO, January 1977.
8. *Financial Statement and Budget Report 1977–8*, Table 5, HMSO, March 1977.
9. Figures for Great Britain from the *Department of Employment Gazette*.
10. See for instance, Dale W. Jorgenson, 'Econometric Studies of Investment Behavior: A Survey', *Journal of Economic Literature*, Vol. IX, December 1971, for one recent survey of econometric work on the investment function. In his account, the capital stock adjustment models have tested best, but the cost of capital is also influential in the more sophisticated versions of these, where it influences the rate of substitution of capital for labour.
11. The argument that follows is set out in detail in Walter Eltis, 'The Failure of the Keynesian Conventional Wisdom', *Lloyds Bank Review*, October 1976.
12. For instance, from 1962 to 1965, private saving rose by £1756 millions in Britain, while private investment (including investment in stocks) rose by £1452 millions. From 1971 to 1974 private saving rose by £10,409 millions while private investment (again including investment in stocks) rose by £9211 millions. (*National*

Income and Expenditure 1973, Table 70, and 1965–75, Table 14.1).

13. See the Cambridge Economic Policy Group's *Economic Policy Review*, University of Cambridge Department of Applied Economics, No. 1, February 1975; No. 2, March 1976; and No. 3, March 1977.
14. The Cambridge Economic Policy Group has never supported the government's expenditure-reducing policies, and it has at no point advocated increased taxation. Its budgetary recommendations in 1975–7, if accepted, would therefore have produced faster increases in the borrowing requirement until 1976 and slower reductions after this than those which actually occurred. The Group apparently believes that the rapid growth its policies would produce should also correct the budget (which it likes to estimate on a full employment basis – see issue No. 2). But the initial widening of the deficit which it has implicitly or explicitly advocated from time to time must produce unsatisfactory initial balance of payments results in any transition to full employment (with the consequent risk of forced devaluations and extra inflation) – and if there is structural unemployment, the period over which such disasters will occur will be a long one.
15. See reports in the *International Currency Review*, March–April and May–June 1976.

6 The Problem in Canada and the USA

The public sector has expanded rapidly in most Western economies and many have experienced problems similar to Britain's. In this chapter the effects of a growing non-market sector in two countries, Canada and the USA, which publish statistics which can be compared with Britain's are set out. Like Britain, Canada and the USA have had slow rates of growth of productivity in their market sectors, 2.4 per cent annum in Canada and 1.7 per cent in the USA in 1955–74 against 2.7 per cent in Britain in 1956–74.[1] Like Britain also, their non-market spending has risen very rapidly. The result has been that all three countries have diverted a high fraction of the extra resources resulting from economic growth to their non-market sectors, leaving relatively little for their market sectors where all marketed output is produced.

The growth in the shares of marketed output taken by the non-market sectors of Britain, Canada and the USA is set out in Chart 23. The British share increased 5.7 per cent from 31.1 per cent in 1955 to 36.8 per cent in 1975. The Canadian share was lower than the British share but it was not that much lower. It started at 25.6 per cent in 1955, nearly 5 per cent below the British share, but it then increased 10 per cent, far faster than Britain's, and it was a mere 1.2 per cent lower than Britain's at 35.6 per cent in 1975. The USA has also been catching up with Britain. It started 7.3 per cent below in 1955 but it has risen 10.4 per cent since then and in 1975 it was just 2.6 per cent short of the British share at 34.2 per cent. But the 1975 statistics have been much influenced by the world recession which began in 1974. In any economy where stabilisation policies are used, public expenditure

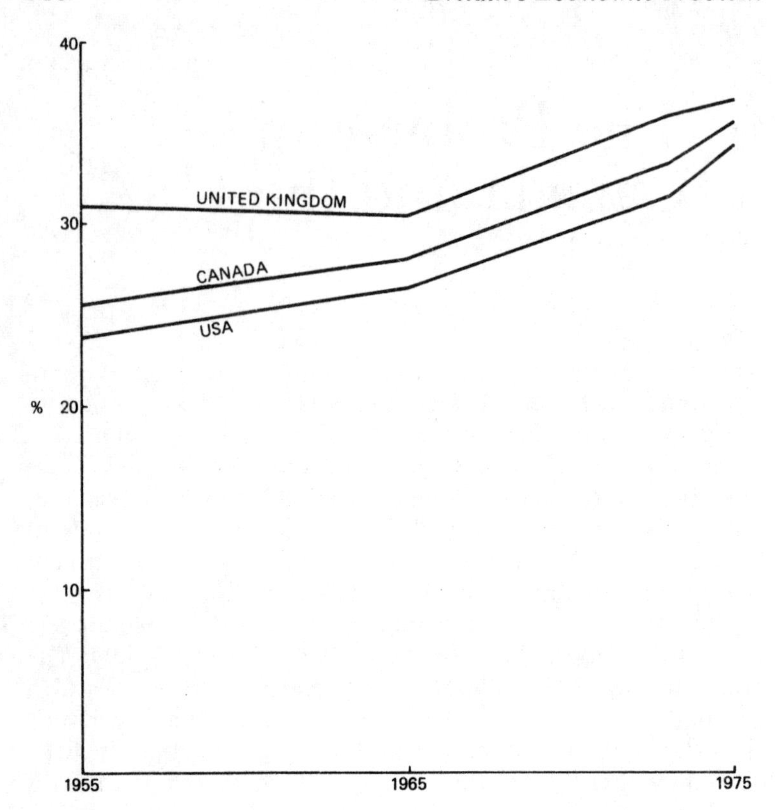

Chart 23 Non-market Purchases of Marketed Output

increases in recessions, and if aggregate output falls, the ratio of public expenditure to output rises merely because there is a recession. For this reason the 1974 figures are likely to reflect long-term trends more closely than the 1975 figures and in 1974 Britain's share of marketed output that went to the non-market sector was 35.9 per cent, Canada's was 33.2 per cent and the USA's 31.4 per cent. It can therefore be said that by that year, the non-market sector took 2.7 per cent more in Britain than in Canada, while it took about 1.8 per cent more in Canada than in the USA. The differences are thus only differences of degree. Any adverse pressures that Britain experienced should have been present in the other

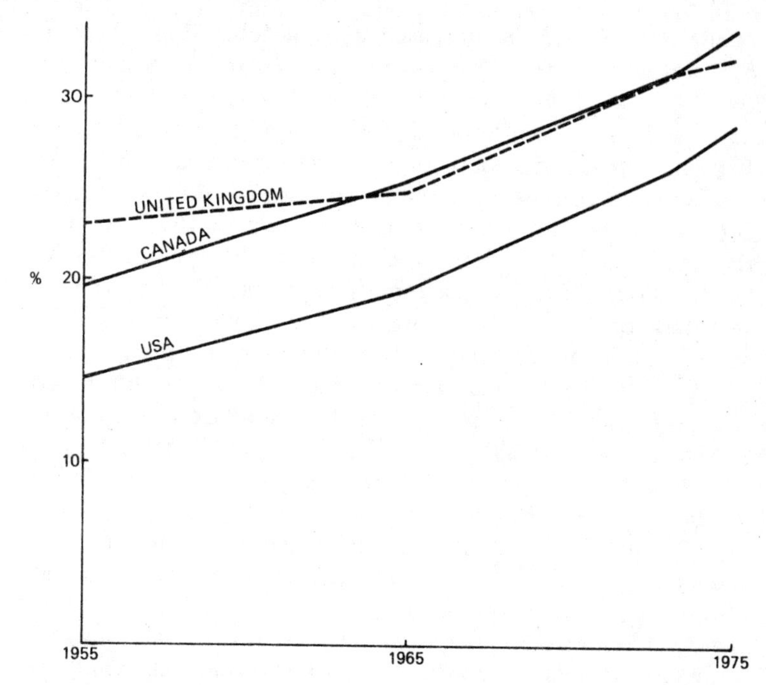

Chart 24 Non-market Purchases of Marketed Output (Excluding Defence)

economies, especially as their non-market spending *increased faster* as a share of output.

The increase in social spending has been especially rapid in the three countries because they each reduced the share of defence spending sharply. Therefore social spending increased far more quickly than the gross spending figures illustrated in Chart 23 indicate. The growth of the non-market share of output with defence spending omitted is illustrated in Chart 24. Here Canada, which reduced defence spending most (from 6.1 per cent of marketed output in 1955 to 1.6 per cent in 1974), increased its non-market purchases apart from defence – mainly social spending – by a staggering 12.1 per cent of output from 19.5 per cent in 1955 to 31.6 per cent in 1974. The USA cut defence spending less than Canada to achieve an 11.8 per cent increase in mainly social spending from 14.4 per cent of marketed output in 1955 to 26.2 per cent in 1974. Britain increased its non-defence purchases by 8.3 per cent from 23.1 per cent of marketed output in 1955 to 31.4 per cent in 1974. Thus Canada and the USA increased their non-defence public spending similarly, while Britain increased its social spending somewhat slower and the non-defence resources taken by the non-market sector were actually higher in Canada than in Britain in 1975. By 1974 the social spending departments in all three countries had become accustomed to extremely rapid rates of growth, and this has been especially the case in Canada where social spending increased fastest of all as a share of output.

The statistics illustrated in the charts do not in fact include all non-market expenditures, and the proportions of spending shown are considerably lower than those in Chart 12 on page 29 above where *all* non-market spending is included in pre-tax government claims on marketed output. This rose to over 60 per cent in Britain in 1975 against the 36.8 per cent shown in Chart 23 – for the share of marketed output *actually purchased* by the non-market sector. There are three principal reasons for the difference in the figures shown in these two kinds of chart. First subsidies of all kinds are excluded from the figures in Charts 23 and 24 because there is no satisfactory way of allocating them between the two sectors which is comparable between the three countries. All three countries will therefore have larger non-market shares than Charts 23 and 24 indicate to the extent that they use subsidies extensively. As Britain now uses subsidies more extensively than Canada and the USA, government spending in Britain is higher in relation to the two other countries than these charts indicate. Second, Chart 12 on page 29, which put the British non-market sector's share at over 60 per cent in 1975, expressed the *pre-tax* ratio of potential non-market sector claims. The charts in this chapter estimate the proportion of output which is actually bought by the non-market sector, and this will be considerably lower. A senior civil servant with an income of £20,000 has a pre-tax claim of £20,000 which is what is entered to produce the 60 per cent public spending figure, but if he pays direct taxes of £7500 and saves one-fifth of the remaining £12,500 he will buy £10,000 of marketed output and not £20,000. The charts in this chapter which show the ratio of British non-market purchases at 36.8 per cent in 1975 against the 62 per cent shown on page 29 include the £10,000 the civil servant actually spends and not the £20,000 he is paid which will be included in all gross aggregate public-spending statistics. Thus the charts in this chapter omit the taxes paid by non-market-sector income recipients and their saving from public spending figures (and these may total something like 34 per cent of all British public sector financed incomes in 1975)[2] as well as all subsidies. They also omit some purely financial capital spending items which are included in gross expenditure statistics. Conversely the charts in this chapter include government investment associated with housing in the non-market spending total because it has not been possible to deduct this comparably between the three economies.

The method of estimation used in this chapter is the one which may come closest to identifying the actual squeeze on market sector resources which is due to growth in non-market expenditures, and this method shows increases in the non-market share of between 6 and 10 per cent of output in twenty years in all three economies. In fact most of the pressure from a growing non-market share occurred in the decade after 1965. In Britain there was a slight decrease in the non-market share from 1955 to 1965 and almost the whole increase that took place occurred from 1965 to 1974. The United States share increased 2.7 per cent in the first decade and a further 4.9 per cent from 1965 to 1974: the Canadian share increased 2.5 per cent from 1955 to 1965 and a further 5 per cent from 1965 to 1974. The shares increased further from 1974 to 1975 in all three countries – partly because of the world recession. The strains from growing non-market expenditures were thus markedly greater after 1965 and the reason for this is brought out in Chart 25.

This shows that the increase in output available to the market sector itself in 1955–65 was almost as great as the actual increase in output in all three economies. Thus in Britain output per worker increased 3.1 per cent per annum in the market sector in 1956–65 and the investment and consumption available to the market sector where these

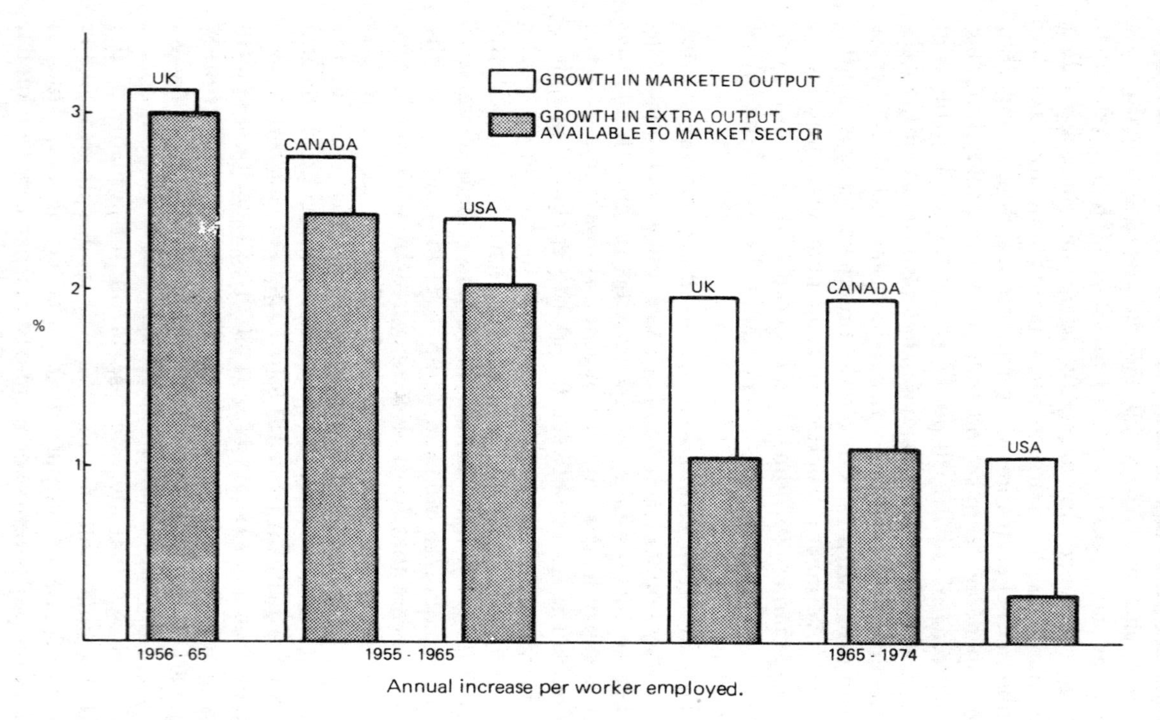

Chart 25 Extra Output Available to Market Sector

improvements were achieved grew 3.0 per cent a year – almost exactly as fast. In Canada output per worker advanced 2.7 per cent per annum in 1955–65 and the extra output available to the market sector after non-market claims had been met increased 2.4 per cent per annum. In the USA output per worker advanced 2.4 per cent in 1955–65, and purchases by the market sector were able to increase almost as fast – 2.0 per cent per annum for each worker employed. The producers of marketed output were therefore able to raise their own consumption and investment almost as fast as marketed output was increasing without damage to the balance of payments. But in 1965 to 1974 the situation was quite different. Firstly productivity advanced less quickly in the market sectors of all three economies. In Britain the rate of growth of productivity fell from 3.1 to 2.0 per cent per annum. It was growing faster in industry but services where productivity rises slowly formed a growing proportion of the market sector. Partly for similar reasons, the rate of growth of productivity in the market sector fell from 2.7 to 1.9 per cent per annum in Canada, and from 2.4 to 1.0 per cent per annum in the USA. There would thus have been a substantial fall in the rate of growth of privately generated incomes in all three economies if the fruits of growth had actually been allowed to go to the producers of marketed output, but this was far from the case. Growing non-market claims were superimposed on this slower productivity growth environment which meant that market-sector incomes could only rise by a fraction of the much diminished rate of growth of productivity. Thus in Britain, where the productivity growth rate fell from 3.1 to 2.0 per cent per annum, the growth of output the market sector could itself purchase without damaging the balance of payments fell from 3.0 to 1.0 per cent per annum for each worker employed. In Canada the output the market sector could buy grew 1.1 per cent per annum against 2.4 per cent in the earlier period, while in the USA the rate of growth of output the market sector could itself purchase fell staggeringly from 2.0 per cent per annum in 1955–65 to 0.3 per cent per annum in 1965–74 despite the vast reduction in the defence burden on the economy.

The market sectors of all three economies thus had to live

with far slower growth rates of output purchased for their own use than they were accustomed to. The British market sector had to manage within a 1.0 per cent growth rate when it had become accustomed to 3.0 per cent. The Canadian market sector had to come down from 2.4 to 1.1 per cent growth, while the United States market sector had to accommodate itself to a situation where there was virtually no per capita growth at all in the output that the market sector could itself purchase.

These great reductions in the rates by which private consumption and capital investment could rise without damaging the balance of payments had very different effects in the three countries, and this is brought out in Table 6.1.[3] It is evident from this table that the rate of growth of private consumption in the British market sector fell much less than the rate of growth of output available for it if trade was to be balanced. In consequence market-sector investment and the balance of payments were bound to suffer and they did. Britain's current account deficit deteriorated from 0.9 per cent of marketed output in 1965 to 6.1 per cent in 1974 and investment fell sharply as a share of marketed output in 1975 when this deficit was reduced. The British situation was in fact far more serious than these figures indicate because the extra per capita output which could be made available to the market sector increased only 0.4 per cent per annum and not 1.0 per cent once capital consumption is allowed for. It is not possible to allow for capital consumption in Table 6.1

Table 6.1

		Rate of growth of output available to the market sector per worker employed	*Rate of growth of market sector private consumption per worker employed*
Britain	1956–65	3.0	2.5
	1965–74	1.0	1.8
Canada	1955–65	2.4	1.8
	1965–74	1.1	0.4
USA	1955–65	2.0	2.0
	1965–74	0.3	0.4

because the official British, Canadian and United States statisticians estimate it in different ways – especially in periods of inflation. Hence any general attempt to deduct it would have produced apparent differences in the three economies which merely reflected different statistical procedures. But with British capital consumption allowed for, the per capita output available to the market sector increased a mere 0.4 per cent per annum from 1965 to 1974. As consumption increased at a per capita rate of 1.8 per cent per annum in the same period, there was a devastating squeeze on the balance of payments, and on net investment as British statisticians measure it. Much has been said about this in previous chapters and more will be said below to explain *why* the British response to a squeeze on the market sector was to continue to raise consumption per worker at almost the same rate as before so that the principal burden fell on the balance of payments and capital investment.

In Canada and the USA the response was different, at least initially. Thus in Canada the fall from 2.4 to 1.1 per cent per annum in the rate at which the output available to the market sector increased resulted in a fall in the rate of increase of market sector consumption per head from 1.8 to 0.4 per cent per annum. Because consumption rose so much more slowly than output, Canada was able to continue to raise its share of investment in marketed output – at least till 1974. But as will become clear below, the slow rate of growth of private consumption led to British-style developments in the Canadian trade union movement which led to accelerating inflation, a rising 'natural' rate of unemployment, and the beginnings of a profit squeeze of the British type. In the USA per capita private consumption rose only a little faster than the extra output available to the market sector, at 0.4 per cent per annum against 0.3 per cent per annum from 1965 to 1974, so there was no significant investment squeeze or balance of payments deterioration. There were abrupt reductions in the rates of growth of both investment and consumption per head without obvious strains of the British type. This appears to throw doubt on the generality of the argument presented in previous chapters, but it will soon be seen that the increase in non-market spending in the USA has had profound effects which are in complete conformity with the theory which has been presented.

What needs to be explained is why the great fall in the rate of growth of marketed output available to the market sector itself which occurred in all three economies produced different basic effects in the USA, Canada and Britain. The actual experience of each country must be examined in detail before this question can be answered.

A great deal has been said about the British case in previous chapters and only that part of the argument which is especially relevant to the explanation of developments in Canada and the USA will be restated here, using the new statistics which show what happened to marketed output in each economy. It has been seen that in Britain the net output actually available to the market sector increased by a mere 0.4 per cent per annum from 1965 to 1974 for each worker employed. The market sector was therefore playing a near-zero sum game for investment and consumption from 1965 to 1974. If workers won, companies were bound to lose and vice versa. In zero sum games conflict is alas inevitable. Any workers who avoided conflict could have expected at best to increase their private consumption in line with the average growth of output available to the market sector, that is by 0.4 per cent per annum. British workers expected far more than this, particularly in view of their experience of an achieved growth rate of 2.5 per cent per annum in private consumption per head in 1956–65.

The outcome was that the workers won the game in the sense that their private consumption rose far more quickly than the aggregate net of tax incomes of the market sector. This occurred because workers were able to raise net of tax wages substantially at the expense of profits. As explained in previous chapters, they achieved this partly because governments of all political colours introduced price and wage controls in their attempts to check accelerating wage inflation, and these restricted profits severely. In addition, at the local level, union pressure reduced the profits which companies were able to earn when they substituted modern for out-of-date plant. With the union leadership appropriate to near-zero-sum game conditions, there were prolonged disputes about manning where new plant was introduced which resulted in less output from that plant in its early years of operation and higher wages and lower profits from it once it started to operate fully. The unions appreciated that they had particular opportunities to achieve above-average earnings increases wherever firms modernised their capital stock, for they needed to use the new plant efficiently to recover the high costs of investment. By exploiting those conditions, workers raised aggregate wages at the expense of profits. Finally union power at the political level changed property rights in favour of labour so that companies were less free than before to equate the marginal cost of labour and its marginal revenue productivity as text-book profit maximisers supposedly do. Firms were legally obliged to continue to employ workers they would have preferred to declare redundant because of high redundancy payments and other changes due to legislation, and this again meant that aggregate wages were raised in relation to aggregate profits. It is because the unions managed to squeeze profits in these three ways that consumption rose so much at the expense of the balance of payments, and from 1975 onwards, at the expense of net investment in the market sector.

Chart 26 shows what happened to marketed output in Britain from 1955 to 1975. It shows that from 1955 to 1975 considered as a whole, market-financed consumption fell as a share of output by 7.4 per cent, actually more than the 5.8 per cent increase in the non-market sector's share. But this disguises the fact that in the vital period, 1965–74 when the economy was destabilised, the consumption share fell only from 53.0 to 51.2 per cent, so that in this period net exports and the share of investment had to give way to accommodate the sharp increase in the government's share. The balance of payments gave way in 1974 with a deficit of 6.1 per cent of marketed output, and net investment fell sharply in 1975.

The fact that there was no fall in the share of gross market-sector investment until 1975 and that even then the share of gross investment was higher than in 1955 disguises an important underlying trend. Net *industrial* investment fell 33 per cent from 1965 to 1974 even though aggregate net

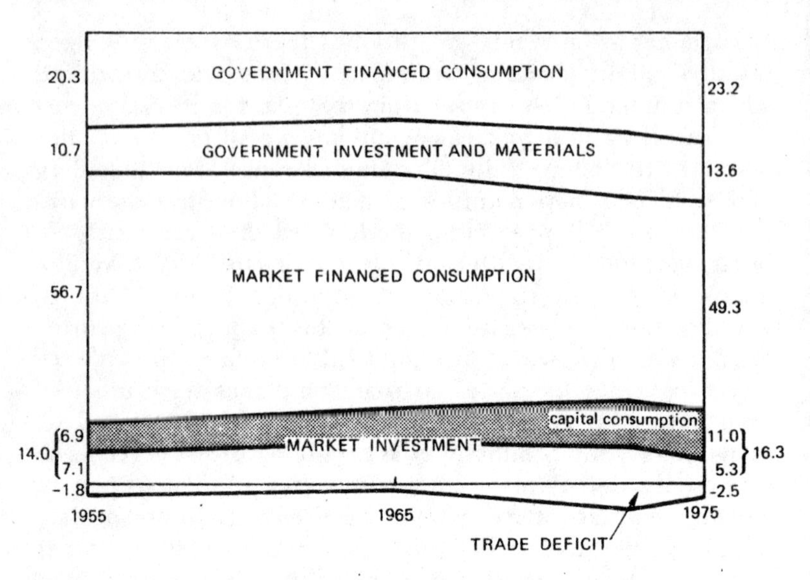

Chart 26 Where marketed Output Went: United Kingdom

market-sector investment rose 3 per cent in this period. There was thus a substantial switch within the market sector from investment in industry to investment in building and in the private service industries. A strong reason why this occurred with all the implications which have been brought out in this book is because the union-induced profits squeeze which has been described reduced profits in manufacturing far more than for companies as a whole. The unions were initially far more powerful in the manufacturing sector, and Charts 11.1 and 11.2 on pages 21 and 22 above illustrate the greater profits squeeze in the manufacturing sector. The fall in industrial investment and the fall in industrial jobs of 250,000 per annum from 1966 onwards followed from this – and of course from the purely static effect of the higher costs of employing labour in manufacturing. These all followed from the zero-sum-game behaviour which became rational after 1965.

The British market sector continued to invest substantially after 1965 and this is brought out in Chart 26, and it invested substantially because money could be borrowed at negative real post-tax interest rates for much of the period, but investment was increasingly diverted away from industry where the trade unions were squeezing profits most sharply to the services where unions were initially less organised. The market sector therefore continued to invest in assets, but to a diminishing extent in the employment-creating assets of the industrial sector. Many of the assets invested in were merely physical assets like buildings which could be expected to rise in price with inflation to justify their purchase with borrowed money at negative real interest rates, and these often provided little extra employment. Centre Point, the famous empty office block which provided no employment at all, is the extreme case of this. With the collapse of industrial profitability, which was very much the consequence of growing non-market expenditure for the reasons which have been outlined, investment was diverted from employment creation to mere asset creation.

The immediate question this account raises is how developments in Britain compare with those in the USA and Canada where non-market expenditures rose still faster as a share of output. The effects in these countries should have been similar but there are in fact considerable differences.

The USA will be considered first. The United States allocation of marketed output between government- and market-financed consumption and investment is shown in Chart 27. This indicates that both market-financed consumption and market-sector investment fell substantially as shares of marketed output from 1955 to 1975, while government-financed purchases increased from 23.8 per cent of marketed output in 1955 to 34.2 per cent in 1975. Why did the market-sector squeeze on the share of consumption fail to produce a British-style reaction in the trade union movement leading to an eventual wage explosion? This was particularly to be expected as the rate of increase of market-financed consumption per worker was only 0.4 per cent per annum from 1965 to 1974. This appears an incredible figure at first sight but closer examination supports it. Weekly earnings in the United States (outside agriculture) increased only 5.5 per cent per annum from 1965 to 1974 and consumer prices rose 5.1 per cent per annum in the same period, so wages *before tax deductions* rose only 0.4 per cent per annum faster than prices in these nine years.[4] It is

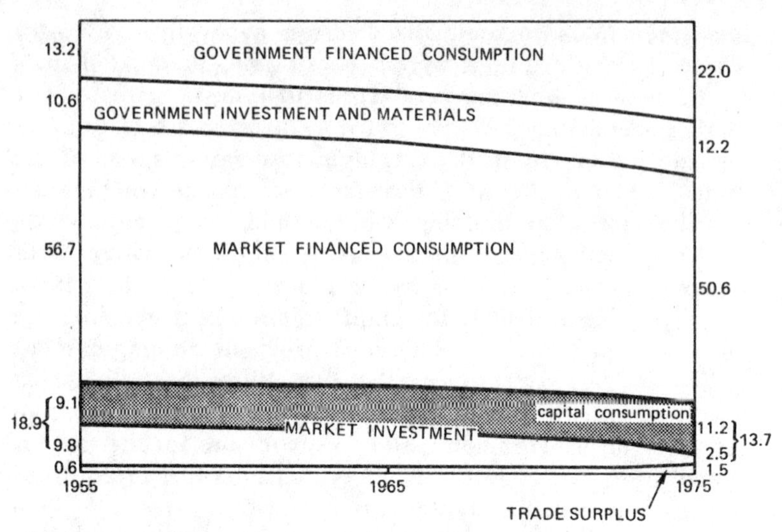

Chart 27 Where Marketed Output Went: USA

therefore perfectly plausible that private consumption per worker increased very little in the USA as a whole from 1965 to 1974. Why then was wage inflation in the USA so restrained?

The answer is partly that wages explode upwards only if unemployment is below the sometimes very high rate that suppresses wage inflation. Growing worker frustration of the British type raises that critical unemployment rate – the 'natural' rate as monetarists call it – so wages will explode upwards if the old low unemployment rate is maintained, but they will not explode if unemployment rises at the same time as worker frustration grows. This has apparently happened in the USA. It has been estimated that the unemployment rate below which wage inflation accelerates increased about 1.5 per cent from 1955 to 1974,[5] and unemployment rates were actually higher in the 1970s than in the 1960s, averaging 5.9 per cent from 1970 to 1974 against 4.1 per cent from 1964 to 1969. Some of the potential inflationary pressures may therefore have been suppressed by the increase in unemployment, and wages might have accelerated far more than they did in the early 1970s if the 1960s unemployment rate of around 4 per cent had been maintained by the Republican administrations of the early 1970s. But that probably explains only a fraction of what occurred. The main explanation is far more startling and unexpected. The great increase in United States public expenditure and taxation that occurred was mainly local and not national, so most of its effects were local effects, influencing particular cities like New York.

From 1955 to 1974 the proportion of United States marketed output which was consumed and invested in the non-market sector increased by 7.6 per cent from 23.8 to 31.4 per cent of marketed output. Now Federal expenditures only increased by 1 per cent of marketed output in this period and the remainder of the increase was local by States, cities, counties and townships. To finance it, federal taxation actually fell as a share of marketed output from 1955–74, but if federal social security charges are included with federal taxes, payments to the federal government showed a small increase. They were 16.7 per cent of marketed output in 1955 and 18.8 per cent in 1974, an increase of 2.1 per cent. The remainder of the 7 per cent increase in non-market spending, over two-thirds of it, was financed from increased local taxation, and this rose from 7.3 to 11.9 per cent of marketed output, an increase of 4.6 per cent.[6] Local taxation therefore increased more than twice as much as federal taxation.

It would be immaterial if increased taxation was local or federal if local taxation increased uniformly throughout the USA, but this is not at all what occurred. Taxation (and public expenditure) increased hardly at all in some areas and a great deal in others. The United States government publishes the statistics set out in Table 6.2, which shows the total local taxes paid in different United States cities in 1974.[7] This table shows that local taxes averaged 14.7 per cent at the $15,000 income level in the four high-tax cities, and only 5.2 per cent in the low-tax ones, and the discrepancy was similar at other income levels. The increase in non-market expenditure and the increased taxation that followed from it evidently occurred extremely unevenly throughout the USA and this had important consequences. Companies and workers together had to pay 9 cents in the dollar more in the high-tax areas. Companies to some extent

Table 6.2 Estimated local taxes paid by a family of four in selected large cities by income level: 1974

	Income Level		
	$10 000	*$15 000*	*$30 000*
	local taxes as a percentage of income		
High tax			
Boston	19.7	19.3	17.7
Buffalo	12.3	12.5	13.5
Milwaukee	13.1	14.0	14.2
New York	12.7	13.2	14.6
Average	8.8	8.9	8.6
Low tax			
Houston	6.1	5.7	4.7
Jacksonville	3.5	3.5	3.0
Memphis	6.5	6.0	4.5
Nashville	6.3	5.8	4.3

compensate their workers for living in high-tax areas like New York, so they earn less profits there, both because they are taxed more heavily themselves and because they have to pay higher salaries. Capital therefore tends to move out of the high-tax neighbourhoods, so these acquire a diminishing ratio of market-sector jobs. The expensive local non-market sector therefore has a diminishing productive base to support it, exactly as in Great Britain. In New York City, for instance, market-sector employment fell from 3,130,000 in 1960 to 2,664,000 in 1976, a reduction of 15 per cent. In the same period, non-market employment increased over 30 per cent from 408,000 to 532,000.[8] From 1960–74 non-market employment actually increased by 42 per cent to 581,000. Then came New York City's crisis, and in the next two years public sector jobs had to be cut back by 50,000 at the very time that market sector jobs were declining by over 200,000. The extra rapid initial expansion of non-market jobs with consequent tax increases therefore forced subsequent cuts in market sector employment, and in the end in public sector employment also, as in Britain.

There is a further important effect. United States evidence suggests that the better paid salaried workers move out of the high-tax areas towards low-tax ones. At the same time, the poor move into the high-tax and high public-benefit areas. As the rich move out and poor move in a vast unstable movement begins.[9] The potential high-tax payers congregate in areas where there is a wealth of skill in the population, and few poor people to support. In other areas, the unskilled and the deprived congregate, and there are a diminishing number of skilled workers to pay the taxes to support them, and to provide a magnet to productive industry and commerce. These trends are slow but they are socially devastating.

An indication that the high-tax areas are declining, and that the low-tax areas are growing is given by the population figures for the eight cities from Table 6.2. In the four low-tax cities population increased 65 per cent from 1960 to 1973 which indicates that capital was expanding rapidly and that jobs were being created on a substantial scale. In the four high-tax cities population fell 7 per cent in the same period,[10] and unemployment rose. In New York City, for instance, unemployment increased from 4.8 per cent in 1970 to 10.6 per cent in 1976. Employment in the 16–19 age group fell from 30 per cent to a socially disastrous 22 per cent in 1976. In expanding low-tax Houston it rose from 41 to 47 per cent in the same period.[11]

It is to be noted that if a combination of high non-market expenditure and high taxation was attractive to the skilled and highly paid, they would move into the high-tax areas and not away from them. The studies quoted suggest that what deters the high-income earner from living in a high-tax area is the redistributive element in the taxation he pays. He can finance his own social services and have something left over in a low-tax area. A further point is that as in Britain, high taxation and high public expenditure often involves a proliferation of administrative expenditures and not the output of more public goods. The social wage may be almost as high in Florida as it is in New York when it is measured by the output of social services provided instead of the cost of providing them.

The fact that workers in the United States have been able to avoid financing the growing non-market sector by simply moving to the suburbs of their cities, the sun-belt or the west helps to explain the relative lack of national trade union pressure. National pressure to resist increased taxation was rational in Britain because it was national taxation that rose. Only about 10 per cent of British public expenditure is financed locally against almost 40 per cent in the USA. But the rational response to an increase in local taxation without a commensurate improvement in services is migration, and this has occurred on a massive scale in the USA. There was therefore no need to turn to the zero-sum-game approach of the British unions except in cities like New York where the public employees have become aware with the departure of some of the capital that finances them that they are indeed living in a zero or negative sum environment. In those areas conflicts of the British kind are developing.

The principal United States problem has thus been the tendency for non-market spending to soar locally and not nationally to produce the unstable result of a series of mini-Britains with growing numbers of public workers and fewer producers to support them, and the situation deteriorating because there is instability. Producers have continuing incentives to leave these areas, and the poor to enter them, to produce areas of poverty, deprivation and urban violence. A restoration of the productive base of these areas is desperately needed, but the high local taxation inhibits it. That is close to the essence of the British problem.

In comparison with these difficulties, the small increase in the 'natural' rate of unemployment which the remainder of the USA has had to live with, due partly to the increase in taxation that has been national rather than local is a minor problem. But reactions to this with a tendency for governments to run the economy with less pressure of demand on resources than in the past may have contributed to the fall in the share of United States investment in the market sector in the 1970s that Chart 27 indicates. There was not a significant fall in the share of gross investment until 1975, a year when the economy was in deep recession, but net investment has been falling according to official United States capital consumption data. The situation will become difficult for the economy as a whole if this reflects an underlying long-term trend, for the United States has a considerable rate of

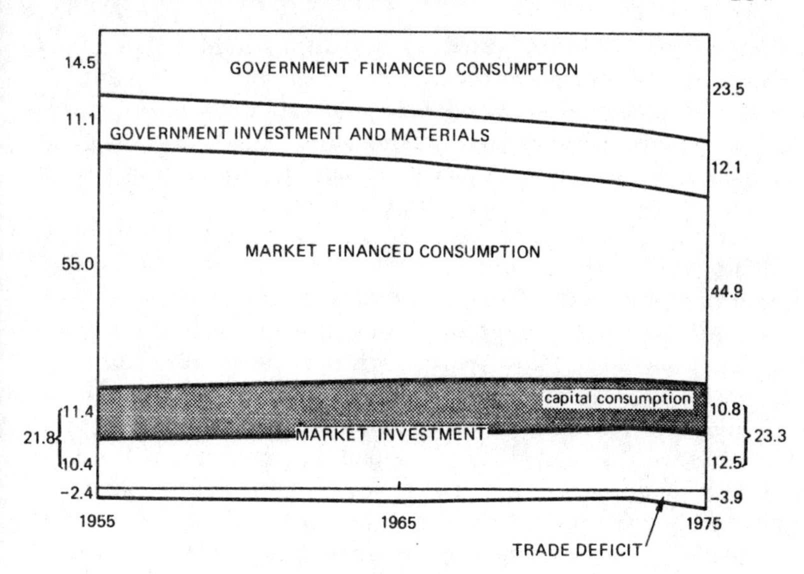

Chart 28 Where Marketed Output Went: Canada

population growth and therefore it needs to maintain a substantial rate of job creation in its market sector. Otherwise it will face the problem of growing nationwide structural unemployment. But these problems are possible future ones. In 1965–74 the United States market sector increased the employment it provided at an annual rate of 1.8 per cent, which suggests that there was no difficulty in maintaining an adequate rate of growth of employment in this period. The lack of job creation in the urban ghettoes is present and real, while a problem of long-term structural unemployment is future and hypothetical – but it may become a reality if recent US capital consumption statistics are accurate.

In Canada also there is no direct and immediate evidence of any trend towards structural unemployment. At the start of the world recession in 1974, unemployment was lower than its average rate in 1955–64. What happened to Canadian marketed output is set out in Chart 28, and this suggests that non-market spending grew entirely at the expense of private consumption. Market-sector investment increased substantially from 1955 to 1974, both when it is measured gross and when it is measured net of capital consumption (as computed by Statistics Canada). There was a fall in investment from 1974 to 1975, but that is plausibly associated with the world recession rather than with long-term trends. What is most striking about Chart 28 is the great decline in the share of market-financed consumption from 55.0 per cent of output in 1955 to 43.8 per cent in 1974 and 44.9 per cent in 1975. During the vital period, 1965–74, it fell 6.4 per cent from 50.2 to 43.8 per cent, and this reduced the rate of growth of output available to the market sector to 1.1 per cent per worker employed. But private consumption grew still more slowly than this because the share of investment increased and Canada's current account trade deficit was reduced. The result was that private consumption increased at a rate of only 0.4 per cent per annum for each worker employed in the market sector. Canadian workers had become accustomed to a rate of increase of private consumption of 1.8 per cent per annum from 1955 to 1965 and they reacted adversely to the developing squeeze on consumption. An aggregate rate of growth of 0.4 per cent per annum produces near zero sum game conditions so, as in Britain, unions increasingly came to realise that they needed larger wage increases than other unions and non-unionised labour if the private consumption of their members was to increase at an adequate rate. They therefore turned more and more to the conflict behaviour appropriate to zero sum game conditions. It has been noted that this did not occur on a significant scale in the USA because most of the increased taxation there was local and not national. In Canada federal taxation which rose 244 per cent from 1965 to 1974 in current money terms and provincial and local taxation which rose 248 per cent increased about equally. All Canadians were therefore being asked to contribute to the growing non-market sector, and trade union action increased throughout Canada in the attempts that were made to maintain the rate of growth of private consumption.

In 1956–65 an average of 1,611,000 working days a year were lost through strikes in Canada, and the number of disputes a year averaged 306. In 1966–72 the number of working days lost increased over three times to 5,592,000 a year and the average number of disputes rose to 574. In 1973–5 the number of working days lost rose further to an

Table 6.3 The annual increase in non-agricultural earnings

	Canada %	USA %
1958–65	3.73	3.43
1965–73	7.35	5.46
1973–76	12.59	6.60

average of 8,641,000 a year and the average number of disputes increased to 665.[12] There was thus strong evidence of increasing trade union activity and this produced results, at least so far as the rate of increase of money wages was concerned. The growth of Canadian weekly earnings in the whole economy apart from agriculture is set out against the same series in the USA for the period 1958–76, in Table 6.3.[13] From 1958 (the first year for which the United States series is available) until 1965 Canadian wages increased only 0.3 per cent faster than United States wages, and as productivity was advancing 0.4 per cent per annum faster in Canada, this was compatible with common inflation rates in Canada and the USA. However from 1965 onwards Canadian wages started to rise 1.9 per cent per annum faster than United States wages, and the Canadian authorities did not let unemployment rise sufficiently to check this faster increase in wages. The acceleration of wage inflation plausibly resulted from the increase in industrial conflict and the squeeze on Canadian market-sector consumption. Monetarists would say that this raised the 'natural' rate of unemployment to produce accelerating inflation if unemployment was not allowed to rise sufficiently to check it. The extra wage inflation of 1.9 per cent per annum did not seriously undermine Canadian competitiveness at first because Canadian productivity was increasing 0.9 per cent per annum faster than United States productivity. Canadian wage costs per unit were therefore rising only 1.0 per cent per annum faster than United States wage costs, and the Canadian dollar actually rose a few per cent relative to the United States dollar from 1966 to 1973.

The situation from 1973 onwards was more serious for Canada. The time lost through industrial disputes increased again, and Canadian wages started to increase 6 per cent per annum faster than United States wages. Price and wage controls like Britain's were introduced in October 1975 intended to run into 1978, and these limited company profits as in Britain. Several companies have been forced to lower their prices by the Canadian Anti-Inflation Board because their profits were deemed to be excessive. In addition, the 6 per cent excess of Canadian wage increases over United States increases from 1973 onwards reduced the competitiveness of the Canadian dollar by perhaps 15 per cent relative to the United States dollar by 1976, and the Canadian dollar was allowed to fall to US$0.93 in 1977 to make good part of this, but the fall in the Canadian dollar still left Canadian wage costs per unit about 8 per cent higher in relation to United States wage costs than they used to be. Clearly if Canadian wages continue to rise significantly faster than United States wages, Canada will lose the psychological defence barrier of a Canadian dollar that is worth about as much as the United States dollar. If the Canadian dollar once falls significantly below US$0.90, a British-style downward slide with Canadian wages chasing the exchange rate down could begin.

Canada has therefore reached a position which resembles Britain's in several respects. The trade unions have become strong enough to push wages upwards at a pace which obliges the authorities (who consider the very high unemployment which might check wage inflation in these new conditions intolerable) to introduce price and wage controls with the result that profits are being squeezed. Furthermore, as in Britain, the country is faced with possible wage explosions as soon as the controls are removed, as they must be from time to time. Finally, private consumption has risen slowly in relation to workers' aspirations with the result that there is pent-up frustration in the labour market leading to zero sum behaviour by the trade unions which leads to inefficiencies and to discomfort for the public during the disputes which become increasingly frequent.

Fortunately for Canada, these difficulties can only have affected market-sector investment adversely from 1974 onwards, for it is only then that Canadian wage costs per unit began to get seriously out of line with United States costs. Canadian market-sector employment increased at the very high rate of 2.75 per cent per annum from 1965 to 1974 and market-sector investment increased faster than output in this period. The fall in the share of investment after 1974, and there has been a fall, has certainly been largely due to the world recession which has had adverse effects on investment everywhere. The slow growth of workers' private consumption until 1974 underlines the proposition that there is no reason to suppose that profits were inadequate to finance the investment that Canada needed until then. But a British-style profits squeeze almost certainly began with the extra wage inflation of 1975–6 which pushed Canadian wage costs ahead of United States costs by 1974 and was then inadequately compensated by the exchange rate. Profits have been squeezed additionally by the price and wage controls of 1975–7. Statistics Canada does not publish statistics for company profits net of capital consumption and inflationary stock appreciation so no one knows what the real inflation-proof accounting profits of Canadian industry and commerce were in 1976 and 1977 but there is a probability that they may by then have become too low for Canada's needs. The calculation of the true Canadian profits trend is therefore a matter of great importance.

If Canadian market-sector profits have become inadequate for the necessary self-finance of investment and the attraction of United States capital (and in 1977 Canadian risk capital has been moving South of the border and not only from Quebec, while less United States capital has been flowing North) the effects could be extremely serious in the 1980s because demographic factors suggest that Canada will need to continue to expand market-sector employment by over 2 per cent per annum for many years to come. It is therefore essential that profits in the market sector be adequate to finance this and to attract United States capital on the scale which will be needed.

But little damage has yet been done to the productive structure of the Canadian economy, and the stability of the economy can be restored provided that the expansion of market-sector employment at a rate of 2 or 3 per cent per annum can resume. If the extra rise in real wage costs of 1973–7 has left market-sector profits too low for this, then real wages may need to be reduced for a year or two to restore the financial viability of the market sector. A failure to restore the rate of market-sector job creation could lead Canada to travel along Britain's road of 1970–75 where an imbalance in the economy developed leading to growing structural unemployment by 1976 and 1977. In Canada too a future government might find it cannot afford to create jobs at the very time that industry and commerce have insufficient finance for job creation because wages absorb too high a share of value-added.

A question that this account raises is why Canada is this far behind Britain on the road to destabilisation. In the 1960s consumption was squeezed more in Canada than in Britain, but the British response was union pressure which forced consumption up at the expense of profits, while in Canada consumption gave way at first, increasing only 0.4 per cent per worker a year from 1965 to 1974, in spite of growing union pressure. The most plausible answer to this question is that in 1965 the Canadian unions were not sufficiently organised to raise wages at the expense of profits. Less than one-third of the labour force was unionised as against about two-thirds in Britain, and the unions managed to raise wages a little faster than before, but prices rose faster too so that profits did not suffer. It was plausibly only by 1973 that union power reached the point where profits began to be squeezed, and workers managed to raise real consumption considerably faster than output. It is therefore being argued that there was a slow and continuing increase in union power in Canada which allowed workers to start to pass the growing costs of the non-market sector on to companies from 1973 onwards but not before.

This account of the effects of the growing non-market sectors of Canada and the USA has made it clear that what happens in particular countries can vary a great deal. The fact that it was local and not federal taxation that increased in the USA meant that most of the effects were local, but they took the form as in Britain of a loss of productive jobs in the areas where non-market expenditure increased most. In Canada the workers wished to pass the higher costs of government on to other groups in the community long before they had the power to do so in the 1970s, and until then they had to pay for the growing non-market sector. The difference in Britain was that unions had the power to squeeze profits as soon as government spending began to rise rapidly, while in Canada it took time for the trade union movement to acquire this power.

It is possible to summarise the argument by suggesting that where non-market spending rises faster than the rate a population wishes to finance, there will be countervailing action of various kinds by that population. As John Kenneth Galbraith pointed out in the early 1950s,[14] in a democracy concentrations of economic power will lead to the growth of countervailing power groups to keep the first ones in check. Therefore bureaucratic concentrations which attempt to correct an imbalance between private affluence and public squalor by moving rapidly towards public affluence are liable to find that the population has countervailing power at its disposal. Workers and companies can relocate where this succeeds in passing the burden on to others, and if movement within the country fails to reduce taxation as in Britain and Canada, workers and companies will both attempt to pass the burden on. In Canada the companies succeeded at first so that higher taxes merely caused accelerating inflation because the government did not react by letting unemployment increase sufficiently with the rising 'natural' rate.[15] But growing frustration increased the organisation and market power of the working class so that, as in Britain, the situation gradually changed to one where it was companies that were having to pay for higher public spending. From that point onwards, and it came far earlier in Britain, the productive structure of the economy was threatened, and the financial foundations of the public sector moved towards collapse.

If the argument of this book is correct, the structure of the economy will be undermined after a time in any democracy where non-market spending is increased at a faster rate than the one the population wishes to finance.

NOTES

1. See Table 23.1, on p. 247, line (25) (real market-sector output) divided by line (29) (market sector employment).

2. See Table 23.1, line (4) divided by line (12) which suggests that on average 66 per cent of all personal incomes were consumed in 1975.
3. The first column of this table is derived from lines (27) and (29) and the second from lines (28) and (29) of Table 23.1.
4. ILO *Year Book of Labour Statistics*, Tables 18 and 25.
5. See, for instance, Michael L. Wachter, 'The Changing Cyclical Responsiveness of Wage Inflation', *Brookings Papers on Economic Activity*, 1976 (1).
6. These figures are derived from the *Statistical Abstract of the United States*, US Department of Commerce, Bureau of the Census, 1976, Tables 418 and 425.
7. *Ibid.*, Table 450.
8. *Thirteenth Interim Report* of the Temporary Commission on City Finances, New York City, May 1977, p. 15 (Economic and Demographic Trends in New York City).
9. See, for instance, J. Richard Aronson and Eli Schwarz, 'Financing Public Goods and the Distribution of Population in a System of Local Governments', *National Tax Journal*, Vol. XXVI, June 1973; and J. Richard Aronson, 'Financing Public Goods and the Distribution of Population in Metropolitan Areas: An Analysis of Fiscal Migration in the United States and England', published in *Economic Policies and Social Goals: Aspects of Public Choice*, Edited A. J. Culyer, Martin Robertson, 1974.
10. *Statistical Abstract of the United States*, 1976, Table 23.
11. *The New York Times*, 2 and 7 August 1977.
12. ILO *Year Book of Labour Statistics*, Table 27A.
13. *Ibid.*, Table 18.
14. J. K. Galbraith, *American Capitalism: The Theory of Countervailing Power*, Houghton Mifflin, Boston, 1952.
15. See John H. Hotson, *Stagflation and the Bastard Keynesians*, University of Waterloo Press, 1976, for an account of the evidence that there was tax-induced inflation in Canada.

7 The Underlying Economic Theory:

The Implications for Inflation, Employment and Growth of a Fall in the Share of Output that is Marketed

In 1974–5 the present authors,[1] and economists in the Cambridge University Department of Applied Economics,[2] and Mr Benn and those associated with him[3] all drew attention to various aspects of the de-industrialisation that Britain has experienced and is experiencing. In addition Professor J. Johnston set out some of the implications of a shift in employment from industry to the provision of unmarketed public services in a most interesting model.[4]

In the Introduction to the present chapter, something will be said about these contributions in general terms: the implications will be discussed of dividing the economy into (i) industrial and non-industrial sectors; (ii) a sector that produces tradable goods and services and one that produces non-tradables; and (iii) a sector that produces marketed goods and services and one that produces non-marketed outputs. The reasons for preferring the marketed and non-marketed division will be explained, and the theoretical implications of a shift in employment from the market to the non-market sector will then be set out in two stages. In Section 2 two economies in steady growth with different ratios of marketed output will be compared, to identify some of the long-term implications of very different ratios of marketed output in total output. In Section 3 the problems involved in moving from a low to a high share of non-marketed output will be set out, including the possibility that there may be no viable growth path the economy can move to, with the result that inflationary pressures grow and the productive base of the economy runs down at an accelerating rate from year to year.

1. INTRODUCTION

The model which will be used to analyse the effects of a lower ratio of marketed output is an elaboration of the growth model with which the classical economists argued that the rate of growth depended on the proportion of an economy's activities that were 'productive' and the rate of surplus earned in the 'productive' sector.[5] In a simple classical growth model it can be assumed that the output of the productive sector where all growth-producing activities originate is O_p of which C_p is consumed by productive workers, C_u is consumed unproductively (by workers who do not work in the productive sector and by non-workers), while the remaining output of the productive sector, I_p, is invested. Then the surplus of the productive sector, i.e. its output less the consumption of its own workers, is $O_p - C_p$, and this must equal C_u plus I_p. Hence

$$\frac{O_p - C_p}{O_p} \equiv \frac{C_u}{O_p} + \frac{I_p}{O_p}$$

Now $(O_p - C_p)/O_p$ is the surplus earned in the productive sector as a fraction of its own output, and e_p can be written for this, while c_u can be written for C_u/O_p, the proportion of the output of the productive sector that is consumed unproductively. If i_p is written for I_p/O_p, the proportion of productive sector output that is invested, then

$$i_p \equiv e_p - c_u \qquad (1)$$

It can be assumed that the output of the productive sector will be constant in the absence of investment (and both output and investment must be defined net of capital consumption to produce this result), while it will grow if there is accumulation and decline if there is decumulation. (1) shows that a classical economy will grow if e_p exceeds c_u, while output will decline if c_u, the proportion of output consumed uproductively, exceeds e_p, the rate of surplus in the productive sector. A stationary state will be achieved if e_p equals c_u, for instance if a 'corn' economy produces a surplus of 50 per cent of output in the 'corn' sector, while one-half of each harvest is diverted to the civilised and/or wasteful activities of the unproductive sector. If the rate of surplus was only 25 per cent, just one-quarter of each year's output could be diverted to the unproductive sector, while a rate of surplus of 75 per cent would allow three-quarters of output to be used in unproductive activities. Growth requires that the unproductive sector be smaller so that part of the surplus of the productive sector can be invested.

The classical economists differed about the correct practical dividing line between the productive and unproductive sectors. There must clearly be something arbitrary in where the borderline is drawn, but there is also an important element of sense in the classical proposition that the economy's ability to support non-surplus-producing activities depends on the ratio of outputs to inputs in the sector of the economy where surpluses are produced. Typical positions taken up by the classical economists were Malthus's that only the activities that produced physical and therefore investable outputs were productive, and that of Smith who came close to saying that all profit-making activities were productive, with the result that his productive sector included many marketed services.[6] These differences are echoed in recent analyses of de-industrialisation where the economy has been divided between an industrial and a non-industrial sector: a sector producing tradable goods and services and a sector producing non-tradables: and a sector producing marketed goods and services and one producing non-marketed outputs.[7]

Where the economy is divided into an industrial and a non-industrial sector, industrial output net of capital consumption is O_i, and C_i of this is consumed by the industrial workers who produce it so the industrial sector's surplus of industrial production is $(O_i - C_i)$. Of this C_u will be consumed by non-industrial workers and by non-workers such as pensioners, I_u will be used up outside industry in the form of investment and material purchases, I_i will be net investment in industry itself, and B_i will be the trade surplus of industrial output. With consistent definitions, and the measurement of sales of industrial production so that these exclude sales of intermediate products to industrial producers to avoid double counting, this is an identity so that:

$$\frac{O_i - C_i}{O_i} \equiv \frac{C_u}{O_i} + \frac{I_u}{O_i} + \frac{B_i}{O_i} + \frac{I_i}{O_i}$$

Now e_i can be written for $(O_i - C_i)/O_i$ as in the basic classical formula (here e_i is the proportion of industrial output that is surplus to the consumption of industrial workers), while c_u, i_u, i_i and b_i can be written for C_u/O_i, I_u/O_i, I_i/O_i and B_i/O_i. Hence:

$$i_i + b_i \equiv e_i - c_u - i_u \qquad (2)$$

This equation is clearly very similar to the classical equation (1). Here the proportion of industrial output that can be reinvested in industry (net of capital consumption), plus the proportion that can be exported net is identically equal to the rate of surplus of industrial production achieved in industry, less the fractions of industrial output that are personally consumed and used up as raw materials and investment outside industry.

In the United Kingdom there was a substantial increase in the size of the non-industrial relative to the industrial sector in 1961–74. Non-industrial employment rose 34 per cent relative to industrial employment in this period, while the fraction of GNP produced outside industry rose 26.1 per cent relative to the value-added in industry. This influenced the terms in the equation. Personal consumption and direct purchases outside industry, i.e. $c_u + i_u$, increased from 63.9 per cent of final sales of net industrial production to 76.6 per cent with the increase in the relative size of the non-industrial sector. This would have had no adverse effects on net industrial investment and the export surplus if e_i, the proportion of industrial output that was surplus to the consumption of industrial workers, had also risen by 12.7 per cent of industrial production, from 84.9 per cent to an *impossible* 97.6 per cent of this. In the event it rose only 2.5 per cent, so i_i and b_i fell by 10.2 per cent of industrial production. The export surplus fell by 8.2 per cent from 13.7 per cent to 5.5 per cent of industrial production, and net investment in industry fell by the remaining 2.0 per cent from 7.3 per cent to 5.3 per cent of industrial production.[8]

An account of this kind omits basic causation but it says very clear things about the necessary *effects* of de-industrialisation. It has tempted the present authors and Mr Benn to apply an argument based on an equation like (2) fairly directly to the British economy.[9]

There are however obvious weaknesses in the industry and non-industry dividing line. Transport, communications and distribution, which are all services, are part of any process by which inputs are transformed into final outputs in the hands of domestic or foreign producers and consumers, and a line drawn between the manufacturing and distribution stages of this process must be an arbitrary one – and this is especially the case as some companies handle manufacturing, transport, and distribution, while others concentrate on just one of these. Hence any attempt to deal with companies according to the sector of the economy within which they work, and this was attempted with Lord Kaldor's Selective Employment Tax, must lead to distortions. In addition, the balance of trade shown in (2) is simply the balance of trade in industrial products, which is merely one component of the current account of the balance of payments. A country could have deteriorating trade in industrial products and improving trade in services and an improving balance of payments, but an equation like (2) would simply suggest that such a country had a deteriorating balance of trade about which something had to be done.

These problems are partly solved if economic activities are divided into the categories tradable and non-tradable. Tradable output is any good or service which can be sold overseas, so this category will include the services that are marketed to foreigners such as shipping, insurance, banking, etc. If O_x is net tradable output while C_x is the consumption of this by those who produce it, $(O_x - C_x)$ will be the surplus of tradable output available to the remainder of the economy, and of this I_x will be invested in the tradable sector, B_x will be net exports, while C_u will be personally consumed and I_u

will be invested or used as materials outside the tradable sector. Hence:

$$\frac{O_x - C_x}{O_x} \equiv \frac{I_x}{O_x} + \frac{B_x}{O_x} + \frac{C_u}{O_x} + \frac{I_u}{O_x}$$

and therefore:

$$i_x + b_x \equiv e_x - c_u - i_u \qquad (3)$$

where the terms in this equation all refer to fractions of tradable output. In the United Kingdom, incomes from generally untradable activities such as central and local government administration, education, health and retirement rose as substantially in relation to incomes from tradable activities as non-industry in relation to industry. This happened because the basic manpower shift that occurred from industry to the public sector services[10] was also a shift from the production of tradables to non-tradables. With this shift, c_u and i_u rose substantially while e_x failed to rise commensurately, so investment in the tradable sector and net exports of tradables both fell as fractions of tradable output. An account of the general deterioration in productive investment and the balance of payments in the United Kingdom would therefore be virtually identical to that arrived at with the categories industrial and non-industrial, and the use of the categories tradable and non-tradable would remove one of the fundamental objections to the previous approach. Thus equation (3) includes all exports and imports and not just the balance of trade in industrial products in b_x, so a change in this must point to a similar change in the current account of the balance of payments. For these reasons one of the present authors preferred the tradable/non-tradable approach in February 1975.[11]

However, some of the other disadvantages of the industry and non-industry division remain. Thus retail distribution is largely untradable, and so is domestic transport and most building and construction activity. Hence i_x will not be net investment as this is ordinarily measured. Indeed the division again draws an arbitrary dividing line between processes that are an indispensable part of the transformation of raw materials into finished goods in the hands of producers and consumers.

These remaining difficulties are removed if economic activities are divided between those that produce marketed outputs and those that do not. A marketed output is one that is marketed at home or overseas, so this automatically includes all tradable outputs, but it includes construction, transport and retail distribution in addition. The economy's market sector must produce all exports (for these are all marketed), all investment, and all the goods and services that workers buy. It is to be noted that the market sector will include the nationalised industries in so far as these cover their costs through sales of output, as well as the private sectors of modern economies. It will exclude public services which are provided free of charge. Using the dividing line between market and non-market sectors of the economy, the basic equation (arrived at as above) becomes:

$$i_m + b_m \equiv e_m - c_u - i_u \qquad (4)$$

where these are all fractions of marketed output. These terms all correspond to easily defined and well-understood totals. The equation shows that the proportion of marketed output that can be reinvested in the market sector (net of capital consumption), plus the proportion that can be exported net is identically equal to the rate of surplus of marketed output achieved in the market sector, less the fractions of marketed output that are personally consumed and used up as raw materials and investment outside the market sector.

There was a large shift from industry to public sector service employment in the United Kingdom in 1961–75 and this increased both the ratio of non-marketed to marketed output and the entitlement to consume marketed output by those who did not produce it directly. The latter also increased because there was a large increase in pensions and social security benefits which entitled non-producers to buy an increasing proportion of marketed output. The pre-tax entitlement to buy United Kingdom marketed output by those who did not produce it directly increased from 41.4 per cent of marketed output in 1961 to 62.1 per cent in 1975. This increased c_u and i_u substantially, and because e_m

did not rise commensurately, b_m and i_m necessarily fell. As all traded goods and services are marketed, b_m is the current account of the balance of payments (expressed as a fraction of marketed output). Similarly as all investment is marketed, i_m is simply total market-sector net investment (expressed as a fraction of marketed output). In Chapter 1 it was argued that a squeeze on b_m and i_m resulted from the increase in the pre-tax entitlement to consume market sector output by non-market sector producers from 41.4 per cent to 62.1 per cent and that this put pressure on the current account of the balance of payments and market-sector investment.

It is universally agreed that many of the most indispensable and civilised activities of a modern society produce unmarketable outputs. The argument is not that increasing unmarketed activities in relation to total output is in any way wrong, but that this must have effects compatible with equation (4), which must always hold as it is an identity. Hence the consumption and investment involved in the provision of unmarketed activities can only be increased without damage to investment and the balance of payments if e_m, the rate of surplus in the market sector, rises commensurately. This happens in any society that achieves a successful transition from a peacetime to a wartime economy, when workers often accept greatly increased rates of taxation without explosive wage inflation. If resources are transferred to the provision of unmarketables on a similar scale in peacetime, and people still wish to buy growing quantities of goods in the shops, one of two things must happen. Either e_m will stay unchanged (i.e. governments fail to apply wartime rates of taxation or the share of wages and salaries fails to fall drastically) and in this case an increase in c_u and i_u must squeeze i_m and/or b_m. Alternatively taxation will be raised enough to prevent this, but ex-ante wage demands may still be based on the marketed goods and services workers expect to be able to buy, and when these ex-ante demands are frustrated ex-post because of higher taxation, etc., wage demands in the next period can be that much higher, producing a continuing acceleration of inflation (at given rates of unemployment) so long as the economy fails to meet workers' ex-ante wage demands in terms of marketed output.[12] A substantial shift from marketed to non-marketed output of the kind that has taken place in Britain since 1961 may therefore have far-reaching effects on the functioning of the economy. This much is apparent from the simple equations so far presented.

It is now time to develop the argument more fully, and show first how basic economic interrelationships such as money flows and factor shares will differ in economies in steady growth with different ratios of marketed output. Following this, the precise form of the problems of transition from a low to a high share of unmarketed output will be outlined.

2. A STEADY-GROWTH COMPARISON BETWEEN TWO ECONOMIES WITH DIFFERENT RATIOS OF MARKETED OUTPUT

An economy with two sectors is assumed. One, the market sector, has companies which produce outputs that they sell. The other, the public sector, produces non-marketed outputs.[13] The argument will be set out in two stages. First, a number of basic relationships which must always hold – whether there is steady growth or not – will be set out. After this, the further relationships which must hold in steady growth will be added, to produce a complete account of the long-term effects on economies of different ratios of marketed to non-marketed output.

(i) RELATIONSHIPS WHICH MUST ALWAYS HOLD

The market sector produces outputs which sell for O_m (which is defined net of the depreciation of the market sector's own capital stock), and the corresponding pre-tax incomes are profits of $\pi.O_m$, and wages of $(1-\pi).O_m$, where π is the share of profits in the market sector. The government taxes all incomes at the same proportional rate of T. Fractions s_π of net tax profits and s_w of net-of-tax wages are saved, and saving from profits is wholly in the form of company saving. All market sector investment, $i_m.O_m$, is done through companies, and i_m, the fraction of marketed output invested, is defined net of capital consumption. The basic relationships of the market sector can be derived very easily from these assumptions, and they are set out in the tables on pp. 203–4 at the end of the chapter.

The government spends $G_o.O_m$ directly on marketed output, and in addition, it pays $G_p.O_m$ to persons for services, or simply as transfers. Hence total non-market expenditure is $(G_o + G_p)O_m$. The $G_p.O_m$ that is paid to persons is taxable at the uniform rate of T, and the recipients save a fraction, s_w, of the net of tax incomes they receive from the government.[14] $G_o.O_m$, total direct public expenditure on marketed output, includes public-sector investment and all purchases of currently used materials by the public sector, and these have identical effects on the equations.[15] The basic public-sector equations are also set out in the tables.

Moving on to international trade, there are two basic equations which state the size of $b_m.O_m$, the current account surplus of the balance of payments, in terms of the economy's other relationships. First, in terms of Marketed Output Balances:

Current account surplus = Sum of Marketed Output Balances of the economy's various sectors,

i.e. the current account surplus must equal the market sector output that is surplus to that sector's investment and consumption, less the marketed output that is purchased by the government and the recipients of public-sector incomes.

Second, as the New Cambridge school has reiterated:[16]

Current account surplus = Sum of financial balances of the economy's various sectors.

The Marketed Output Balance equation is in fact the same as the Cambridge Financial Balance equation. Using the tables, both equations can be written as:

$$\begin{aligned} b_m &= T\{1 + G_p - \pi s_\pi - s_w(1 - \pi + G_p)\} \\ &\quad - i_m - G_o - G_p + \pi s_\pi + s_w(1 - \pi + G_p) \qquad (5) \end{aligned}$$

It is to be noted that b_m is the *ratio* of the current account surplus to marketed output.

(ii) A STEADY GROWTH COMPARISON

Two economies in steady growth will be compared where one has a substantially higher $(G_o + G_p)$ than the other, i.e. one uses up a substantially higher fraction of marketed output in the public sector. To focus attention on this difference and its consequences, it will be assumed initially that both economies have the same rate of Harrod-neutral technical progress, a, in their market sectors. This assumption will be relaxed later, as it is plausible that the size of the public sector will influence the rate of technical progress, for instance because education and defence spending may have some favourable long-term effects on this; but so long as it holds, both economies will be assumed to have the same rate of growth of productivity in their market sectors. With constant rates of taxation, and unchanging income distribution, wages net of tax will increase at the same rate as productivity. Then wages will increase at rate a in both economies in terms of marketed output, and this rate of increase of private consumable income will apply to the workers of both sectors, and it will be assumed that these receive the same wage. It will also be assumed that the labour force grows at rate n in both economies. Then with constant shares of employment in the market and non-market sectors, employment will grow at rate n in both sectors of both economies. As output per worker grows at rate a, total market sector output will grow at rate $(a + n)$ in both economies. Non-market expenditure will also grow at rate $(a + n)$, and this will allow the government to increase the *goods* that it buys for investment, etc., at rate $(a + n)$, but in steady growth it will only increase its direct employment at rate n, the rate at which the labour force grows, and the cost of this rises at an annual rate of $(a + n)$ because wages (in terms of marketed output) rise at rate a.

Up to this point, the growth paths of the two economies appear extremely similar. Both have the same rates of growth of public and private sector output and employment, and the same rate of growth of living standards in terms of both marketed and non-marketed outputs. The sole difference is that in the case of one economy a higher fraction of what is provided (and this grows at the same rate in both economies) is not marketed. It is now time to turn to the differences.

First, the two economies will have very different rates of taxation. These can be calculated very easily as the natural first assumption to make in a steady growth comparison is that the budgets of both economies balance.[17] As exports can be assumed continually equal to imports in steady growth, there will be no financial surplus or deficit in transactions with foreigners.

With the budgets of both economies balanced, governments which spend $(G_o + G_p)O_m$ and receive $T(1 + G_p)O_m$ will need to set the rate of taxation at:

$$T = \frac{G_o + G_p}{1 + G_p} \tag{6}$$

For the United Kingdom it can be said conservatively that $(G_o + G_p)$ increased from 45 per cent in 1961 to 60 per cent in 1974. This slightly understates the increase in $(G_o + G_p)$ that took place. In both years approximately five-ninths of non-market expenditure was in the G_p category (payments to persons) and four-ninths in the G_o category (investment and material purchases).[18] The uniform rate of tax needed to balance the budget would then have been of the order of 36 per cent in 1961 and 45 per cent in 1974, so a 9 per cent increase in taxation on all incomes would have sufficed to allow an extra 15 per cent of marketed output to be used by the government. Substantially less extra taxation than 15 per cent is needed because with the present assumptions the government gets tax back at the uniform rate of T on all its payments to persons. Indeed it follows from (6) that if G_o and G_p always increase in the same proportion:

$$\frac{dT}{d(G_o + G_p)} = \left(\frac{1}{1 + G_p}\right)^2 \tag{7}$$

This was about 0.64 in the United Kingdom in 1961 when G_p was about 0.25 and 0.56 in 1974 when G_p was about 0.33, so an increase in non-market expenditures of 10 per cent of marketed output may now require an increase in overall taxation of less than 6 per cent, because civil servants' salaries, like those of others, are taxed.*

* In the examples in Chapter 4 where a country with an initial national income, all marketed, of £8000 million either moved

It might be thought that the above equations would suffice to show how workers' living standards in terms of marketed output would be affected by various different ratios of public expenditure to marketed output. Thus it might be believed that if one economy required a T of 45 per cent while another required a T of only 36 per cent, then workers and profit receivers in the first economy would keep 55 per cent of the marketed output they produced, while those in the second economy would keep 64 per cent, with the result that in any given year both workers and profit-receivers would be 9/64, or about 14 per cent, worse off in terms of marketed output in the economy with a T of 45 per cent. This calculation only holds if the share of profits is the same in both economies. If a larger non-market sector is associated with a higher or a lower share of profits this will obviously have crucial effects on how living standards, etc., differ between the two economies.

A first approach to how income distribution will be affected is to follow through the effects of the condition that the private sectors of both economies have balanced financial transactions, which follows from the assumptions that foreign trade is balanced and that the governments' budgets are balanced. With no private-sector financial surpluses or deficits, it can be inferred from the tables at the end of the chapter that:

$$\pi = \left(\frac{1}{1-T}\right)\left\{\frac{i_m}{s_\pi - s_w} - (1 - G_o)\frac{s_w}{s_\pi - s_w}\right\} \tag{8}$$

This is close to $1/(1-T)$ times the share of profits in Lord Kaldor's celebrated equation for the share of profits,[19] and the equation shows that with the present assumptions the share of profits is of the order of $1/(1-T)$ times what it

---

workers earning £2000 million to the non-market sector or paid pensions of £2000 million (see pp. 94–5 above), G_p is £2000 million/£6000 million = 0.33 in the first case, and £2000 million/£8000 million = 0.25 in the second, so these will require different tax rates. Hence extra payments to non-market sector workers (drawn from the market sector) would have different long-term effects on G_p and the required rate of taxation from those produced by equal extra payments to pensioners.

would be in the absence of public expenditure and taxation. As companies then pay a rate of tax of T on these profits, they keep about $(1 - T)$ times $1/(1 - T)$ of the profits they would have obtained in the absence of public expenditure and taxation, so their net-of-tax profits will be only slightly influenced by the rate of public expenditure. This means that the entire cost of the public sector is borne by labour. A simple example illustrated in Chart 29 shows how this comes about.

The share of profits in marketed output is 25 per cent (net of capital consumption) in the left-hand block, approximately the British percentage in 1961, and the uniform rate of tax is the hypothetical 36 per cent needed to balance the British budget in that year. Thus 16 per cent of the 25 per cent share of profits is left after tax, and for simplicity it is assumed that this is half invested and half consumed. It is also assumed that all saving comes from profits and s_π is one-half, so profit-receivers also consume half of profits net of tax. With all saving coming from profits, workers consume the entire net-of-tax incomes that they receive, and these amount to the share of wages and salaries (75 per cent) less taxation at 36 per cent, or 48 per cent of marketed output.

In the right-hand block the rate of taxation is 45 per cent, the hypothetical rate needed for a 60 per cent share of non-market expenditure in 1974. Companies pass this on, so the entire 9 per cent cost of the larger public sector is financed at the expense of workers' consumption – partly through the higher taxation of wages (at 45 per cent instead of 36 per cent), and partly through the lower share of wages (71 per cent instead of 75 per cent) that results from the passing on of profits taxation.

A crucial assumption in the above analysis is the one that the proportion of marketed output invested in the market sector is unaffected by the rate and share of profits. In steady growth this will equal $V(a + n)$, where V is the capital-output ratio in the market sector. It has been assumed that $(a + n)$, the 'natural' rate of growth, will be the same with all rates of non-market expenditure, but it is far from clear that V, the capital-output ratio, will be unaffected by this. Pasinetti has suggested that since factor prices have such uncertain effects on V, it is best to assume (where something must be assumed) that V depends mainly on technical factors, and that it is independent of relative factor prices.[20] This result would be arrived at with neo-classical analysis where ϕ, the elasticity of substitution between labour and capital, is zero. With this assumption, V will be the same whatever the rate of non-market expenditure, and as $(a + n)$ is also independent of this, i_m will be the same in two economies in steady growth, whatever the rate of taxation and the relative size of their non-market sectors. Then the above calculation will be correct, and *in steady growth* the entire cost of the larger non-market sector will be financed by labour.

Suppose however that *faute de mieux* the capital-output ratio depends in an old-fashioned way on the relative cost of labour and capital. The simplest example to take first is the one where $\phi = 1$, the Cobb-Douglas case, where the share of

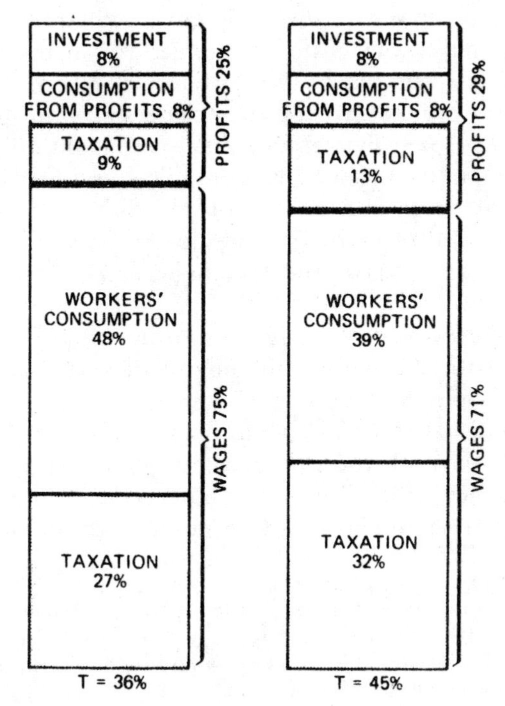

Chart 29 The Passing-on of Profits Taxation

profits will be the same, whatever the size of the non-market sector. With $\phi = 1$, the economy with a larger non-market sector will have a higher rate of profit,* a correspondingly lower capital-output ratio, and the same share of profits as another with a smaller non-market sector. With the same share of profits in both economies, workers and profit receivers will each contribute equal fractions of unchanged income shares to finance a larger non-market sector. Thus, for instance, if this required a doubled rate of tax, workers and profit-receivers would both need to give up twice as much from lower output levels (since the capital-output ratio is lower) to finance it. There would be no difficulty in financing investment from the lower net-of-tax profits, because the capital-output ratio and therefore the share of investment which needs to be financed in steady growth (which is $V(a + n)$) will be reduced in precisely the same proportion.

There are thus two limiting cases. Where $\phi = 0$, as in Chart 29, the whole cost of a larger non-market sector is borne (directly or indirectly) by labour. Where $\phi = 1$, both labour and capital give up the same extra proportion of unchanged income shares. Where ϕ exceeds 0 but is less than 1, as is generally supposed by those who consider it relevant, labour will bear most but not all the cost of a larger non-market sector – and it will do so from lower output levels than in the fixed production coefficients case set out in Chart 29.[21]

It will be evident that the assumption that the budget is balanced, with the result that the private sector has neither a financial surplus nor deficit, makes it virtually certain that workers will have to finance (in one way or another) almost the whole cost of the non-market sector. This is because something very like Kaldor's income distribution equation must hold with this assumption, and profits taxes are then

* The net of tax rate of profit of an economy in steady growth must always be $(a + n)/s_c$ (where s_c is the net-of-tax propensity to save of those with no earned incomes). The rate of profit before tax will be $1/(1 - T)$ times this, so an economy with a larger non-market sector than another similar economy will have a higher rate of profit before tax.

largely passed on. To assume that they are passed on is implicitly to assume that workers acquiesce in any share of profits that results – an assumption that will be relaxed below. Taxation is wholly passed on to labour where V is independent of relative factor prices, and partly passed on where there is some substitutability of capital and labour (with $\phi < 1$) – when workers lose additionally because output per worker is lower. It follows that workers' living standards in terms of marketed output must always be lower to a rather greater extent than that indicated by the tax rate. At the same time, profit-receivers are largely protected from the high taxation that must result from a large non-market sector. With Kaldor's equation, their ability to finance investment is independent of the rate of tax, because profits always generate a rate of saving from companies and workers that is sufficient to finance the steady growth share of investment. With these assumptions, therefore, net-of-tax profits are never squeezed relatively to investment, with the result that companies face no financing problems when the non-market sector is large that they do not face equally where it is small. The sole pressure is on labour.

It is perhaps unrealistic to set up a model where workers are certain to give way to this pressure, as has been assumed so far. It is true that the analysis of this section is based on the assumptions of steady growth where the workers of different economies consume (and have always consumed) different fractions of the marketed output they produce. There is therefore never pressure on workers to move down to a growth path where private consumption per head is lower – pressure which trade unions might be expected to resist. Nevertheless it may be worth while to set out the implications of an alternative set of assumptions where the shares of wages and profits in marketed output depend on the relative market power of labour and capital. It could for instance be assumed that the 'degree of monopoly' in Kalecki's sense is independent of the rate of taxation and the relative size of the non-market sector. Then the ratio of prices to direct costs of production will always be the same, with the result that π, the share of profits in marketed output, will be a constant and not a variable.[22]

With this assumption, the cost of the non-market sector will be shared by workers and profit receivers. The latter will receive π times marketed output before tax, where π is a constant, depending on the degree of monopoly, and workers will receive $(1 - \pi)$ times marketed output before tax. After tax they will receive $(1 - T)\pi$ and $(1 - T)(1 - \pi)$ times marketed output respectively. As the share of profits and pre-tax relative factor prices will then be the same in different economies with different rates of taxation etc., the capital-output ratio and therefore the share of investment will also be the same at all rates of taxation. The different economies with different sized non-market sectors but the same degree of monopoly will all have the same share of profits before tax, the same rate of profit, the same capital-output ratio, and the same share of investment. The principal differences between economies with large and small non-market sectors will simply be that the former will have higher rates of taxation, with the result that their workers and profit receivers will be entitled to consume and invest (with internal finance) smaller fractions of marketed output. As the steady growth share of investment in the market sector will be the same in low- and high-tax economies, while high-tax economies will have less net-of-tax company saving, the latter will have to use more outside finance to invest the fraction $V(a + n)$ of marketed output that all must invest in steady growth. With the previous assumptions, π adjusted to tax rates and investment requirements, with the result that the ratio of investment to internal finance was the same at all rates of taxation. A low π (due to a low degree of monopoly) might however now create the problem that companies could only invest $V(a + n)$ if they were prepared to use a very high ratio of external finance – and it will be evident after the next stage of the argument that this might have to come from the government.

This emerges when the second principal effect of the assumption that π depends on the degree of monopoly is analysed. It is a consequence of this that the budget will no longer be balanced (apart from a fluke). With π given independently of investment requirements and saving propensities, the market sector of the economy may have a financial deficit or surplus so the assumption of a balanced budget which has been made hitherto cannot be retained. However, the assumption of balanced trade on a steady growth path can be retained, and this produces the condition that the market sector and the government taken together must have neither a surplus nor a deficit.[23] This condition will be fulfilled where the tax rate is (from (5)):

$$T = \frac{G_o + G_p + i_m - \pi(s_\pi - s_w) - (1 + G_p)s_w}{1 + G_p - \pi(s_\pi - s_w) - (1 + G_p)s_w} \tag{9}$$

Now when this tax rate is compared with the balanced budget tax rate, $(G_o + G_p)/(1 + G_p)$, it emerges that:

T is lower than the balanced budget tax rate, producing a consequent budget deficit, where:

$$\pi > \left(\frac{1 + G_p}{1 - G_o}\right) \left\{\frac{i_m}{s_\pi - s_w} - (1 - G_o)\frac{s_w}{s_\pi - s_w}\right\} \tag{10}$$

and conversely, T is higher and the budget is in surplus where π is less than this.

It will be evident when (10) is compared with (8) that, not unexpectedly, the crucial point is whether the degree of monopoly share of profits exceeds or falls short of Kaldor's π, which is what the right-hand side of (10) is equivalent to. If the degree of monopoly share of profits is greater, the market sector of the economy will generate unnecessarily high profits and excessive saving with the result that a budget deficit is needed in full employment equilibrium. Conversely, if the degree of monopoly factors produce a lower share of profits than Kaldor's equation (in the modified form appropriate to the present model), the government must run a budget surplus to generate the savings that are not coming from profits. Companies must then continuously borrow this surplus from the government to finance the fraction of the steady growth investment of $V(a + n)$ that company saving and workers' saving will not finance. Thus, where the degree of monopoly produces a 'low' share of profits, companies must be prepared to borrow from the government to finance investment, and where it produces a 'high' share of profits, the private sector must be prepared to invest a fraction of its saving in government bonds. The balance of payments can only be in equilibrium if these rules are followed.

Where two economies with different rates of non-market expenditure and similar saving propensities, etc., are compared, the one with a higher ratio of non-market expenditure, i.e. a higher $(G_o + G_p)$, will have a higher Kaldor share of profits, i.e. a higher share of profits from equation (8). If both economies have the same degree of monopoly share of profits, which is what their shares of profits will have to be with Kalecki-like assumptions, the one with a high $(G_o + G_p)$ could well be in the situation where a budget surplus is needed, and the one with low non-market expenditure could need continuous deficits. Then the economy with high non-market expenditure could well require institutions to channel government tax revenues to the finance of company investment, while the economy with low non-market expenditure would require continuous budget deficits with private sector subscriptions to public debt. Certainly with the degree of monopoly π given, higher non-market expenditure must be associated with a lower required budget deficit or a higher required surplus, so at a certain point it is bound to place an economy in the budget surplus situation where companies must borrow from the government to finance the steady-growth share of investment.

It is now time to summarise some of the basic implications of the argument. Where the share of profits is determined independently of the degree of monopoly, steady growth with a high rate of non-market expenditure requires that workers give up consumption to finance almost the entire cost of the non-market sector, while the size of this has no adverse effects on the availability of private-sector finance. The economy simply generates whatever profits are needed net of tax to produce sufficient private-sector saving to finance investment. On the other hand, where the share of profit depends on the degree of monopoly, workers' consumption is reduced by the uniform rate of tax needed to finance the non-market sector, and it is reduced no more than this. But company savings are squeezed net of tax in relation to the required steady-growth investment ratio in the market sector, and this means that companies may need to invest much more than their savings, and borrow from the government as well as from workers to do so. There are therefore two kinds of obstacle which may set an upper limit to the ratio of non-market expenditure which is compatible with steady growth: a certain minimal *share* or else *quantity* of marketed output may be required for workers' private consumption, and companies may be unwilling to increase their borrowing beyond a certain point. These potential constraints will be considered in turn, and the possibility that there might be a lower limit to workers' consumption will be considered first.

All would agree that there must be a Malthusian lower limit to workers' consumption of marketed output, i.e. workers will need a minimum wage in terms of marketed output if the labour force is not to decline. It is usually assumed that this classical minimum wage is fixed as an absolute quantity of goods and not a proportion of marketed output per head, so an economy could always overcome this constraint if its output per worker was sufficiently high. Thus if the classical minimum wage was w_s, and a society's desired rate of public expenditure left workers only 25 per cent of what they produced per head in the form of marketed output, there would be a feasible steady growth path once output per worker reached $4w_s$. Until then the workers in the market sector would need to consume more than 25 per cent of market sector output. Clearly in this case a steady growth path can exist provided that

$$(1-\pi)(1-T) \geqslant w_s \qquad (11)$$

where w_s is the classical subsistence wage expressed as a fraction of output per worker in the market sector.* In poor societies (or rich societies with extraordinary rates of non-market expenditure) this condition will set an upper limit to T and therefore to non-market expenditure as a fraction of marketed output.

* Expressed as a *quantity* of output, (11) would be: $(1-\pi)(1-T)(O_m/L_m) \geqslant w_s$ where O_m/L_m is output per worker in the market sector.

In rich societies there is a modern version of the classical subsistence minimum, and this has been most clearly described by Joan Robinson:

> There is a limit to the level to which real-wage rates can fall without setting up a pressure to raise money-wage rates. But a rise in money wage-rates increases money expenditure, so that the vicious spiral of money wages chasing prices sets in. . . . Either the system explodes in a hyper-inflation, or some check operates to curtail investment.[24]

She argues that workers, through trade union pressure, have the power to set an 'inflation barrier' of this kind which sets a lower limit to wages in terms of marketed output. An 'inflation barrier' at a wage of w_q expressed as a fraction of output per worker in the market sector would impose the condition that:

$$(1-\pi)(1-T) \geqslant w_q \tag{12}$$

which would set an upper limit to T, and therefore to $(G_o + G_p)$ in exactly the same way as the classical subsistence wage. Again, the 'inflation barrier' minimum wage might need to be sufficient to purchase a particular quantity of output and not a fraction of marketed output per worker, so that an economy with high output per worker could get past this barrier and have a large non-market sector.* In contrast, an economy with lower output per worker could have minimum private consumption demands (including perhaps sufficient post-tax income to finance car ownership, etc.) which could set the 'inflation barrier' so high in relation to output per worker that T had to be relatively low. An economy in this situation would have to wait until output per worker was high enough to provide both for workers' private consumption at rate w_q and desired non-market activities before non-market expenditure could be raised to the desired fraction of marketed output. From this point onwards, steady growth with the desired non-market expenditure ratio would be practicable.

* Expressed as a *quantity* of output (12) would read

$$(1-\pi)(1-T)(O_m/L_m) \geqslant w_q.$$

While all would accept the validity of the classical constraint that $(1-\pi)(1-T) \geqslant w_s$. it would not be as universally agreed that $(1-\pi)(1-T) \geqslant w_q$ will also set a constraint in a modern developed economy. It would be argued by some that balanced budgets and money supply growth at a rate of $(a+n)$ would ensure stable prices, whatever the aspirations of workers. With this view of the problem, workers would have to accept any real wage in excess of w_s, and this would set the only effective constraint (and advanced economies would hardly need to concern themselves with it, so for them virtually any tax rate would be compatible with steady growth at stable prices). A difficulty with this line of argument is that it is universally admitted that trade unions, influenced by the fact that private consumption per worker is less than the inflation barrier minimum, can *temporarily* raise money wages rather rapidly. Monetarists would assume however that the unemployment this caused (when the money supply was increased only at rate $(a+n)$) would arrest such inflation, and make it impossible that it should persist in the long term. If this is accepted, it could still be supposed that there will always be substantial upward wage pressure *at full employment* whenever workers cannot buy w_q of marketed output. Then steady growth *at full employment* requires that workers be able to purchase w_q with their wages, so that $(1-\pi)(1-T) \geqslant w_q$ will be a constraint that must be satisfied on any steady growth path. Monetarists might prefer to allow that private consumption per employed worker of less than w_q will produce a 'natural' rate of unemployment that exceeds the merely frictional rate. Thus steady growth will be incompatible with just frictional unemployment where $(1-\pi)(1-T)$ is less than w_q.

The second obstacle that may set an upper limit to the ratio of non-market expenditure in steady growth is that companies may require a minimum ratio of net of tax profits to marketed output, if they are to invest the fraction $V(a+n)$ that they must invest in steady growth. Where outside finance is borrowed on fixed interest terms, companies may go bankrupt while they are still achieving an operating surplus, for this must be sufficient to pay interest on all debt. A company which has no fixed interest debt is less likely to face bankruptcy where things go wrong than a company which has much debt and therefore a high gearing ratio; and the higher the gearing ratio (i.e. the higher the ratio of debt to equity) the greater will be the danger that outsiders will obtain control of the company. This means that risk is always involved in borrowing on fixed interest terms, and companies are therefore likely to set upper limits to the ratio of fixed interest debt to equity that they are prepared to make use of. The risks involved in accepting government finance are likely to be particularly great unless there are financial institutions which make this available to companies without the risk of increasing government managerial interventions. Obviously none of these difficulties will arise with nationalised companies, which do not face risks of takeover if they borrow too heavily and then make inadequate surpluses to service the loans. However non-nationalised companies will face increasing risk as they increase their ratio of debt to equity,[25] and this means that it may be right to assume that there will be an upper limit to the investment they will undertake which will be a multiple of their own undistributed profits net of tax. There are, of course, no risks to companies in general on a steady growth path, but it can still be assumed, sensibly, that companies will refuse to borrow more than a particular fraction of the capital they use. Company profits net of tax are $(1 - T)\pi$, and companies save a fraction, s_π, of these, so the internal finance available to them will be the fraction $s_\pi(1 - T)\pi$ of total market sector output. If it is assumed for simplicity that only fixed interest finance can be obtained externally (and it forms most outside finance) and that the external debt which companies as a whole are prepared to incur each year is D times the increase in their equity, i.e. D times the profit they can themselves put into their businesses, then the maximum investment that companies can finance is the fraction $s_\pi(1 + D).(1 - T)\pi$ of marketed output. Hence, the achievement of steady growth is subject to the constraint that:

$$s_\pi(1 + D)(1 - T)\pi \geqslant V(a + n) \qquad (13)$$

If profits taxes are passed on as is the case with Kaldor's equation, this constraint will be equally easy to meet at all levels of T, because $(1 - T)$ times π will not vary inversely with T – but if instead π is determined by 'degree of monopoly' factors, there may be trouble. A higher T (as a result of higher non-market expenditure as a ratio of marketed output) will then reduce the left-hand side of (13) and increase the likelihood that companies will be unable to invest the fraction $V(a + n)$ of marketed output because to do so would involve excessive fixed interest borrowing. Too low a share of profits, or too high a rate of taxation, may then prevent the achievement of steady growth because companies will fail to undertake the investment in the market sector necessary for this.

The argument has suggested that two obstacles may stand in the way of steady growth (in addition to the usual ones that stand in the way of steady growth in any model). First, workers may set off inflation if consumption per head in terms of marketed output is less than a certain minimum. Second, companies may have inadequate internal finance for the steady growth share of investment if their profits net of tax do not reach a certain minimum proportion of this. Either of these constraints, or both together, may set upper limits to the ratio of non-market expenditure to marketed output that is compatible with steady growth. If neither constraint operates, economies with very different ratios of non-market expenditure will be able to grow at rate $(a + n)$ with the effects that have been outlined.

There is one further point that must be discussed before the next part of the argument where the problems of transition from a low to a high ratio of non-market expenditure will be outlined. It has been assumed so far that the economy's long-term rate of growth will be the same $(a + n)$, whatever its ratio of non-market expenditure to marketed output. It has thus been assumed that the long-term rate of growth of productivity is independent of the size of the non-market sector and the rate of taxation. In fact the size of the non-market sector can be expected to have two general effects, one favourable and one unfavourable, on the long-term rate of growth of productivity. First, many public-sector activities which do not result in marketed outputs are likely to have favourable effects on the rate of growth of productivity. Of these, education, government-financed research and defence spending can all be expected to have favourable though sometimes severely lagged effects on technical progress that are not easily quantifiable.[26] On the other hand, the larger the ratio of employment in the non-market sector, the smaller will be the aggregate amount of market sector output in any given year, and this means that market-sector investment (which is a *fraction* of market sector output) will be less. Growth models have been put forward by Arrow and others which make technical progress a function of the amount of investment,[27] and if there is less market sector investment, there will be less 'learning by doing', and research and development departments may be smaller with the result that they discover less per annum. On this line of argument, productivity will rise faster where the market sector is larger in relation to the non-market sector. Kaldor has suggested that returns to scale will be more favourable in industry than in services, and industry is likely to form a high though historically diminishing fraction of the market sector, and it might be thought that this would be a further factor leading to a strong association between the size of the market sector and productivity growth.[28]

However, where economies of scale and Verdoorn effects have been formulated so that they can play a part in growth models, it has been shown that they apply a multiplier to growth from other sources. This means that two economies with equal rates of labour growth, n, and equal rates of technical progress, a, in their industrial sectors will both have growth rates of $(a + n).\psi$ where ψ is the 'economies of scale' multiplier, even if the size of their industrial sectors is very different.[29] Thus an economy with a larger market sector will not have a faster *steady-growth rate* of output than another with the same $(a + n).\psi$ which has a larger non-market sector. It will obviously have a higher *level* of output, but it will only enjoy faster growth if it has a higher a or n (Kaldor himself has attached particular importance to the industrial n, but this must be the same as the economy's n in steady growth comparisons). The crucial advantage of a large market sector is then that this will be associated with high industrial investment which will have favourable effects on research and development and 'learning by doing'. The crucial advantage of a large non-market sector is that this will include education, much research, defence, and so on. It is not possible to say at present which of these can be expected to provide the greater stimulus to the long-term rate of growth of productivity, so the assumption that has been made throughout this section that $(a + n)$ will be the same in economies with different rates of non-market expenditure that are being compared may well be the best working assumption to make for the time being.

This means that the basic results that have been arrived at can be carried forward to the next section without further modification. Thus, it is not clear that a larger non-market sector will be associated with faster or slower growth in the long term, but it will certainly be associated with higher taxation – and it may be associated with a higher share of profits also (provided that $\phi < 1$) if this is not determined primarily by degree of monopoly factors. Finally a minimum wage in terms of market sector outputs, and minimum required profits net of tax, may both set upper limits to the proportion of marketed output that can be diverted to the non-market sector in the very long run.

3. THE PROBLEMS INVOLVED IN INCREASING THE SIZE OF THE NON-MARKET SECTOR

It has been shown in the previous section that it may or may not be possible to increase the relative size of the non-market sector of the economy in the very long run. It will be possible to do this in principle in a growing economy if the new and larger non-market sector is compatible with steady growth, and it will be impossible if it is not. The case where steady growth can be achieved with the new and larger non-market sector will be considered first. After this, the case where the larger non-market sector is incompatible with steady growth will be outlined, and just how the economy breaks down as attempts are made to maintain an 'impossible' ratio of non-market expenditure will be explained.

If steady growth can be achieved with the new and larger non-market sector, neither of the constraints outlined in the last section operate. Hence the workers in the market sector are prepared to consume a lower fraction of marketed output, and companies are if necessary prepared to finance a larger fraction of investment through borrowing. The simplest case which will be considered first is the one with fixed coefficients, where companies pass on their share of the larger cost of the non-market sector through an increase in the share of profits with the result that workers bear the entire cost of this. Then if, as a result of a larger non-market sector, T (which equals $(G_o + G_p)/(1 + G_p)$) has to be increased from T_1 to T_2, the fraction of marketed output that the workers in the market sector will be able to receive net of tax will need to fall by $(T_2 - T_1)$. As they originally receive the fraction $(1 - \pi_1)(1 - T_1)$, where π_1 is the original share of profits, they will have to forgo the fraction

$$\frac{T_2 - T_1}{(1 - \pi_1)(1 - T_1)}$$

of their net of tax incomes. These grow at an annual rate of a on any steady growth path, but workers must lose the above fraction to move from one steady growth path to another where there is less private consumption. If this transition takes z years, private consumption per worker will increase at less than rate a in this period when its growth rate, g_c, will be (on the assumption of a constant propensity to save from wages so that workers' consumption rises at the same rate as their net of tax incomes) approximately

$$g_c \simeq a - \frac{1}{z}\left(\frac{T_2 - T_1}{(1 - \pi_1)(1 - T_1)}\right) \tag{14}$$

In the United Kingdom in 1961–74 the hypothetical budget-balancing tax rate had to rise from about 36 per cent to 45 per cent, so $(T_2 - T_1)$ was 0.09, while $(1 - \pi_1)$ was about 0.75 and $(1 - T_1)$ was 0.64. With these hypothetical figures, and a thirteen-year transition period from 1961 to 1974, equation (14) would be:

$$g_c \simeq a - 1.44\%$$

The United Kingdom's growth in output per worker in the market sector (i.e. a) was about 2.5 per cent per annum in

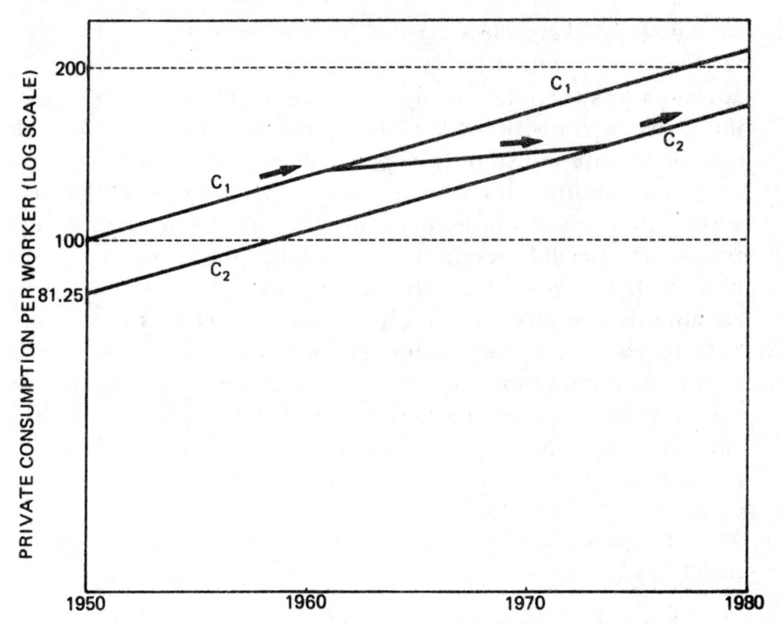

Chart 30 The Transition to a Larger Non-market Sector

1961–74 so the growth of private consumption per worker would have had to be limited to about 1.06 per cent per annum if the entire extra cost of the non-market sector had been financed at the expense of workers' consumption as in equation (14).[30]

This example is illustrated in Chart 30. The line C_1C_1 shows what consumption per worker would be if the hypothetical uniform 1961 tax rate of 36 per cent was maintained continuously, and this line rises at an annual rate of 2.5 per cent which is the assumed increase in marketed output per worker from 1961 to 1974. The line C_2C_2 shows what consumption per worker would be if the hypothetical 1974 tax rate of 45 per cent was maintained continuously and the whole extra cost of the higher tax rate was met from workers' private consumption as is being assumed. C_2C_2 is drawn 18.75 per cent below C_1C_1 because that is the extent to which a higher tax rate of 9 per cent reduces workers' private consumption in the conditions assumed. From 1961 to 1974 workers move from C_1C_1 to C_2C_2 so in this thirteen-year transition period their private consumption advances less than half as quickly as on C_1C_1 and C_2C_2. Once the costs of transition have been paid (in 1974), the growth rate of private consumption per worker can return to 2.5 per cent per annum and it can follow the growth path C_2C_2 which advances at this annual rate. Clearly the more rapid the transition period required to attain the new ratio of non-market expenditure the larger the fall in the ratio of consumption relative to that in steady state growth.*

With the complete passing on of profits taxation that is being assumed, companies in the market sector can invest the fraction $V(a + n)$ of marketed output on both the original and the new steady growth paths without any increase in gearing, i.e. any increase in fixed interest borrowing as a ratio of their own net of tax profits.

In terms of the basic equation (4) with $V(a + n)$ substituted for i_m,

$$V(a + n) + b_m = e_m - c_u - i_u \quad (15)$$

An increase in $(c_u + i_u)$, the proportion of marketed output required in the non-market sector, calls for an equivalent increase in e_m, the proportion of marketed output that is surplus to consumption in the market sector. That is what is required if there is to be no reduction in the share of investment in the market sector, or deterioration in the balance of payments. In the full passing-on case with fixed coefficients, the whole cost of the higher $(c_u + i_u)$ is borne by labour with the result that e_m rises by the same amount as $(c_u + i_u)$ and workers' consumption as a fraction of marketed output falls by exactly the extent to which $(c_u + i_u)$ rises.

If there are not fixed coefficients, V will be lower on the new steady growth path where $(c_u + i_u)$ is higher to an extent

* This example serves to show what will happen to consumption during a transition period of given length which attains a new ratio of non-market expenditure. It is possible to analyse the optimal path to a new ratio and the choice of an optimal ratio itself given an appropriate utility function for society, using the methods developed by Kenneth J. Arrow and Mordecai Kurz in *Public Investment: the Rate of Return, and Optimal Fiscal Policy*, Johns Hopkins Press, 1970.

depending on the elasticity of substitution between labour and capital. Then e_m would not need to rise as much as $(c_u + i_u)$ because the left-hand side of equation (15) would be lower to the extent that $V(a + n)$ was lower. Hence workers would not have to give up as great a fraction of marketed output as has so far been assumed. This would not mean that the growth of consumption per worker would necessarily be more favourable in the transition period than that indicated in equation (14).[31]

The assumption that profits taxes are passed on (which follows from the balanced-budget assumption on which this case like the last is based) ensures that companies will face no liquidity problems at high rates of taxation that they do not face equally at low rates. Hence the effect the larger non-market sector has on workers' consumption is what primarily needs to be considered.

This is not the case where the share of profits is determined by 'degree of monopoly' factors which are unaffected by the size of the non-market sector. In this situation workers and companies must both give up the extra fraction $(T_2 - T_1)$ of their incomes to the government, while the distribution of incomes between wages and profits is unchanged. As workers receive $(1 - \pi)(1 - T_1)$ times marketed output before the increase in the size of the non-market sector, and $(1 - \pi)(1 - T_2)$ after the transition is completed, private consumption per worker falls by the proportion

$$\frac{T_2 - T_1}{1 - T_1}$$

in the z-year transition period. Hence over the transition period, consumption per worker grows at approximately the rate given by

$$g_c \simeq a - \frac{1}{z}\left(\frac{T_2 - T_1}{1 - T_1}\right) \tag{16}$$

It will be observed that consumption now increases less slowly in the transition period. Taking the approximation to the British 1961–74 case as an example where $a = 2.5$ per cent per annum, T_1 is 0.36 and T_2 0.45, g_c is 1.42 per cent per annum in the transition period with equation (16) in place of the 1.06 per cent rate suggested by equation (14).

The growth of net of tax profits, g_π, is $(a + n)$ on any steady growth path, but like wages it will fall short of this by

$$\frac{T_2 - T_1}{1 - T_1}$$

during a z-year transition period in which the rate of taxation rises from T_1 to T_2 and the distribution of income is unchanged. Thus:

$$g_\pi \simeq a + n - \frac{1}{z}\left(\frac{T_2 - T_1}{1 - T_1}\right) \tag{17}$$

Consumption from profits will grow at this rate, but the case of investment is more complex. Once steady growth is resumed with a higher ratio of non-market expenditure, investment will need to be the fraction $V(a + n)$ of marketed output that it must be on all steady-growth paths, and V will be unchanged with constant income distribution, but company saving will have fallen from the fraction $\pi(1 - T_1)s_\pi$ to $\pi(1 - T_2)s_\pi$ of marketed output. Companies will therefore need to borrow an extra $\pi(T_2 - T_1)s_\pi$ of marketed output on the steady growth path where non-market expenditure is higher. If they are prepared to increase their gearing to the required extent, the economy can achieve a new steady growth path with the same share of investment in marketed output, $V(a + n)$, and lower ratios of private consumption from wages and profits than on the old path. Once the new path is achieved, marketed output will grow at rate $(a + n)$, consumption per worker at rate a, and so on.

It can be noted that as the greater cost of the non-market sector is likely to be financed with different rates of taxation on profits and wages, the costs of transition to a larger non-market sector could be borne more by capital or by labour than the previous analysis would indicate. If taxes were increased mainly on profits, and these taxes were only partly passed on, the gearing ratio would need to rise more than has so far been indicated, while if taxes were increased mainly on wages and salaries, the costs of transition could fall predominantly on labour. The result of this would approximate to that shown by equation (14) which described the effects of complete passing on of profits taxation. There it made no difference where higher taxation was actually levied, since workers paid it all in any case.

It has been assumed so far that the constraint that prevents workers' private consumption from falling below a certain fraction of marketed output, and the constraint that sets an upper limit to company borrowing, do not operate. If either constraint operates, the economy will not be able to achieve steady growth with a higher ratio of non-market expenditure, and it will be interesting to see what form this failure will take if the government raises public expenditure to the desired extent.

If company taxes are completely passed on, only the wage constraint can operate. If it does, money wages will start to rise rapidly at full employment as soon as $(1 - \pi)(1 - T)$ becomes less than w_q. It will be immaterial whether the higher taxes that follow too large a non-market sector are levied predominantly on wages or on profits, for higher profits taxes will simply be passed on and so raise π, and therefore reduce $(1 - \pi)(1 - T)$ below w_q. This inflation could presumably be eliminated by a sufficient rate of unemployment which would mean that economies with a larger non-market sector either had more inflation or more unemployment than economies with a smaller non-market sector, once the w_q constraint began to operate. It is to be noted that an economy with a larger non-market sector and therefore more unemployment (if this is preferred to extra and perhaps accelerating inflation)[32] would for this reason have a still higher ratio of non-market expenditure since the market sector could be expected to have to produce whatever unemployment was needed to stabilise prices. Thus if the market sector produced 100 at full employment of which the non-market sector took 60 and this was sufficient to set off a rapid wage-price spiral because the 'inflation barrier' was breached, and the authorities reacted by creating market-sector unemployment while leaving non-market expenditure uncut, market sector output might fall to for instance 96, with the result that the ratio of non-market expenditure to this became 60/96 or 62.5 per cent in place of 60 per cent. This would accentuate the effect of the high ratio of non-market expenditure with the result that still higher unemployment would be needed, both to compensate for the original failure to give the workers w_q at full employment, and for the fact that still less could be given as a result of the inability of the economy to allow the market sector to use the share of resources available to it at full employment. With full passing on of any profits taxes, investment would be adequate in the long term to produce growth in marketed output at a rate of $(a + n)$.

It is to be expected that the policy options of rapid and perhaps accelerating inflation or high unemployment which followed failure to meet the w_q constraint might lead governments in societies in this situation (which did not wish to reduce the size of their non-market sectors) to attempt to introduce prices and incomes policies to contain the inflation that resulted from a net of tax wage of less than w_q in terms of marketed output. Such policies often seek to control profits as well as wages, with the result that the assumption of complete passing on of profits taxes could hardly be made in these circumstances. This means that the constraint of a limit to investment set by undistributed profits net of tax plus the fixed interest borrowing firms are prepared to undertake could begin to operate. It could operate in any event, even if the real wage constraint did not, in the case where the share of profits is determined by 'degree of monopoly' factors, so it will be important to see how a failure of investment in the market sector to reach the fraction $V(a + n)$ will affect the economy.

The most direct approach to this problem is the following. If the fraction $V(a + n)$ of marketed output must be invested in the market sector to increase employment in that sector at rate n, less investment than this while new plant has an unchanged capital-output ratio will create fewer employment opportunities. With zero net investment, it could be assumed that the output capacity of the market sector would be constant, and that productivity growth at rate a would make a fraction a of the labour force redundant. This redundant labour, and the extra labour, n, can be employed with new plant if $V(a + n)$ is spent on this, but if, for instance, only $V.a$

is spent, then new plant will be adequate to reabsorb those made redundant by technical progress, but it will be inadequate to provide for growth in employment in addition. It follows from this approach to the problem that the number of workers who can be employed in the market sector will only grow if more than the fraction $V.a$ of marketed output can be invested in that sector. It will grow as fast as the steady growth rate n if $V(a + n)$ is invested, and it will actually decline if less than $V.a$ is invested.

The rationale for this approach – and it has crucially important implications – is as follows. With substitutability between capital and labour with old plant, any number of workers can be fitted into any given capital stock if the wage is low enough. However if, as is being assumed here, there are factors which prevent the share of wages in the market sector from falling, extra workers cannot be found jobs in that sector without new investment. It can be assumed that companies will not employ extra workers if this reduces aggregate profits and as the cost of employing workers in terms of marketed output rises at rate a (with a constant share of profits) fewer workers and not more must be employed in the absence of investment. If V, the capital-output ratio with new plant, were flexible, a halved share of investment would still allow plant to provide employment for the fraction $(a + n)$ of the labour force if V was also halved. But in terms of neo-classical theory companies will only choose to invest in new plant with a lower V if the cost of capital rises in relation to the cost of labour (and non-neo-classics would perhaps prefer to treat V as fixed in any case by the available technology). If competitive conditions in the labour and product markets prevent the share of profits from rising, while the government taxes employment as much as investment, companies will have no incentives of any kind to invest in new plant with a lower V. If employment is taxed more heavily (as in Britain) or wages rise relative to profits, companies might very well choose new plant with a higher V. Any shortfall in the share of investment from the steady growth share will then undoubtedly have the consequence that insufficient employment opportunities will be created in the market sector to permit steady growth.

This will not necessarily do harm in a transition period

from a steady growth path with a small non-market sector to another with a larger one. A smaller fraction of the labour force will need to work in the market sector on the second growth path, so it will be right that investment should be less than $V(a + n)$ in the transition period when the non-market sector is growing relative to the market sector. However, the share of investment in the market sector must be restored to $V(a + n)$ as soon as it is desired that this process of structural change in favour of the non-market sector should cease. If it is not, employment opportunities in the market sector will decline indefinitely, and this means that the full employment ratio of non-market expenditure to market sector output will rise each year. This will require ever-rising tax rates if trade is to be balanced, and this will continuously reduce the proportion of marketed output that workers can consume, and put increasing pressure on company liquidity. In consequence what workers receive in terms of marketed output can be expected to fall short of w_q to an increasing extent if this constraint operates, while at the same time, with rising taxation of profits, companies with constraints on the amount of their borrowing can be expected to invest a diminishing fraction of marketed output since they will receive a falling fraction of this net of tax. Then fewer jobs will be created or more lost in the market sector in each successive year, with the result that the necessary annual increase in taxation will accelerate, as will inflation if workers' private consumption is at all close to w_q. Correspondingly more unemployment or, alternatively, tougher incomes controls will therefore be needed in each successive year to arrest the inflation.

It will be evident that an economy must drift deeper and deeper into this territory in the conditions assumed, namely workers who bargain for private consumption per head of at least w_q, income distribution that does not automatically keep the share of profits net of tax in line with the investment that must be undertaken to maintain market-sector employment, and companies that will not borrow to finance investment to an unlimited extent. Once companies fail to borrow a sufficient amount, the share of investment must become less than $V(a + n)$, and the proportion of the labour force that can be provided with jobs in the market sector of the economy must fall at an accelerating rate if the share of investment in the market sector remains less than $V(a + n)$, and falls with profits net of tax. Moreover prices will also rise at an accelerating rate after a time if Friedman's analysis is correct.

Two points should be noted about this impasse. First, an increase in productivity growth (i.e. an increase in a) will do nothing to relieve the situation if this faster technical progress is Harrod-neutral. This is because faster productivity growth would *increase* the required share of investment, for being Harrod-neutral, it would leave V unchanged at the existing income distribution and so increase $V(a + n)$. Only technical progress or productivity growth with a capital-saving bias would be helpful, and faster neutral or capital-using technical progress would actually increase the rate at which the market sector had to shed labour. It follows that a continuing and accelerating decline of employment in the market sector in relation to the non-market sector with almost inevitably associated inflation could only be arrested through an end to the conditions that led to this state of affairs. Thus the share of investment in the market sector would need to be raised to $V(a + n)$ to prevent further relative decline, and an increase in the proportion of employment provided in the market sector would require a share of investment of more than $V(a + n)$. Either of these would require a lower rate of company taxation, and/or a higher share of profits, and/or an increase in the willingness of companies to finance investment through borrowing. Real resources for these would only become available given the equation:

$$i_m + b_m \equiv e_m - c_u - i_u$$

if a country ran a balance of payments deficit during any transition period in which the capital stock of the market sector was restored, or reduced private consumption in the market sector as a ratio of marketed output, or reduced the proportion of market sector output that was needed in the public sector.

It must be emphasised that the case of extreme and

accelerating instability that has been outlined will only arise as a result of an increase in the proportion of marketed output required by the non-market sector if conditions in the economy are such that the share of profits in marketed output cannot rise correspondingly, and companies will not increase their ratio of investment to net-of-tax profits. These are unfortunately conditions that are rather commonly found, and if nothing is done to maintain market sector investment in the face of them, a proportionately larger non-market sector will produce accelerating inflation and a rising unemployment trend as efforts are made to correct this, together with an accelerating decline in employment opportunities. These are what will be produced if market-sector investment is allowed to fall in the long run, instead of the benefits which it was hoped a larger non-market sector would provide.

Some final comments about the balance of payments are in order. It goes without saying that inappropriately low tax rates will be associated with a balance of payments deficit (for they will leave e_m too low in relation to c_u and i_u, given the need to maintain investment which has been amply discussed). In addition an inappropriate domestic price level in relation to foreign price levels will make it impossible to balance trade at full employment, even if tax rates are correct. Hence both tax rates and relative price levels must be appropriate, and this is well known.[33] It is widely believed that even these two conditions for balance of payments equilibrium are often insufficient because countries that devalue rapidly and have less than full employment also often have substantial deficits. The problem these countries face is generally that they are so much on the 'inflation barrier' that the competitive advantages that a falling exchange rate should produce are rapidly eroded by domestic inflation. Hence devaluations do not succeed in lowering domestic prices in relation to foreign prices for a sufficient length of time.[34] The difficulty is really that in the equation

$$i_m + b_m \equiv e_m - c_u - i_u$$

e_m is prevented from rising by the 'inflation barrier', while $(c_u + i_u)$ is kept high by a very large non-market sector. With this situation, balance of payments deficits or insufficient investment leading to still greater future difficulties are inevitable, whatever the exchange rate policies that are pursued. If developed economies like Britain with elasticity pessimism, because devaluations generally fail, bring the size of their non-market sectors under control, they might well find that devaluations started to produce the desired results. If the excess of e_m over $(c_u + i_u)$ is sufficient, they should only find particular difficulty in exchanging some of their marketed output for that of others on mutually acceptable terms if the relevant international trade elasticities are extraordinarily perverse.

TABLES

THE INCOMES AND EXPENDITURES OF COMPANIES, WORKERS, THE GOVERNMENT, ETC.

Companies

Profits	$\pi.O_m$
Taxes paid	$T.\pi.O_m$
Profits net of tax	$(1-T).\pi.O_m$
of which: saved	$s_\pi(1-T).\pi.O_m$
consumed	$(1-s_\pi)(1-T)\pi.O_m$
Investment	$i_m.O_m$
Financial surplus (saving – investment)	$[s_\pi(1-T)\pi - i_m]O_m$

Workers in the Market Sector

Wages	$(1-\pi).O_m$
Taxes paid	$T(1-\pi).O_m$
Wages net of tax	$(1-T)(1-\pi).O_m$
of which: saved	$s_w(1-T)(1-\pi).O_m$
consumed	$(1-s_w)(1-T)(1-\pi).O_m$
Financial surplus (saving – investment)	$s_w(1-T)(1-\pi).O_m$

Total Market Sector – Workers and Companies

Output	O_m
Taxes paid	$T.O_m$
Incomes net of tax	$(1-T).O_m$
of which: saved	$[s_\pi.\pi + s_w(1-\pi)](1-T).O_m$
consumed	$[1 - s_\pi\pi - s_w(1-\pi)].(1-T).O_m$
Investment	$i_m.O_m$
Financial surplus	$[(s_\pi\pi + s_w(1-\pi))(1-T) - i_m].O_m$
Marketed output balance (market sector output available to other sectors)	$[1 - i_m - \{1 - s_\pi.\pi - s_w(1-\pi)\}(1-T)]O_m$

Recipients of Incomes from the Government

Incomes received	$G_p.O_m$
Taxes paid	$T.G_p.O_m$
Incomes net of tax	$(1-T).G_p.O_m$
of which: saved	$s_w(1-T).G_p.O_m$
consumed	$(1-s_w)(1-T).G_p.O_m$
Financial surplus	$s_w(1-T).G_p.O_m$
Marketed output balance (market sector output produced less that consumed)	$-(1-s_w)(1-T).G_p.O_m$

Government

Taxes received	$T.O_m + T.G_p.O_m$
Expenditure	$(G_o + G_p).O_m$
Financial surplus	$[T(1+G_p) - (G_o + G_p)].O_m$
Marketed output balance	$-G_o.O_m$

NOTES

1. R. W. Bacon and W. A. Eltis, 'A Budget Message for Mr Healey: Get More People into Factories', *Sunday Times*, 10 November 1974; and 'Stop–Go and De-industrialization', *National Westminster Bank Quarterly Review*, November 1975; and Walter Eltis, 'How Public Sector Growth Causes Balance of Payments Deficits', *International Currency Review*, vol. 7, no. 1, January–February 1975.
2. See Vivian Woodward, 'The Need to Avoid Higher Government Employment', *The Times*, 7 July 1975; and (an article based on research by R. J. Tarling, C. J. Allsopp, V. Woodward, J. Morley and D. A. C. Heigham), 'A View of Industrial Employment in 1981', *Department of Employment Gazette*, May 1975.
3. See 'Tony Benn Writes About Industrial Policy', *Trade and Industry*, 4 April 1975.
4. J. Johnston, 'A Macro-Model of Inflation', *Economic Journal*, vol. 85, June 1975.
5. The basic account of the classical theory of economic growth is set out in Book II of Adam Smith, *An Inquiry into the Nature and Causes of the Wealth of Nations* (1776). See J. R. Hicks, *Capital and Growth* (Oxford University Press, 1965), Chapter IV; and W. A. Eltis, 'Adam Smith's Theory of Economic Growth' (in *Essays on Adam Smith*, ed. A. Skinner and T. Wilson, Oxford University Press, 1975) for modern restatements of the theory.
6. The case for the various possible dividing lines between 'productive' and 'unproductive' and who used them is set out very comprehensively by Malthus in *Principles of Political Economy* (2nd ed., 1836) Chapter 1, 'Of the Definitions of Wealth and of Productive Labour'.
7. The distinction between industrial and non-industrial activities is the one favoured by Mr Benn and by the present authors in their

first joint publications. Walter Eltis, 1975 (*op. cit.*), however, used the tradable/non-tradable distinction and J. Johnston (*op. cit.*) the one between marketables and non-marketables.

8. These figures are taken from table 10.3 on pp. 228–9. They differ slightly from those in Chapter 1, because for the purposes of equation (2), i_u must include all purchases of capital goods by the non-industrial sector, so it will include capital consumption in that sector. This was excluded from non-industrial investment which was shown as net investment in Chapter 1.
9. See R. W. Bacon and W. A. Eltis (*op. cit.*, 1974), and Tony Benn (*op. cit.*).
10. See 'A View of Industrial Employment in 1981', (*op. cit*).
11. See Walter Eltis 1975 (*op. cit.*).
12. This possibility is clearly and fully set out in J. Johnston (*op. cit.*).
13. Public sectors produce some marketed outputs, but it will obviously simplify the argument to have a complete dichotomy between a private sector that markets its output and a public sector that does not.
14. The proportion of marketed output that is consumed *by persons* outside the market sector is $G_p(1 - T)(1 - s_w)$, and this equals c_u in equation (4).
15. G_o is equivalent to i_u in equation (4)
16. See *National Institute Economic Review*, no. 64, May 1973, pp. 20–4, for an account of some of the propositions of the New Cambridge School.
17. If the budgets were not balanced and trade was balanced, the private sectors of the two economies would have persistent financial surpluses or deficits. This would have monetary implications that are best avoided in the initial statement of the argument.
18. In 1962 58.7 per cent of non-market expenditure went to persons: wages and salaries 27.1 per cent, debt interest 12.8 per cent, and grants to the personal sector 18.8 per cent. In 1974 these totalled 56.5 per cent (wages and salaries 27.0 per cent, debt interest 9.5 per cent and grants 20.0 per cent). *National Income and Expenditure*.
19. N. Kaldor, 'Alternative theories of distribution', *Review of Economic Studies*, vol. XXIII, 1955–6. Equation (8) would give precisely $1/(1 - T)$ times Kaldor's share of profits if G_o was zero, or s_w was zero.
20. L. L. Pasinetti, *Growth and Income Distribution*, Cambridge University Press, 1974, pp. 133–4.
21. The actual equations are set out in detail in R. W. Bacon and W. A. Eltis, 'The Implications for Inflation, Employment and Growth of a Fall in the Share of Output that is Marketed', *Bulletin of the Oxford University Institute of Economics and Statistics*, Vol. 37, November 1975.
22. M. Kalecki, 'The Determinants of Distribution of the National Income', *Econometrica*, vol. VI, April 1938.

23. Equality between exports and imports requires that there be no financial surplus nor deficit when all domestic financial accounts are added. Similarly, there must be no surplus nor deficit when the domestic 'marketed output balances' are added.
24. Joan Robinson, *The Accumulation of Capital*, Macmillan, 1956, p. 48.
25. See M. Kalecki, 'The principle of increasing risk', *Essays in the Theory of Economic Fluctuations*, London, 1939.
26. The positive feedback from non-market expenditure to the rate of growth of labour productivity in the market sector is an important element in Professor J. Johnston's model (*op. cit.*).
27. K. J. Arrow, 'The economic implications of learning by doing', *Review of Economic Studies*, vol. XXIX, June 1962. See W. A. Eltis, *Growth and Distribution*, Macmillan, 1973, ch. 6, for an account of further arguments which lead to this result.
28. N. Kaldor, *Causes of the Slow Rate of Growth of the United Kingdom* (inaugural lecture), Cambridge University Press, 1966.
29. See F. H. Hahn and R. C. O. Matthews, 'The theory of economic growth; a survey', *Economic Journal*, vol. LXXIV, December 1964, p. 833, and W. A. Eltis, *Growth and Distribution*, ch. 11.
30. Equation (14), which suggests that private consumption per worker increases at an annual rate of 1.06 per cent in the transition from C_1C_1 to C_2C_2, is only an approximation because of the assumption that precisely the fraction, $1/z$, of the cost of transition is paid each year. With a geometric rate of expansion this is not quite accurate, and the calculation of the cost of transition in chapter 4 (p. 99), which shows workers' consumption rising at 0.9 per cent per annum in the thirteen years, gives the accurate answer.
31. The lower capital-output ratio on the new steady-growth path would be associated with less output per worker in the market sector. Workers would be able to consume a higher fraction of this lower output because e_m would not need to rise as much, but it is not clear on *a priori* grounds whether they would gain or lose from the lower share of investment. They might gain because less marketed output was needed for investment, and they might lose because marketed output per worker was lower, see p. 180 above.
32. The rate of inflation will accelerate if Professor Friedman's theory of the effect of unemployment below the 'natural' rate is correct. See 'The role of monetary policy', *American Economic Review*, vol. LVIII, March 1968.
33. See W. M. Corden, 'The geometric representation of policies to attain internal and external balance', *Review of Economic Studies*, vol. XXVIII, October 1960, for *the* account of the underlying theory.
34. See T. Wilson, 'Effective devaluation and inflation', *Oxford Economic Papers*, vol. 28, no. 1, March 1976.

The Statistical Background and the Derivation of the Charts

The following pages present the data on which the charts in the preceding chapters are based. In some cases it has been possible to use figures already published elsewhere – for example the indicators of Britain's comparative economic performance since 1961. In other cases it has been necessary to use well-known methods to derive a series suitable for the purposes of this book – examples of this are the calculation of 'real' net-of-tax earnings for an average worker, and the calculation of the ratio of non-market expenditure to marketed output. The only methodological problems involved here were those of definition.

However, two of the detailed calculations should be noted. The estimation of a 'net' profit series on pp. 231–8 differs from some of the other work in this area, partly because the concept of profit required is a liquidity one – the funds available for reinvestment – and partly because an estimate was needed that brought in all the relevant information, such as investment grants. Moreover it was easily calculable from the National Accounts.

The second calculation was the major task of producing a time series for the sales and purchases of industrial products classified by the categories relevant to the economic model used in this book. This novel exercise (in pp. 217–31 below), which would have been simpler if there were an input–output table for every year, necessitated the blending of data from the few input–output tables with data from the yearly National Accounts. The resulting estimates of the sales and purchases of industrial products cannot be claimed to be perfect, but they do constitute an advance in methodology that would be capable of further refinement if desired.

The plan of this section is to present the data, the sources of the data and the detailed calculations, where these are necessary, in the order in which the charts appear in the text. Within each section about a given chart there may be several tables, and these have been labelled with the first number indicating the chart number. Charts 16–21 are explained in the notes for Chart 10.

In the second edition we have updated all the tables by one year, using the most recently available source of data. The publication of revised figures for earlier years in *National Income and Expenditure* 1965–1975 has meant that Tables 10 and 11 have been revised from 1969 onwards.

Table 8.2 has been replaced by a new table because of the discontinuation of a series. A new calculation has been added which we number as Table 11.4.

THE DERIVATION OF CHARTS 1, 2, 3, 4 AND 5: THE COMPARISON OF BRITAIN'S ECONOMIC PERFORMANCE WITH THAT OF OTHER COUNTRIES

CHART 1 GROSS DOMESTIC PRODUCT AT CONSTANT MARKET PRICES

Table 1.1

	1961	*1973*	*1974*
U.K.	100	140	141
U.S.A.	100	170	167
France	100	197	205
W. Germany	100	171	172
Italy	100	177	183
Japan	100	318	315

Sources

Data for 1961–72 are taken from *National Accounts for O.E.C.D. countries 1961–1972* (OECD) and are at constant 1963 prices.

Data for 1973 and 1974 are taken from *National Accounts for O.E.C.D. countries 1962–1973, 1963–1974* (OECD) and are at constant 1970 prices.

The two series have been spliced together to yield a single series at 1963 prices, using 1972 as a link year.

CHART 2 THE CONSUMER PRICE INDEX WITH 1963 WEIGHTS

Table 2.1

	1961	*1974*	*1975*
U.K.	100	212	263
U.S.A.	100	165	180
France	100	196	219
W. Germany	100	162	172
Italy	100	210	246
Japan	100	255	285

Sources

Data for all countries are taken from the *National Institute Economic Review*, February 1971, August 1973, November 1975 and November 1976. The series are all converted to a 1963 base by using 1969 as a link between data on the 1963 base and data on the 1970 base.

CHART 3 INDICES OF OUTPUT PER MAN-HOUR AT CONSTANT 1963 VALUES

Table 3.1

	1961	*1974*	*1975*
U.K.	100	166	165
U.S.A.	100	154	157
France	100	218	208
W. Germany	100	199	206
Italy	100	236	225
Japan	100	329	319

Source

The data measure output per man-hour in manufacturing. Data for all countries are taken from the *National Institute Economic Review*, February 1971, November 1975 and November 1976. The data are all at constant 1963 values obtained by linking at 1969.

CHART 4 THE SHARE OF GROSS DOMESTIC CAPITAL FORMATION IN GROSS DOMESTIC PRODUCT

Table 4.1

	1961	*1973*	*1974*
U.K.	0.173	0.198	0.205
U.S.A.	0.163	0.182	0.175
France	0.215	0.244	0.251
W. Germany	0.252	0.247	0.225
Italy	0.278	0.212	0.234
Japan	0.332	0.367	0.343

Source

Data for all countries are taken from the *National Accounts of O.E.C.D. countries 1961–1972* and *National Accounts of O.E.C.D. countries 1962–1973* and *1963–1974.* Gross domestic product is measured at market prices.

CHART 5 SHARES OF WORLD TRADE IN MANUFACTURES (MEASURED IN VALUE TERMS)

Table 5.1

	1961	*1974*	*1975*
U.K.	0.164	0.088	0.093
U.S.A.	0.205	0.172	0.177
France	0.094	0.093	0.102
W. Germany	0.202	0.217	0.203
Italy	0.057	0.067	0.075
Japan	0.068	0.145	0.136

Source

All data are from *National Institute Economic Review* November 1973, November 1975 and November 1976.

CHART 6 THE RELATION BETWEEN GROSS PAY IN MONEY TERMS AND NET PAY IN CONSTANT PRICE TERMS FOR AN AVERAGE WORKER

The purpose of this table is to show how a figure for after-tax income is derived. The assumptions made are that the worker is male, is married, has no children and has no other source of income.

There is no time series for the absolute amount of average earnings for the category of 'all workers' (as opposed to 'manual workers') but there is a series based on an index number (January 1970 = 100). This series is converted to absolute values by using the same technique as in the *National Institute Economic Review*, May 1974. From 1970 onwards there is a separate series on earnings of all male workers given in actual values. This series is taken at April in each year and it is assumed that the two series coincide in absolute values for April 1970 with an average earnings figure of £29.70 (*Department of Employment Gazette*, November 1975). This yields a series from 1963 to 1974 for the level of average earnings of all male workers in full-time employment for a week in April.

The deductions from gross pay are of three types: income tax, social security contributions and rates. The amount of income tax paid is calculated for each April by taking the tax rates for a couple with no children and no other income for the year starting that April. The social security contributions include the weekly flat rate contribution paid by an employee in April each year (assuming he is contracted in) and also the total graduated pension contribution. Both of these are income-related. The amount of rates paid by a couple with average gross earnings is not directly available. However, it is possible to estimate the average rates paid by taking rates plus rateable value paid on all owner-occupied housing by families of the given income. Rateable value is then subtracted and the residue is an estimate of rates. There are no separate figures for rates paid on rented property so it is also necessary to assume that rates paid at a given level of income are the same for all types of housing.

The estimate of rates paid is clearly subject to some error but to ignore this compulsory deduction from income would overstate disposable income.

The cost of living index used to convert net earnings in current prices to net earnings at constant prices is the retail price index for April of each year based on 1961. The index is reconverted to 1963 = 100 so that the real series given at 1961 prices equals the money value at 1963.

Table 6.1 Calculation of real disposable

	1963	*1964*	*1965*	*1966*	*1967*
(1) Gross Earnings	18.00	19.57	20.92	22.52	23.03
(2) Tax	2.17	2.65	3.17	3.69	3.84
(3) Social Security	0.33	0.58	0.68	0.68	0.68
(4) Graduated Pension	0.25	0.38	0.38	0.38	0.45
(5) Rates	0.60	0.66	0.74	0.76	0.80
(6) Net Earnings	14.45	15.30	15.95	17.01	17.26
(7) Price Index	100.0	102.0	107.8	111.6	115.0
(8) Real Net Earnings	14.45	15.00	14.80	15.24	15.00
(9) Net Earnings (before deducting rates)	15.05	15.96	16.69	17.77	18.06
(10) Real Net Earnings (before deducting rates)	15.05	15.65	15.48	15.92	15.70

The numbers in brackets refer to the rows of Table 6.1:

(1) Estimate of average weekly gross earnings in April for 'All Male Workers' in full-time employment, taken from the *Department of Employment Gazette* Index and set to a value of £29.70 in April 1970.
(2) Estimate of tax paid per week by a married couple with no children and no other source of income, taken from *Inland Revenue Statistics.*
(3) Flat Rate Social Security Contribution for a week in April paid by a contracted-in employee. Data are taken from *Social Security Statistics Yearbook 1973.*
(4) Graduated Pension paid by a contracted-in employee for a week in April.
(5) Rates plus rateable value less rateable value paid per week by the average of all family sizes living in owner-occupied accommodation. The exact figure for the income level is found by interpolating between levels given by the *Family Expenditure Surveys.*
(6) Net Average Earnings in Current Prices: Gross Average Earnings less all four deductions.
(7) Index of the cost of living using 1961 values as weights and based on 1963 = 100. The source is the *National Institute Economic Review.*

earnings for the average male worker (£)

1968	*1969*	*1970*	*1971*	*1972*	*1973*	*1974*	*1975*
24.72	26.90	29.70	32.90	36.70	41.90	47.70	60.70
4.39	5.09	5.84	6.45	6.59	8.10	10.25	14.82
0.78	0.83	0.88	0.88	0.88	0.88	0.84	0.75
0.45	0.47	0.80	0.82	1.23	1.54	1.92	2.83
0.83	0.87	0.97	1.03	1.24	1.27	1.47	n.a.
18.27	19.64	21.21	23.72	26.76	30.11	33.22	n.a.
120.1	126.7	133.8	146.4	155.7	168.1	193.4	236.0
15.21	15.50	15.85	16.20	17.19	17.91	17.13	n.a.
19.10	20.51	22.18	24.75	28.06	31.38	34.69	42.30
15.90	16.19	16.58	16.91	17.98	18.67	17.94	17.92

(8) Net Average Earnings at 1961 prices based on the level at 1963 equalling the money value in 1963.
(9) Net Average Earnings in Current Prices before deducting rates.
(10) Net Average Earnings before deducting rates at 1961 prices.

CHART 7 THE RATIO OF INDUSTRIAL TO NON-INDUSTRIAL EMPLOYMENT (EXCLUDING AGRICULTURE)

Table 7.1 *Numbers of civilians employed by sector*

		Industry	*Non-industry less agriculture*	*Agriculture*
U.K.	1961	11 989	11 624	972
	1975	10 096	13 812	667
U.S.A.	1961	21 564	38 982	5 200
	1975	24 565	56 837	3 381
France	1961	7 132	7 540	4 044
	1975	8 022	10 391	2 351
W. Germany	1961	12 965	9 824	3 449
	1975	11 460	11 546	1 822
Italy	1961	7 646	6 155	6 207
	1975	8 305	7 549	2 964
Japan	1961	13 460	18 490	13 030
	1975	18 550	26 650	6 580

Table 7.2 Ratio of non-industrial to industrial employment

	1961	*1974*	*% change*	*1975*	*% change*
U.K.	0.970	1.299	33.9	1.368	41.0
U.S.A.	1.808	2.086	15.4	2.313	27.9
France	1.057	1.254	18.6	1.295	22.5
W. Germany	0.758	0.866	14.2	1.007	32.8
Italy	0.806	0.889	10.3	0.908	12.6
Japan	1.374	1.353	−1.5	1.436	4.5

Sources
The data for all countries are taken from *O.E.C.D. Labour Force Statistics: Quarterly Supplement to the Yearbook*, August 1975 and August 1976 and from *O.E.C.D. Labour Force Statistics 1961–1972.*

The figure for the U.K. in 1974 was supplied by the Department of Employment.

The coverage of the series is for total civilian employment which equals total employees in employment plus employers plus the self-employed.

Industry is defined as mining plus manufacturing plus construction plus gas, electricity and water.

CHARTS 8 AND 9 INCREASES IN EMPLOYMENT BY CATEGORY IN GREAT BRITAIN 1961–1975

Table 8.1 Numbers employed in various sectors – grouping A(thousands)

		1961	*1974*	*1975*
Total	Male	14 202	13 363	13 240
	Female	7 586	8 933	8 973
	Total	21 789	22 297	22 213
Industry	Male	8 148	7 153	6 951
	Female	2 772	2 526	2 349
	Total	10 920	9 679	9 300
Non-industry less agriculture	Male	5 503	5 913	6 002
	Female	4 674	6 300	6 523
	Total	10 177	12 214	12 525

Table 8.1 Numbers employed in various sectors – grouping A (thousands)

		1961	*1974*	*1975*
Transport and communication	Total	1 649	1 483	1 495
Distributive trades	Total	2 705	2 707	2 709
Insurance, banking, finance	Total	675	1 101	1 088
Professional and scientific services	Total	2 080	3 284	3 465
Miscellaneous services	Total	1 788	2 088	2 157
Public administration and defence	Total	1 280	1 551	1 608

Sources

Data for 1961 are taken from the *Department of Employment Gazette*, March 1975. Data for 1974 are taken from the *Department of Employment Gazette*, June 1975 and June 1976. The three years have been classified in an entirely comparable way.

Data refer solely to employees in employment and thus exclude employers, the self-employed and members of the armed forces. However the series do include part-time employment and some of the changes must be due to a changing incidence of such employment.

Table 8.2 The growth in numbers employed in various service categories in the United Kingdom

	1961	*1975*	*% increase*
Local authorities	1782	3024	69.7
Central government	1776	2246	26.5
Other services	7298	8062	10.5

Sources

Data for local authorities and central government cover the total working population in employment which includes the armed forces (but not public corporations). These two series are taken from *National Income and Expenditure 1972* and *1965–1975* (Table 1.10).

The data for other services include employees in employment and are taken from the *Department of Employment Gazette* October 1975 and September 1976. Services include all of the non-industrial sector less education, health and public administration.

This table replaces the version in the first edition of the book where government employment did not make full allowance for those in the state health and education sectors.

Table 9.1 Numbers employed in selected service categories – grouping B (thousands)

	1961	*1964*	*1967*	*1970*	*1973*	*1974*	*1975*
Total employment	21789	22362	22347	21993	22182	22297	22213
Transport	1649	1629	1591	1549	1501	1483	1495
Distribution	3356	3531	3437	3238	3340	3312	3312
Insurance, banking etc.	985	1104	1173	1324	1459	1532	1530
Education services	960	1100	1291	1412	1620	1693	1776
Medical services	779	863	962	1007	1104	1130	1219
Leisure	897	975	958	950	1057	1067	1091
Public administration	1280	1325	1439	1446	1544	1551	1608

Sources
The basic source of the employment data is the same as for Table 8.1 above but categories have been regrouped so as to highlight certain trends. The new groups are derived from the ones given in the *Gazette* as follows:

(*a*) Transport is the same as transport and communication.
(*b*) Distribution is distributive trades plus the following categories taken from miscellaneous services: hairdressing, laundries, dry cleaning, motor repairs and shoe repairs.
(*c*) Insurance, banking, etc., is insurance, banking and finance plus the following categories from professional services: accountancy, legal services, research and development, and other professional and scientific services.
(*d*) Education is taken from professional and scientific services.
(*e*) Medicine is taken from professional and scientific services.
(*f*) Leisure is the residue of miscellaneous services less the category 'other services'.

Before comparing the 1975 and 1974 figures it is important to note the *Department of Employment Gazette's comments* (1976):

'Both the results for June 1975 and the changes compared with previous years have been affected by the reclassification of some local authority establishments. When the results of the June 1974 census were published mention was made of the problems encountered in analysing the local authority figures . . .

In the 1975 census, more detailed information about local authority employment was obtained . . . The consequent industrial reclassification would affect most industries and services where local authority employees are engaged. Precise estimates of the changes cannot be made, but one MLH particularly affected was local government service. A very appropriate estimate would suggest that around 30,000 employees who were classified in 1974 to this general heading were, in 1975, reclassified to other industries and services.'

THE DERIVATION OF CHARTS 10, 16, 17, 18, 19, 20 AND 21: SALES AND PURCHASES OF INDUSTRIAL PRODUCTS

The purpose of these charts is to show the total amount of industrial products available to the U.K. economy and the fractions of this amount purchased by various categories of buyer.[1]

The charts used in Chapters 1, 2 and 3 are derived from the detailed tables presented below. To understand these tables it is necessary to start from the following identities (which are independent of the precise definition of the industrial sector):

Total sales of industrial products for final use by domestic and foreign firms

= Total purchases of industrial products by final buyers (1)

∴ Sales of industrial products for final use by domestic firms plus imports of industrial products for final use less all imports of industrial products

= Total purchases of industrial products by final buyers less total imports of industrial products (2)

The second identity is the one used in the text because it allows the overall trade balance in industrial products to be identified as a component of the right-hand side and to be calculated as a fraction of the left-hand side (along with purchases by consumption, investment and the government).

Data on all four of these broad categories of purchase of industrial products and for total sales exist for the five years (1963, 1968, 1970, 1971 and 1972) for which there is an input–output table for the U.K. economy. Hence it is necessary to find a method of using the annual national accounts data to estimate a complete run of all these series.

As well as the estimation problem there are two problems of definition to be resolved. 'Industry' is conventionally defined as 'mining and quarrying' plus 'manufacturing' plus 'construction' plus 'gas, electricity and water'. The trade data, as presented in secondary sources, group processed and unprocessed items together in the category 'food, drink and tobacco'. The processed items are in industry while the unprocessed items are not. Rather than reclassify the trade data for each year from the primary source, the category of 'food, drink and tobacco' has been moved from the industry sector to the non-industry sector throughout the ensuing calculation. The second problem of definition arises because 'mining and quarrying' includes 'crude petroleum products'. Now in the period 1961–74 the U.K. did not produce any crude petroleum and virtually none was purchased by final buyers. However a great deal was imported for intermediate use and this would be reflected in trade data taken on the same coverage as the definition of industrial production. Hence the trade data has excluded 'crude petroleum' and the detailed calculations relating industrial imports to the size of the domestic industrial and non-industrial sectors have treated 'crude petroleum' as a non-industrial import.

KEY TO TABLES 10.1–5 (pp. 224–31)

The bracketed numbers on the left below refer to the rows numbered serially in the same way through the five tables. Other references to tables are to those in *National Income and Expenditure 1964–1974* (HMSO), except that the five input–output tables are from the Central Statistical Office's

Studies in Official Statistics, nos 16 and 22, and from *Business Monitor PA1004*, 1970, 1971 and 1972 (all HMSO).

The table has been completely revised from 1969 onwards using the revised data published in *National Income and Expenditure 1965–1975* and the 1972 Input–Output table.

The implicit assumptions used to derive consumption figures for individual categories from the pre-tax income data are that the average tax rate is the same for each group, that the average propensity to consume industrial products is the same for each group, and that the sole determinant of consumption is current incсme.

The method of interpolation used is the same in all cases. There is linear interpolation between known years, and for years outside the data period the figure is set at that of the nearest known year.

10.1 The calculation of the macro-economic aggregates of industrial products

(1) Value-added of industry including 'food, drink and tobacco' (FDT) and including stock appreciation, all at factor cost (Table 18).
(2) Stock appreciation of all manufacturing less that of FDT (Tables 76 and 77).
(3) Wages plus salaries of FDT (Table 20).
(4) Ratio of value-added of FDT net of stock appreciation to wages plus salaries of FDT (Tables 19 and 20). This ratio is directly available for 1963, 1968, 1970, 1971 and 1972. For other years it is obtained by interpolation.
(5) Estimated value-added of FDT net of stock appreciation: (3) x (4).
(6) Estimated value-added by industry net of FDT and net of stock appreciation all at factor cost: (1)–(2)–(5).
(7) Ratio of total final sales by domestic firms of industrial products (net of FDT) to value-added by industry (net of FDT). This ratio is directly available for the four years of the input–output tables and is interpolated for the other years.
(8) Estimated final sales of industrial products (net of FDT) at factor cost. (6) x (7).

(9) Ratio of gross domestic product at market prices to gross domestic product at factor cost (Table 12).
(10) Estimated final sales by domestic firms of industrial products (net of FDT) at market prices: (8) x (9).
(11) Value-added by non-industry (including FDT) excluding stock appreciation at factor cost (Table 11).
(12) Ratio of imports of industrial products (excluding FDT) for intermediate use by the non-industrial sector to value-added by non-industrial sector. For the four years of the input output tables the amount of such imports is directly available but does not correspond exactly in coverage to the import figures available on an annual basis. Hence in these years the intermediate imports from the input–output tables are scaled by the ratio of total industrial imports from the annual source to total industrial imports from the input–output tables. This yields the required ratio for the four years and the ratios for other years are obtained by interpolation.
(13) Estimated imports of industrial products for intermediate use by the non-industrial sector: (11) x (12).
(14) Ratio of imports of industrial products (excluding FDT) for intermediate use by the industrial sector to the value-added by the industrial sector (excluding FDT). This ratio is available directly for the four input–output table years and the intermediate imports are again scaled by ratio of total industrial imports from the annual source to total industrial imports from the four tables. The ratio is interpolated for other years.
(15) Estimated imports of industrial products for intermediate use by the industrial sector: (6) x (14).
(16) Total imports of industrial products c.i.f. (*Monthly Digest of Statistics*) – defined as imports of S.I.T.C. categories 5–8.
(17) Estimated imports of industrial products for final use: (16) – (15) – (13).
(18) Ratio of government current purchases of industrial products to government current purchases of all goods not provided by the government. This ratio is taken from the four input–output tables and is interpolated for the other years.

(19) Current expenditure by the public authorities on 'other payments net' (Table 53). This is that part of the government current expenditure on goods and services which is not wage and salary payments.
(20) Estimated current purchases of industrial products by the public authorities: (18) x (19).
(21) Exports of industrial products f.o.b. (*Monthly Digest of Statistics*) – defined as S.I.T.C. categories 5–8.
(22) Investment purchases of industrial products – defined as the total of all gross domestic fixed capital formation and the value of the physical increase in stocks and work in progress of manufacturing less FDT (Tables 1, 76 and 77). There are no separate stock data for the rest of the industrial sector.
(23) Estimated total sales of industrial products to final purchasers: (10) + (17).
(24) Estimated final purchases of industrial products excluding purchases by consumption: (20) + (21) + (22).
(25) Estimated purchases of industrial products (net of FDT) by consumption: (23) – (24).

10.2 The allocation of consumption of industrial products between the various classes of consumer and the allocation of investment between categories of investor

(26) The ratio of total wage plus salary income (including employers' contributions) from employment and self-employment to all personal income (Table 2).
(27) The ratio of income from rent, interest and dividends to all personal income (Table 2).
(28) The ratio of income from national insurance benefits and other current grants from public authorities (transfers) to total personal income (Table 2).
(29) Total income from employment and self-employment (Table 2).
(30) Wages plus salaries plus employers' contributions paid by the non-trading activities of the public authorities (Table 53).
(31) Wages plus salaries plus employers' contributions paid by industry including FDT (Table 18).
(32) Ratio of employers' contributions to wages plus salaries in manufacturing (Table 18).

(33) Estimated employers' contributions by FDT: (32) x (3).
(34) Estimated wages plus salaries plus employers' contributions of industry less FDT: (31) – (33) – (3).
(35) Wages plus salaries plus employers' contributions of non-industry, non-government employees: (29) – (30) – (34).
(36) Share of industrial workers' consumption in the total consumption of industrial products: (34) ÷ (29).
(37) Share of government-employed workers' consumption in the total consumption of industrial products: (30) ÷ (29).
(38) Share of other workers' consumption in the total consumption of industrial products: (35) ÷ (29).
(39) Net investment by industry including FDT (Table 71).
(40) Capital consumption by industry including FDT (Table 68).
(41) The ratio of capital consumption by industry to the gross investment by industry: (40) ÷ [(39) + (40)].
(42) Gross investment by FDT (Table 65).
(43) Estimated capital consumption by FDT: (42) x (41).
(44) Estimated net investment by FDT: (42) – (43).
(45) Estimated net investment by industry less FDT: (39) – (44).
(46) Estimated capital consumption by industry less FDT: (40) – (43).
(47) Net investment by non-industry excluding FDT (Table 71).
(48) Estimated net investment by non-industry including FDT: (47) + (44).
(49) Capital consumption by non-industry excluding FDT (Table 68).
(50) Estimated capital consumption by non-industry including FDT: (49) + (43).
(51) Net investment by social and other public services (Table 71).
(52) Net investment by non-industry, non-government sector (Table 71).
(53) Change in the physical value of stocks plus work in progress of manufacturing less FDT (Tables 76, 77).

10.3 Shares of the purchases of industrial products in total final sales less total imports

(54) Total sales of industrial products to final purchasers less total imports of industrial products: (23) – (16).
(55) Total exports less total imports of industrial products (balance of trade in industrial products): (21) – (16).
(56) The share of total consumption: (25) ÷ (54).
(57) The share of gross fixed domestic capital formation: [(22) – (53)] ÷ (54).
(58) The share of the physical change in stocks: (53) ÷ (54).
(59) The share of government purchases: (20) ÷ (54).
(60) The share of the trade balance: (55) ÷ (54).
(61) The share of consumption by industrial workers: (36) x (56) x (26).
(62) The share of consumption by government workers: (37) x (56) x (26).
(63) The share of consumption by other workers: (38) x (56) x (26).
(64) The share of consumption by recipients of rent, interest and dividends: (27) x (56).
(65) The share of consumption by recipients of transfer incomes: (28) x (56).
(66) The share of net industrial investment: (45) ÷ (54).
(67) The share of capital consumption by industry: (46) ÷ (54).
(68) The share of net investment by social and other public services: (51) ÷ (54).
(69) The share of net investment by the non-industry non-government sector: (52) ÷ (54).
(70) The share of capital consumption of non-industry: (50) ÷ (54).

10.4 Shares of purchases of industrial products in the total of final sales less total imports less all capital consumption less the change in stocks (grouping A)

The new total, symbolised by (x), is equal to: (54) – (46) – (50) – (53).

(71) The share of industrial net investment: (45) ÷ (x).
(72) The share of non-industrial net investment: (48) ÷ (x).
(73) The share of the balance of trade: (55) ÷ (x).

Table 10.1 The macro-economic aggregates of industrial product

VARIABLE NUMBER	1961	1962	1963	1964	1965	1966	1967
(1)	11399	11744	12346	13702	14711	15298	15551
(2)	60	45	79	203	172	205	96
(3)	479	506	525	557	606	659	690
(4)	1.834	1.834	1.834	1.830	1.826	1.822	1.817
(5)	878	928	936	1019	1107	1201	1254
(6)	10461	10771	11421	12480	13432	13892	14201
(7)	1.214	1.214	1.214	1.230	1.245	1.260	1.275
(8)	12699	13075	13865	15350	16722	17503	18106
(9)	1.125	1.129	1.128	1.134	1.140	1.146	1.148
(10)	14286	14761	15639	17406	19063	20058	20785
(11)	13630	14436	15404	16569	17816	19108	20433
(12)	0.007	0.007	0.007	0.007	0.007	0.008	0.008
(13)	95	101	108	116	125	153	163
(14)	0.083	0.083	0.083	0.093	0.103	0.113	0.123
(15)	868	894	948	1161	1383	1569	1746
(16)	1404	1440	1572	2160	2256	2472	2796
(17)	441	445	516	883	748	750	887
(18)	0.644	0.644	0.644	0.630	0.610	0.590	0.570
(19)	1815	1936	1974	2052	2339	2489	2777
(20)	1168	1246	1271	1292	1426	1468	1582
(21)	3084	3156	3372	3768	4092	4392	4380
(22)	4902	4757	5102	6526	6854	7161	7561
(23)	14727	15206	16155	18289	19811	20808	21672
(24)	9154	9159	9747	11586	12372	13021	13523
(25)	5573	6047	6408	6703	7439	7787	8149

1968	1969	1970	1971	1972	1973	1974	1975
16933	18053	19875	21663	24402	29459	35007	41347
265	469	657	575	684	1699	3750	3101
735	802	894	1014	1111	1279	1501	1966
1.812	1.797	1.782	1.793	1.857	1.827	1.827	1.827
1332	1441	1593	1818	2063	2336	2742	3591
15326	16143	17625	19270	21655	25424	28515	34655
1.289	1.310	1.333	1.340	1.273	1.273	1.273	1.273
19755	21147	23494	25821	27566	32364	36299	44115
1.157	1.175	1.173	1.160	1.147	1.136	1.113	1.108
22856	24847	27558	29952	31618	36765	40400	48879
22064	23372	26000	29918	33516	38365	45581	59089
0.008	0.013	0.018	0.021	0.022	0.022	0.022	0.022
177	303	468	628	737	844	1002	1299
0.134	0.146	0.158	0.147	0.122	0.122	0.122	0.122
2053	2356	2784	2832	2641	3101	3478	4227
3624	3948	4560	5002	6093	8909	11928	12805
1394	1289	1308	1542	2715	4964	7448	7279
0.551	0.546	0.541	0.540	0.537	0.537	0.537	0.537
2878	2756	2969	3313	3731	4400	5451	7209
1585	1504	1606	1789	2003	2362	2927	3871
5412	6252	6804	7825	8257	10455	13685	16464
8412	8855	9767	10340	11504	14559	17627	19873
23980	26136	28866	31494	34333	41729	47848	56158
15409	16611	18177	19954	21764	27376	34239	40208
8571	9525	10689	11540	12569	14353	13609	15950

Table 10.2 Allocation of consumption and investment purchases to individual sectors

VARIABLE NUMBER	1961	1962	1963	1964	1965	1966	1967
(26)	0.810	0.809	0.799	0.800	0.793	0.792	0.786
(27)	0.115	0.113	0.118	0.118	0.121	0.120	0.120
(28)	0.075	0.078	0.083	0.082	0.086	0.088	0.094
(29)	18529	19554	20402	22038	23806	25456	26553
(30)	2501	2717	2923	3154	3466	3770	4084
(31)	8099	8435	8680	9451	10242	10849	10989
(32)	0.062	0.066	0.070	0.071	0.074	0.077	0.082
(33)	30	33	37	40	45	51	57
(34)	7590	7896	8118	8857	9591	10139	10242
(35)	8438	8941	9361	10030	10749	11547	12227
(36)	0.410	0.404	0.398	0.402	0.403	0.398	0.386
(37)	0.135	0.139	0.143	0.143	0.145	0.148	0.154
(38)	0.455	0.457	0.459	0.455	0.452	0.454	0.460
(39)	969	890	849	1103	1271	1404	1406
(40)	921	988	1055	1118	1226	1345	1425
(41)	0.487	0.526	0.554	0.503	0.490	0.489	0.503
(42)	157	143	148	170	178	175	203
(43)	76	75	82	86	87	85	102
(44)	81	68	66	84	91	90	101
(45)	888	822	783	1019	1180	1314	1305
(46)	845	913	973	1032	1139	1260	1323
(47)	1502	1576	1667	2271	2365	2410	2831
(48)	1583	1644	1733	2355	2456	2500	2932
(49)	1283	1366	1449	1549	1640	1758	1858
(50)	1359	1441	1531	1635	1727	1843	1960
(51)	333	422	455	578	611	663	807
(52)	1169	1154	1212	1693	1754	1747	2024
(53)	234	-43	90	504	374	243	73

1968	1969	1970	1971	1972	1973	1974	1975
0.781	0.780	0.789	0.793	0.793	0.796	0.796	0.803
0.118	0.117	0.109	0.105	0.098	0.100	0.099	0.089
0.101	0.101	0.101	0.101	0.108	0.103	0.104	0.107
28467	30537	34199	37889	43013	49998	60391	76886
4382	4690	5394	6351	7393	8356	10515	14992
11669	12613	14058	15580	16576	19480	23217	29438
0.084	0.081	0.085	0.087	0.090	0.090	0.099	0.113
62	64	75	88	99	115	148	222
10872	11747	13089	14478	15360	18086	21568	27250
13213	14100	15716	17060	20260	23556	28308	34644
0.382	0.384	0.382	0.382	0.357	0.361	0.357	0.354
0.154	0.153	0.157	0.167	0.171	0.167	0.174	0.195
0.464	0.463	0.461	0.451	0.472	0.472	0.469	0.451
1228	1259	1307	1131	766	1022	1742	2389
1553	1684	1900	2165	2388	2711	3355	4476
0.558	0.572	0.592	0.656	0.757	0.726	0.658	0.652
220	221	246	272	305	374	457	441
122	126	146	178	231	271	301	288
98	95	100	94	74	103	156	153
1130	1164	1207	1037	692	919	1586	2236
1431	1558	1754	1987	2157	2440	3054	4188
3377	3423	3701	4292	5091	6229	6500	7214
3475	3518	3801	4386	5165	6332	6656	7367
2030	2224	2545	2927	3435	4186	5036	6431
2152	2350	2691	3105	3666	4451	5337	6719
946	970	1133	1277	1501	1763	1852	2123
2431	2548	2668	3109	3664	4569	4804	5244
234	265	1133	-165	-176	411	994	-637

Table 10.3 Shares of purchases of industrial products in total final sales less imports

VARIABLE NUMBER	1961	1962	1963	1964	1965	1966	1967
(54)	13323	13766	14583	16129	17555	18336	18876
(55)	1680	1716	1800	1608	1836	1920	1584
(56)	0.418	0.439	0.439	0.415	0.424	0.425	0.432
(57)	0.351	0.349	0.345	0.375	0.370	0.377	0.398
(58)	0.017	-0.004	0.006	0.030	0.020	0.013	0.002
(59)	0.088	0.091	0.087	0.080	0.081	0.080	0.084
(60)	0.126	0.125	0.123	0.100	0.105	0.105	0.084
(61)	0.139	0.144	0.140	0.134	0.136	0.134	0.131
(62)	0.046	0.049	0.050	0.047	0.049	0.050	0.052
(63)	0.154	0.162	0.161	0.151	0.152	0.153	0.156
(64)	0.048	0.050	0.052	0.049	0.051	0.051	0.052
(65)	0.031	0.034	0.036	0.034	0.036	0.037	0.041
(66)	0.067	0.060	0.054	0.063	0.067	0.072	0.069
(67)	0.064	0.066	0.067	0.064	0.065	0.069	0.070
(68)	0.026	0.032	0.032	0.037	0.036	0.037	0.044
(69)	0.092	0.087	0.087	0.109	0.104	0.099	0.111
(70)	0.102	0.104	0.105	0.102	0.098	0.100	0.104

Table 10.4 Shares in total, net of all capital consumption and change in stocks (grouping A)

VARIABLE NUMBER	1961	1962	1963	1964	1965	1966	1967
(71)	0.082	0.072	0.066	0.078	0.082	0.088	0.084
(72)	0.144	0.143	0.145	0.181	0.171	0.166	0.188
(73)	0.154	0.150	0.150	0.124	0.128	0.128	0.102
(74)	0.170	0.173	0.170	0.167	0.166	0.164	0.159
(75)	0.450	0.462	0.469	0.450	0.453	0.454	0.467

1968	1969	1970	1971	1972	1973	1974	1975
20356	22188	24306	26492	28240	32820	35920	43353
1788	2304	2244	2823	2164	1546	1757	3659
0.421	0.429	0.440	0.436	0.445	0.437	0.379	0.368
0.402	0.387	0.388	0.396	0.413	0.431	0.463	0.473
0.011	0.011	0.012	-0.006	0.006	0.012	0.027	-0.014
0.078	0.067	0.066	0.067	0.070	0.071	0.081	0.089
0.088	0.103	0.092	0.106	0.076	0.047	0.048	0.084
0.125	0.125	0.133	0.132	0.126	0.126	0.108	0.105
0.051	0.051	0.055	0.058	0.060	0.058	0.052	0.058
0.153	0.155	0.160	0.156	0.167	0.164	0.141	0.133
0.049	0.050	0.048	0.046	0.044	0.044	0.038	0.033
0.043	0.043	0.044	0.044	0.048	0.045	0.039	0.039
0.055	0.070	0.072	0.075	0.076	0.074	0.085	0.096
0.070	0.052	0.049	0.039	0.024	0.028	0.044	0.051
0.048	0.043	0.046	0.048	0.053	0.053	0.051	0.048
0.122	0.114	0.109	0.117	0.129	0.139	0.133	0.120
0.106	0.105	0.110	0.117	0.129	0.135	0.148	0.154

1968	1969	1970	1971	1972	1973	1974	1975
0.069	0.065	0.062	0.048	0.031	0.036	0.060	0.068
0.209	0.195	0.194	0.203	0.229	0.248	0.251	0.223
0.108	0.128	0.115	0.131	0.096	0.061	0.066	0.111
0.154	0.153	0.165	0.162	0.157	0.162	0.146	0.137
0.460	0.459	0.464	0.456	0.487	0.493	0.477	0.461

Table 10.5 Shares in total, net of all capital consumption

VARIABLE NUMBER	1961	1962	1963	1964	1965	1966	1967
(76)	0.082	0.072	0.066	0.078	0.082	0.088	0.084
(77)	0.154	0.150	0.150	0.124	0.128	0.128	0.102
(78)	0.170	0.173	0.170	0.167	0.166	0.164	0.159
(79)	0.301	0.299	0.302	0.323	0.313	0.308	0.324
(80)	0.059	0.056	0.063	0.061	0.062	0.062	0.063
(81)	0.234	0.250	0.249	0.247	0.249	0.250	0.268

(74) The share of the consumption by industrial workers: (61) x (54) ÷ (x).
(75) The share of all other consumption and government current purchases: 1 – (71) – (72) – (73) – (74).

10.5 Shares of purchases of industrial products in the total of final sales less total imports less all capital consumption less the change in stocks (grouping B)

(76) The share of industrial net investment: (71).
(77) The share of the balance of trade: (73).
(78) The share of consumption by industrial workers: (74).
(79) The share of consumption by workers in the non-industry, non-government sector and net investment by the non-industry and non-government sector: [(63) + (69)] x (54) ÷ (x).
(80) The share of consumption from rent, interest and dividends: (64) x (54) ÷ (x).
(81) The share of consumption by government employees plus consumption from transfer incomes plus government current purchases plus net investment of government non-trading sector: 1 – (76) – (77) – (78) – (79) – (80).

and change in stocks (grouping B)

1968	1969	1970	1971	1972	1973	1974	1975
0.069	0.065	0.062	0.048	0.031	0.036	0.060	0.068
0.108	0.128	0.115	0.131	0.096	0.061	0.066	0.111
0.154	0.153	0.165	0.162	0.157	0.162	0.146	0.137
0.388	0.331	0.334	0.335	0.369	0.389	0.370	0.331
0.060	0.061	0.059	0.056	0.054	0.056	0.051	0.043
0.271	0.262	0.265	0.268	0.293	0.296	0.307	0.310

THE DERIVATION OF CHART 11.1 THE SHARE OF POST-TAX PROFITS NET OF STOCK APPRECIATION AND CAPITAL CONSUMPTION IN THE VALUE-ADDED OF MANUFACTURING (EXCLUDING METAL MANUFACTURING) NET OF STOCK APPRECIATION

The purpose of this chart is to show post-tax profits, net of stock appreciation and capital consumption, as a fraction of value added by manufacturing net of stock appreciation. Such calculations have been carried out by others, notably King,[2] and hence the major differences between the methods of calculation used are worth noting. The way in which taxation, and investment grants are calculated below is on a payments basis rather than an accruals basis. The payments of bank interest, etc., are deducted from profits to yield a figure which reflects the *liquidity* aspect rather than the *change in wealth* aspect of profits. The details of the costs which are subtracted are given in *National Accounts Statistics: Sources and Methods*, edited by Rita Maurice (HMSO), 1968, pp. 223–6.

KEY TO TABLES 11.1–3 (pp. 234–6)

The same numbering principles apply here as to Tables 10.1–5, and other references to tables are again to those in *National Income and Expenditure 1964–1974* (HMSO). The implicit assumption is that taxes are paid proportionately to current gross trading profits, and that investment grants and capital taxes are proportionate to expenditure on investment in plant and machinery.

11.1 The calculation of value added by companies in manufacturing less metal manufacturing

(1) Value added in manufacturing (Table 18).
(2) Trading surplus plus rent of iron and steel industry (Table 44).
(3) Trading profits of metal manufacturing (MM) (Table 40).
(4) Wages plus salaries in MM (Table 20).
(5) Wages plus salaries in manufacturing (Table 20).
(6) Ratio of wages plus salaries in MM to wages plus salaries in manufacturing; (4) ÷ (5).
(7) Employers' contributions in manufacturing (Table 18).
(8) Estimated employers' contributions in MM: (6) x (7).
(9) Gross profits of companies plus trading surplus of public corporations in manufacturing (Table 18).
(10) Gross profits of companies in manufacturing: (9) – (2).
(11) Gross trading profits of companies in manufacturing (Table 40).
(12) Ratio of gross profits to gross trading profits in manufacturing: (10) ÷ (11).
(13) Estimated gross profits of MM: (3) x (12).
(14) Estimated gross profits of manufacturing less MM: (10) – (13).
(15) Value added by manufacturing less MM (including stock appreciation): (14) + (5) – (4) + (7) – (8).
(15a) Value added less stock appreciation: (15)–(20).

11.2 The calculation of profits, investment grants, tax payments, stock appreciation and capital consumption for manufacturing less metal manufacturing

(16) Gross trading profits of manufacturing less MM: (11) – (3).
(17) Estimated tax deductable interest, etc., for manufacturing less MM: (14) – (16).
(18) Stock appreciation in manufacturing (Tables 76, 77).
(19) Stock appreciation in MM (Tables 76, 77).
(20) Stock appreciation in manufacturing less MM: (18) – (19).
(21) Capital consumption in manufacturing (Table 68).
(21a) Proportion of capital stock in manufacturing that is in

iron and steel manufacturing (Table 73). This is set at 0.1 for the period.

(22) Estimated capital consumption in manufacturing less MM: (21) x 0.9.

(23) Investment grants plus other net capital transfers less capital taxes for all companies (Table 35).

(24) Gross domestic fixed capital formation in plant and machinery for all industry (Table 65).

(25) Gross domestic fixed capital in plant and machinery for manufacturing less MM (Table 65).

(26) Ratio of GDFC in manufacturing less MM to all industry: (25) ÷ (24).

(27) Estimated investment grants, etc., paid to manufacturing less MM: (26) x (23).

(28) Total taxes on companies received by U.K. government (Table 56).

(29) Ratio of trading profits of manufacturing less MM to trading profits of all companies (Table 40).

(30) Estimated tax paid by manufacturing less MM: (29) x (28).

(31) Residual profits after deducting taxes, stock appreciation and capital consumption and adding investment grants for manufacturing less MM: (16) – (20) – (22) – (30) + (27).

11.3 Shares in value-added of manufacturing less MM sector

(32) Share of residual profit in value added: (31) ÷ (15a).

(33) Share of tax payments in value added: (30) ÷ (15a).

(34) Share of stock appreciation in value added: (20) ÷ (15a).

(35) Share of capital consumption in value added: (22) ÷ (15a).

(36) Share of trading profits plus investment grants in value added: [(16) + (27)] ÷ (15a).

THE DERIVATION OF CHART 11.2 THE SHARE OF POST-TAX PROFITS NET OF STOCK APPRECIATION AND CAPITAL CONSUMPTION IN THE VALUE ADDED NET OF STOCK APPRECIATION OF ALL COMPANIES

This new chart is designed to give similar information to that in Chart 11.1, but based on all companies rather than the manufacturing sector.

Table 11.1 The calculation of value added by companies in

VARIABLE NUMBER	1961	1962	1963	1964	1965	1966
(1)	8454	8605	9084	10021	10821	11240
(2)	16	7	8	13	14	13
(3)	269	224	241	261	279	218
(4)	473	465	477	542	589	599
(5)	5499	5678	5817	6349	6914	7346
(6)	0.086	0.082	0.082	0.085	0.085	0.082
(7)	344	380	411	451	517	572
(8)	30	31	34	38	44	47
(9)	2489	2427	2728	3080	3233	3147
(10)	2473	2420	2720	3067	3219	3134
(11)	2343	2337	2628	2933	3025	2812
(12)	1.055	1.035	1.035	1.045	1.064	1.114
(13)	284	232	249	273	297	243
(14)	2189	2188	2471	2794	2922	2891
(15)	7529	7750	8188	9014	9760	10163
(15a)	7454	7686	8067	8902	9582	9978

Table 11.2 The calculation of profits, investment grants,

(16)	2074	2113	2387	2672	2746	2594
(17)	115	75	84	122	176	297
(18)	80	67	110	166	197	237
(19)	5	3	-11	54	19	52
(20)	75	64	121	112	178	185
(21)	556	599	636	669	731	791
(22)	500	539	572	602	658	712
(23)	9	12	9	13	15	19
(24)	1763	1807	1920	2222	2475	2749
(25)	648	661	651	779	924	1022
(26)	0.367	0.365	0.339	0.350	0.373	0.371
(27)	3	4	3	5	6	7
(28)	682	867	759	622	538	544
(29)	0.569	0.588	0.582	0.588	0.579	0.563
(30)	388	510	442	366	312	306
(31)	1114	1004	1255	1597	1604	1398

manufacturing (less metal manufacturing)

1967	1968	1969	1970	1971	1972	1973	1974
11302	12343	13286	14833	16062	17748	21618	25764
47	98	96	147	69	78	157	224
156	170	256	226	231	246	291	327
579	606	681	806	826	861	1007	1171
7392	7919	8738	9929	10741	11481	13481	16007
0.078	0.077	0.078	0.081	0.077	0.075	0.075	0.073
609	670	716	847	935	1043	1222	1592
48	52	56	69	72	78	92	116
3126	3550	3620	3829	4120	4908	6522	7697
3079	3452	3524	3682	4051	4830	6365	7473
2786	3140	3362	3468	3883	4475	5206	5367
1.105	1.099	1.048	1.061	1.043	1.079	1.222	1.392
172	187	268	240	241	265	356	455
2907	3265	3256	3442	3810	4565	6009	7018
10281	11196	11973	13343	14318	16150	19613	23330
10195	10864	11583	12674	13700	15419	18002	19663
tax payments and capital consumption							
2630	2970	3106	3242	3652	4229	4905	5040
277	295	150	200	158	336	1104	1978
103	347	473	713	634	774	1873	4001
17	15	83	44	16	43	262	334
86	332	390	669	618	731	1611	3667
826	892	966	1090	1243	1372	1557	1907
743	803	869	981	1119	1235	1401	1716
228	422	544	404	492	319	271	267
2885	2985	3197	3658	3938	4007	4854	5664
1013	1088	1272	1422	1414	1296	1567	1962
0.351	0.364	0.398	0.389	0.359	0.323	0.323	0.346
80	154	217	157	177	103	88	92
866	973	1024	1283	1276	1269	1379	2005
0.564	0.563	0.584	0.571	0.554	0.546	0.497	0.467
488	548	598	733	707	693	685	936
1393	1441	1466	1016	1385	1673	1296	-1187

Table 11.3 Shares in value-added of the manufacturing

VARIABLE NUMBER	1961	1962	1963	1964	1965	1966
(32)	0.149	0.131	0.155	0.179	0.168	0.140
(33)	0.067	0.070	0.071	0.068	0.069	0.071
(34)	0.010	0.008	0.015	0.013	0.019	0.019
(35)	0.052	0.066	0.055	0.041	0.033	0.031
(36)	0.279	0.275	0.296	0.301	0.287	0.261

Table 11.4 The calculation of net profit by all companies

(1)	3803	3762	4275	4723	4927	4811
(2)	13	16	14	17	20	26
(3)	878	938	989	1062	1160	1274
(4)	123	105	163	242	252	298
(5)	682	842	733	577	539	546
(6)	2133	1893	2404	2864	2996	2719
(7)	13999	14505	15444	16796	17925	18814

Table 11.5 Shares in value added of all companies

(8)	0.152	0.131	0.156	0.171	0.167	0.144
(9)	0.049	0.058	0.047	0.034	0.030	0.029
(10)	0.009	0.007	0.010	0.014	0.014	0.016
(11)	0.063	0.065	0.064	0.063	0.065	0.068
(12)	0.272	0.260	0.278	0.282	0.276	0.257

KEY TO TABLES 11.4 AND 11.5 (p. 236–7)

The same numbering principles apply here as to Tables 10.1–5, and other references to tables are those in *National Income and Expenditure 1965–1975.*

11.4 The calculations of net profit by all companies

(1) Gross Trading Profits plus rents of companies (Table 1.10).

(less metal manufacturing) sector

1967	1968	1969	1970	1971	1972	1973	1974	
0.137	0.133	0.125	0.080	0.101	0.108	0.072	-0.060	
0.073	0.074	0.075	0.077	0.082	0.080	0.078	0.087	
0.008	0.031	0.034	0.053	0.045	0.047	0.089	0.186	
0.048	0.050	0.052	0.058	0.052	0.045	0.038	0.048	
0.266	0.288	0.287	0.268	0.279	0.281	0.277	0.261	
4886	5527	5602	5996	6965	8172	10386	11372	11061
239	460	606	537	609	416	378	368	531
1324	1414	1562	1778	2044	2312	2677	3323	4454
148	470	590	891	831	1067	2546	4908	4107
873	989	1072	1392	1371	1351	1472	2088	1555
2782	3114	2984	2472	3328	3858	4069	1411	1476
19363	20626	21740	23844	26454	29732	34027	37727	45917
0.144	0.151	0.132	0.104	0.126	0.130	0.120	0.037	0.032
0.045	0.048	0.049	0.058	0.052	0.045	0.043	0.055	0.034
0.008	0.023	0.027	0.037	0.031	0.036	0.074	0.130	0.089
0.068	0.069	0.072	0.075	0.077	0.078	0.079	0.088	0.097
0.265	0.290	0.286	0.274	0.286	0.289	0.316	0.311	0.252

(2) Capital transfers to companies (Table 5.2).
(3) Capital consumption of companies (Table 12.9).
(4) Stock appreciation of companies (Table 13.4).
(5) Tax paid by companies on profits in UK on current and capital accounts (Tables 5.1 and 5.2).
(6) Net Profits: (1) + (2) – (3) – (4) – (5).
(7) Gross value added by companies less stock appreciation (Table 1.10).

Table 12.1 Pre-tax non-market sector claims and marketed

VARIABLE NUMBER	1961	1962	1963	1964	1965	1966	1967
(1)	9050	9756	10380	11405	12686	13765	15819
(2)	1104	1114	1257	1257	1348	1465	1573
(3)	897	925	1012	1177	1284	1445	1649
(4)	273	321	365	495	545	655	743
(5)	8984	9624	10260	10990	12205	13130	15000
(6)	1383	1458	1551	1681	1812	1983	2129
(7)	427	460	498	539	606	665	710
(8)	549	662	685	733	817	899	981
(9)	179	203	229	252	274	304	341
(10)	2538	2743	2963	3205	3509	3851	4161
(11)	24218	25279	26887	29255	31237	33139	34956
(12)	21680	22536	23924	26050	27728	29288	30795
(13)	0.414	0.427	0.429	0.422	0.440	0.448	0.487

11.5 Shares in value added of all companies

(8) Share of residual profit in value added: (6) ÷ (7).
(9) Share of tax payments in value added: (5) ÷ (7).
(10) Share of stock appreciation in value added: (4) ÷ (7).
(11) Share of capital consumption in value added: (3) ÷ (7).
(12) Share of gross profits in value added: (1) ÷ (7).

THE DERIVATION OF CHART 12 PRE-TAX NON-MARKET SECTOR CLAIMS AS A RATIO OF MARKETED OUTPUT FOR THE UNITED KINGDOM 1961–75

The purpose of this chart is to compare the spending power before tax created by the non-market sector with the size of the domestic market sector. To the extent that public activities are paid for directly such activities should be excluded. In fact all trading activities of the central and local government are excluded by the source of data utilised, with the exception of local authority housing. All expenditure on *output (£ million)*

1968	1969	1970	1971	1972	1973	1974	1975
17206	17729	19721	22114	24955	29363	38093	49952
1794	1929	2026	2089	2298	2710	3410	3957
1599	1476	1666	1846	1753	2046	2521	3455
783	798	744	670	713	1059	1757	2035
16618	17384	19337	21687	24787	28968	37225	48419
2268	2461	2761	3270	3688	4124	5210	7107
771 1069	1995	2256	2641	3180	3590	4669	7154
377	430	496	543	630	715	779	904
4485	4886	5513	6454	7498	8429	10658	15165
37475	39483	43489	49071	54968	63447	73511	93146
32990	34597	37976	42617	47470	55018	62853	77981
0.504	0.502	0.509	0.509	0.522	0.527	0.592	0.621

local authority housing is subtracted, which clearly removes too much rather than too little from the total of public-sector-created claims on marketed output.[3]

KEY TO TABLE 12.1

The bracketed numbers on the left refer to rows. As before, references to other tables are to those in *National Income and Expenditure 1964–1974*. Data are all in current prices and GDP is measured net of stock appreciation throughout. Data from 1969 on have been revised from the latest National Accounts.

(1) Public expenditure net of debt interest (Table 58).
(2) Debt interest less debt interest of public corporations (Tables 57, 58).
(3) Gross domestic fixed capital formation of public corporations (Table 58).

(4) Gross domestic fixed capital formation of local authorities on housing (Table 58).
(5) Public-sector created claims: (1) + (2) – (3) – (4).
(6) GDP of public administration and defence (Table 11).
(7) GDP of public health services (Table 11).
(8) GDP of local authority educational services (Table 11).
(9) Income from services to private non-profit-making bodies (Table 13).
(10) Total non-marketed output at factor cost: (6) + (7) + (8) + (9).
(11) Total GDP at factor cost (Table 11).
(12) Total marketed output at factor cost: (11) – (10).
(13) Ratio of non-market sector-created claims to marketed output: (5) ÷ (12).

THE DERIVATION OF CHART 13 THE GROWTH OF MAJOR ITEMS OF NON-MARKET EXPENDITURE 1961–75

Table 13.1

	1961	*1975*	*1961 Fraction of marketed output*	*% change*
	(£million)			
Defence	1 725	5 173	0.080	200
Roads, transport, industry	592	6 121	0.027	934
Housing	260	1 986	0.012	664
Environment	620	4 100	0.029	561
Education	1 104	7 237	0.051	556
Health	996	6 310	0.046	534
Social security	1 628	8 918	0.075	448
Debt	1 104	3 957	0.051	258
Marketed output	21 680	77 981	1.000	260

Source

All data on items of public expenditure are taken from Table 10.2 of *National Income and Expenditure 1965–1975*. The categories above are obtained by reclassifying that table as follows:

(*a*) Defence – as in Table 10.2.
(*b*) Roads, transport and industry. The three major categories are roads and public lighting plus transport and communication plus other industry and trade. Activities of the public corporations have been netted out.
(*c*) Housing – as in Table 10.2 less public corporation and local authority expenditure on gross domestic fixed capital formation.
(*d*) Environment. This contains the two major categories environmental services and law and order.
(*e*) Education. This is taken from the detailed breakdown of expenditure on social services and school meals.
(*f*) Health. This covers the two sub-categories national health and personal social services.
(*g*) Social security – as in Table 10.2.
(*h*) Debt – as in Table 10.2.
(*i*) Marketed output – as defined in the notes on Chart 10.

The data are all taken at current prices so as to reflect changes in expenditure caused by relative price changes.

THE DERIVATION OF CHART 14 NATIONAL PLAN PROJECTIONS AND ACTUAL ECONOMIC PERFORMANCE 1964–74

The purpose of this chart is to compare what would have happened if the growth rates of the National Plan had been achieved with what actually happened. The period of comparison is 1964–74. The National Plan looked at the period 1964–70 so the annual growth rates have been continued until 1974.

Table 14.1 Percentage increase in various sectors 1964–70 given by the Plan

Gross national product	25
Private investment	40
Public investment	41
Public consumption	19
Personal consumption	21

Table 14.2 Percentage increase in various sectors 1964–74 extending the Plan period

Gross national product	46
Private investment	75
Public investment	77
Public consumption	34
Personal consumption	37

Sources

The data are taken from Table 1.1 of *The National Plan*, Cmnd. 2764 (HMSO, 1965).

Private investment includes manufacturing and construction plus other private industries and services.

Public consumption includes current spending on defence as well as on social and other public services.

All data are at constant 1964 prices.

Table 14.3 The actual percentage increase in various sectors 1964–74

Gross national product	28
Private investment	41
Public investment	21
Public consumption	28
Personal consumption	26

Sources

The data are all taken from the *National Institute Economic Review*, August 1975.

The figures for investment are taken from Table 10 and all the other data from Table 1. The data for gross domestic product are calculated on an expenditure basis and it is assumed that GNP grew at the same rate as GDP. All data are in constant 1970 prices.

The above calculations may be slightly too favourable to the National Plan in that it was assumed that employment would grow at 0.5 per cent per annum during the planning period. In fact in 1964–74, the period used in this comparison, it fell by 0.03 per cent per annum.

Charts 15, 22, 29 and 30 are explained where they appear in the text.

THE DERIVATION OF CHARTS 23, 24, 25, 26, 27 AND 28: WHERE COMPARISONS BETWEEN THE UNITED KINGDOM, CANADA AND THE UNITED STATES ARE PRESENTED

Comparable data are needed, and the official national income accounts of each country have been used to provide the basis for this. These are published in *National Income and Expenditure* for the United Kingdom, and in Statistics Canada's *National Income and Expenditure Accounts*, and in the United States Department of Commerce's *Statistical Abstract of the United States*. Use has been made of other officially published data.

Table 23.1 below gives the basic data from which Charts 23, 24, 25, 26, 27 and 28 are derived. The actual figures used in these charts are all derived from Table 23.1, and they are presented in Tables 23.2, 24, 25 and the composite Table 26–7–8 below. The derivation from Table 23.1 of the precise data for each chart is explained with the presentation of Tables 23.2, 24, 25 and 26–7–8.

The concept that is new in these charts is the division of the marketed output of each country between its various purchasers (as opposed to the division of *industrial* output which was set out in Charts 10, 16, 17, 18, 19, 20 and 21). The authors have greatly benefited from correspondence with Dr Ralph Turvey of the International Labour Office, Geneva, about the problems involved in this, and from being able to see his estimates of similar tables from various countries including Britain and Canada (but not the United States) for the period 1964 to 1974.

23.1 The derivation of the basic data for the United Kingdom, Canada and the United States of America for 1955, 1965, 1974 and 1975

The 1965–75 edition of *National Income and Expenditure* provides the British data apart from 1955 (and 1956 where 1955 is unavailable). The 1961–75 edition of Canada's *National Income and Expenditure Accounts* provides the Canadian data for 1965, 1974 and 1975, and the 1976 edition of the *Statistical Abstract of the United States* provides virtually all the United States data that are needed.

The references to tables that are given below for the three countries are to these official publications. The United Kingdom data for 1955 and 1956 are derived similarly from *National Income and Expenditure* 1966 (for 1955) and 1967 (for 1956). The Canadian data for 1955 are derived from the 1926–74 edition of *National Income and Expenditure Accounts*. Such United States data as are not published in the 1976 *Statistical Abstract* are derived from the most recent previous edition in which 1955 data appears, The few other sources for data which have been needed are specifically mentioned below.

Thc term 'general government' where it is used below refers to the central and all state and local government units, but not to government controlled companies.

23.1 The basic data for comparison

(1) Gross domestic product at market prices (UK Table 1.8; Canada Table 2; USA Table 630).
(2) Income from employment in general government (UK Table 1.10; Canada Table 8; USA Table 636).
(3) Gross marketed output: (1)–(2).
(4) Consumers expenditure (UK Table 1.8; Canada Table 2: USA Table 630).
(5) General government expenditure on goods and services – current only for the UK and Canada; current and capital for the USA (UK Table 1.8; Canada Table 2; USA Table 630).
(6) General government gross domestic investment (UK Table 11.3; Canada Table 2; USA included in (5) above).
(7) General government expenditure on materials and gross investment: (5) + (6) – (2).
(8) Exports less imports (UK Table 1.8; Canada Table 2, USA Table 630).
(9) Total market-sector gross investment in fixed capital and inventories (UK Table 11.3 and 1.8 for inventories; Canada Table 2; USA Table 630).
(10) Market-sector capital consumption (UK Table 12.9; Canada Table 8; USA Tables 638 and 636 to exclude 'capital consumption adjustment').

(11) Market-sector net investment: (9) – (10).
(12) Total personal incomes (UK Table 4.1; Canada Table 4; USA Table 638).
(13) Transfers from general government to persons (UK Table 4.1; Canada Table 4; USA Table 638).
(14) General government debt interest (UK Table 10.1; Canada Table 43; USA Table 422 with 1975 assumed to increase over 1974 by the same amount as Federal government interest from Table 401).
(15) General government financed personal incomes: (2) + (13) + (14).
(16) Proportion of personal incomes derived from general government: (15) ÷ (12).
(17) Private consumption from incomes derived from general government on the assumption that the propensity to consume from these incomes and from market-generated incomes is the same: (16) x (4).
(18) Private consumption from market-generated incomes: (4) – (17).
(19) Gross marketed output derived from market-sector purchases: (7) + (8) + (9) + (17) + (18).
(20) Statistical discrepancy between (19) and (3) as a proportion of (3).
(21) Total defence spending (UK Table 10.2; Canada *Canadian Statistical Review* Table 11, section 13 in 1976 editions; USA Table 630).
(22) Total general government-financed personal incomes and investment and material purchases: (7) + (15).
(23) Consumption and material purchases for defence on the assumption that its proportion of marketed output is the same as its proportion of gross general government expenditures: ((17) + (7)) x (21) ÷ (22).
(24) Official deflators needed to convert UK into 1970 prices (Table 2.4 – total 'final expenditure' index), Canada into 1971 prices (Table 7 the Gross National Expenditure index) and USA into 1972 prices (Table 630).
(25) Real marketed output: (19) ÷ (24).
(26) Real marketed output invested and consumed by non-market sector: ((7) + (17)) x (25) ÷ (19).

(27) Real marketed output that remains for the market sector: (25) – (26).

(28) Real marketed output consumed privately from market-generated incomes: (25) x (18) ÷ (19).

(29) Market-sector employment (UK Table 1.10; USA civilian employees [Table 571] – Government civilians [Table 452]: Canada, a series provided by the Institute for Policy Analysis of the University of Toronto from its computer print-out. A series differing by 2 per cent at most from this can be derived by assuming that the ratio of government employment to total civilian employment equals the ratio of government civilian payrolls to total civilian payrolls (including 'persons'). The series derived by the Institute for Policy Analysis is preferred. The relative figures for 1955, 1965 and 1974 (using Tables 8 and B to derive the alternative series) with the Policy Studies series marked P are: 1955 4,804,000P, 4,739,000; 1965 5,685,000P, 5,667,000; 1974 7,258,000P, 7,113,000.

(30) Non-market employment (UK Table 1.10; USA Military employment [Table 531] plus government civilian [Table 452]; Canada series provided by the Centre for Policy Studies. This series is again close to the totals arrived at by the method outlined in (29) above.

The data for Charts 23, 24, 25, 26, 27 and 28 are derived from Table 23.1 and all figures in brackets below refer to lines of Table 23.1

Table [illegible] The derivation of the basic data for the UK, Canada and the USA for 1955, 1965, 1974 and 1975

	UK					Canada				USA (Billions)			
	1955	*1956*	*1965*	*1974*	*1975*	*1955*	*1965*	*1974*	*1975*	*1955*	*1965*	*1974*	*1975*
(1)	19.103	20.663	35.609	81.859	103.286	28.528	53.364	144.616	161.132	399.3	688.1	1413.2	1516.3
(2)	2.099	2.303	3.821	11.186	15.919	2.058	5.568	18.554	22.398	36.6	69.8	160.4	175.9
(3)	17.004	18.360	31.788	70.673	87.367	26.470	49.796	126.062	138.734	362.7	618.3	1252.8	1340.4
(4)	13.107	13.829	22.845	51.832	63.373	18.388	33.947	82.064	95.018	253.7	430.2	887.5	973.2
(5)	3.171	3.428	6.041	16.578	22.907	4.036	8.358	27.838	32.712	75.0	138.4	303.3	339.0
(6)	0.755	0.788	1.486	4.331	4.914	0.949	2.430	5.488	6.517				
(7)	1.827	1.913	3.706	9.723	11.902	2.927	5.220	14.772	16.831	38.4	68.6	142.9	163.1
(8)	–0.304	0.044	–0.277	–4.328	–2.155	–0.641	–1.159	–2.055	–5.371	2.2	7.5	7.5	20.5
(9)	2.374	2.574	5.514	13.446	14.247	5.759	11.993	30.964	32.405	68.4	112.0	215.0	183.7
(10)	1.171	1.274	2.497	7.351	9.626	3.017	5.887	13.421	15.063	33.0	61.3	134.7	149.9
(11)	1.203	1.300	3.017	6.095	4.621	2.742	6.106	17.543	17.342	35.4	50.7	80.3	33.8
(12)	15.600	16.738	30.083	75.850	95.700	21.265	41.071	114.825	113.114	308.8	537.0	1153.3	1249.7
(13)	1.195	1.193	2.596	7.873	10.208	1.719	3.423	13.799	16.939	16.2	37.6	134.6	168.9
(14)	0.907	0.802	1.456	3.837	4.513	0.664	1.675	5.386	6.335	5.7	11.4	30.1	33.5
(15)	4.121	4.298	7.873	22.896	30.640	4.441	10.666	37.739	45.672	58.5	118.8	325.1	378.3
(16)	0.264	0.257	0.262	0.302	0.320	0.209	0.260	0.329	0.343	0.189	0.221	0.282	0.303
(17)	3.460	3.554	5.985	15.653	20.279	3.843	8.826	26.999	32.591	47.9	95.1	250.3	294.9
(18)	9.647	10.275	16.860	36.179	43.094	14.545	25.121	55.065	62.427	205.8	335.1	637.2	678.3
(19)	17.004	18.360	31.788	70.673	87.367	26.433	50.001	125.745	138.883	362.7	618.3	1252.9	1340.5
(20)	nil	nil	nil	nil	nil	–0.001	+0.004	–0.003	+0.001	nil	nil	nil	nil
(21)	1.537	1.625	2.105	4.131	5.173	1.750	1.595	2.509	2.974	38.4	49.4	77.3	84.3
(22)	5.948	6.211	11.579	32.619	42.542	7.368	15.886	52.511	62.503	96.9	187.4	468.0	541.4
(23)	1.366	1.430	1.762	3.214	3.913	1.608	1.410	1.996	2.352	34.2	43.2	64.9	71.3
(24)	60.1	62.1	78.7	152.0	189.0	65.0	79.1	131.1	145.2	60.98	74.32	116.41	127.25
(25)	28.293	29.565	40.391	46.495	46.226	40.666	63.212	95.915	95.649	594.78	831.94	1076.28	1053.44
(26)	8.797	8.803	12.314	16.695	17.027	10.415	17.757	31.862	34.037	141.52	220.26	337.77	359.92
(27)	19.496	20.762	28.077	29.800	29.199	30.251	45.455	64.053	61.612	453.26	611.68	758.51	693.52
(28)	16.052	16.546	21.423	23.802	22.801	22.377	31.758	42.002	42.994	332.89	447.39	545.14	531.55
													Millions
(29)	n.a.	20 516	21 245	20 129	19 698	4 804	5 685	7 258	n.a.	54 768	60 499	71 308	69 797
(30)	n.a.	3 993	3 957	4 931	5 270	677	1 289	1 960	n.a.	10 319	13 446	16 768	17 070

Table 23.2 Non-market purchases of marketed output as a proportion of marketed output: 1955–75

UK

	1955	1965	1974	1975
$\frac{((7)+(17))}{(19)}$	0.311	0.305	0.359	0.368

CANADA

	1955	1965	1974	1975
$\frac{((7)+(17))}{(19)}$	0.256	0.281	0.332	0.356

USA

	1955	1965	1974	1975
$\frac{((7)+(17))}{(19)}$	0.238	0.265	0.314	0.342

Table 24 Non-market purchases of marketed output excluding defence as a proportion of marketed output: 1955–75

UK

	1955	1965	1974	1975
$\frac{(7)+(17)-(23)}{(19)}$	0.231	0.249	0.314	0.324

CANADA

	1955	1965	1974	1975
$\frac{(7)+(17)-(23)}{(19)}$	0.195	0.253	0.316	0.339

USA

	1955	1965	1974	1975
$\frac{(7)+(17)-(23)}{(19)}$	0.144	0.195	0.262	0.288

Table 25 Extra output available to the market sector: 1955–74

	UK		*CANADA*		*USA*	
	1956–65	*1965–74*	*1955–65*	*1965–74*	*1955–65*	*1965–74*
			percentage rates of growth			
(a) Growth in marketed output	3.53	1.58	4.51	4.74	3.41	2.90
(b) Growth in market-sector employment	0.39	–0.39	1.70	2.75	1.00	1.84
(c) Growth in output per worker	3.13	1.98	2.76	1.94	2.39	1.04
(d) Growth in output available to market sector	3.41	0.66	4.16	3.88	3.04	2.12
(e) Growth in output per worker available to market sector	3.00	1.05	2.42	1.10	2.02	0.27

(a) is derived from line (25) of Table 23.1
(b) is derived from line (29)
(c) is (a) – (b) calculated geometrically
(d) is derived from line (27)
(e) is (d) – (b) calculated geometrically

Tables 26, 27 and 28   Where marketed output went: 1955–75

percentages of marketed output

	UK				*CANADA*				*USA*			
	1955	*1965*	*1974*	*1975*	*1955*	*1965*	*1974*	*1975*	*1955*	*1965*	*1974*	*1975*
(a) Market-financed consumption	56.7	53.0	51.2	49.3	55.0	50.2	43.8	44.9	56.7	54.2	50.9	50.6
(b) Government-financed consumption	20.3	18.8	22.1	23.2	14.5	17.7	21.5	23.5	13.2	15.4	20.0	22.0
(c) Government materials and investment	10.7	11.7	13.8	13.6	11.1	10.4	11.7	12.1	10.6	11.1	11.4	12.2
(d) Market-sector gross investment	14.0	17.3	19.0	16.3	21.8	24.0	24.6	23.3	18.9	18.1	17.2	13.7
of which												
(e) Capital consumption	(6.9)	(7.9)	(10.4)	(11.0)	(11.4)	(11.8)	(10.7)	(10.8)	(9.1)	(9.9)	(10.8)	(11.2)
(f) Exports less imports	−1.8	−0.9	−6.1	−2.5	−2.4	−2.3	−1.6	−3.9	0.6	1.2	0.6	1.5

(a) is (18) ÷ (19).
(b) is (17) ÷ (19)
(c) is (7) ÷ (19)
(d) is (9) ÷ (19)
(e) is (10) ÷ (19)
(f) is (8) ÷ (19)

NOTES

1. Both total sales and total purchases are taken net of intermediate sales of industrial products to the industrial sector, and net of intermediate sales of industrial products to the non-industrial non-government sector.
2. M. A. King, 'The United Kingdom Profits Crisis: Myth or Reality?', *Economic Journal*, Vol. 85, March 1975.
3. The most recent National Accounts do not take account of the latest Treasury calculations on debt interest (see: 13th Report of Expenditure Committee of House of Commons: Session 75/76) and so no alteration has been made to these figures.

Index